John Owen

Travels into Different Parts of Europe in the Years 1791 and 1792

Vol. 1

John Owen

**Travels into Different Parts of Europe in the Years 1791 and 1792**
*Vol. 1*

ISBN/EAN: 9783337345785

Printed in Europe, USA, Canada, Australia, Japan

Cover: Foto ©Andreas Hilbeck / pixelio.de

More available books at **www.hansebooks.com**

# *OWEN*'s
# TRAVELS

INTO

## *DIFFERENT PARTS OF EUROPE*,

In the Years 1791 and 1792.

VOL. I.

# TRAVELS

INTO

## DIFFERENT PARTS OF EUROPE,

IN THE YEARS 1791 AND 1792.

WITH

## FAMILIAR REMARKS

ON

## PLACES—MEN—AND MANNERS.

By JOHN OWEN, A. M.
LATE FELLOW OF CORPUS CHRISTI COLLEGE.

*Mores, et Studia, et Populos*——    VIRG. Georg. Lib. 4.

IN TWO VOLUMES.

VOL. I.

*LONDON:*
PRINTED FOR T. CADELL JUN. AND W. DAVIES,
(SUCCESSORS TO MR. CADELL,) IN THE STRAND.

1796.

# PREFACE.

It is a subject of equal notoriety and regret, that prefaces have funk into general difufe, or loft to a great degree their juft and original character. The abrupt appearance of an author before the bar of the public is an enterprize of moft anxious uncertainty. He feems to be bound by a fort of refpect, to prefent fome credentials or fubmit to fome formalities, before he prefume upon the ready difpofition of fo auguft a judicature to hear and determine his merits. In addition to that duty which refpect impofes, a more important claim attaches upon him,

him, from the abfolute neceffity of fome preliminary arrangements, for the purpofes of a fair and equitable decifion. Yet fuch is the impatience of the bulk of readers, that all which intervenes between the title and the work is confidered as an obftacle in the way of their progrefs, and treated as a flavifh compliance with an obfolete ceremony. The influence of this judgment ftops not with readers. It relaxes the ftrictnefs of authors themfelves; and induces a habit of writing with loofenefs thofe very preliminaries, which feem to demand the moft cautious precifion—an indolence natural to the human mind, which is rarely brought to execute with care, what is not likely to be regarded with attention.

It

It may, however, be affirmed, that the majority of cafes in which the merits of writers have been miſtaken by the public, might be fairly referred to thoſe defects in the outſet of their acquaintance, which a due regard to ſome prefatory ſteps would have ſufficiently ſupplied. Works of travel ſtand particularly expoſed to the danger of an erroneous judgment. Preſenting in many inſtances a picture of the times, and embracing a variety of circumſtances and events, they may be conſidered as bearing upon modern hiſtory; and therefore, like that, encountering the jealouſies, ſuſpicions, and prejudices of minds variouſly intereſted, and affected by different, and yet exiſting, impreſſions. Theſe obſtacles can only be with any colour of expectation diminiſhed, by the eſtabliſhment of some premises, which the reader may adopt, and to which he may refer, as a rule for interpreting the author's mind on points of critical and delicate decision.

The volumes of travel with which the public are now presented profess to stand on more hazardous ground, in respect to a fair and equitable judgment, than any similar work with which they might be compared; and the author is unwilling to commit them to the world, without anticipating, in some premonitory remarks, the leading objections by which they may be attacked.

1. It may be urged, that books of travel have been greatly multiplied, and that the route which the author pursues has in it no chance of novelty. To this the author, with little variation,

PREFACE.	v

tion, concedes. He is ready to admit, that the cabinet is already supplied with a numerous catalogue of entertaining travellers; he is ready to admit, that the outline of his tour differs in very few respects from the ordinary track of fashionable travel; and that the places alluded to in the succeeding volumes are, with few exceptions, such as have been repeatedly viewed and repeatedly described. The attention of the public to travelling journals has however, he presumes, not yet been fatiated by all that has been, nor will probably be satisfied by all that may be said, of foreign countries and foreign manners. The necessity of supplying some species of light and unelaborate reading is felt by all who are acquainted with the public taste: and no productions are,

gene-

generally speaking, more readily digested, than those which conduct the fire-side traveller through an extensive tract of country without disturbing him from his arm-chair; and introduce him to all the beauties of a country without exposing him to any of its storms. Relying upon this passion for travelling journals, and the endless variety of an active mind, the author engaged in a correspondence for furnishing expressly the materials of the present volumes. Whether he has rightly judged of the public feelings, and his own powers—will be hereafter decided.

A second objection may probably arise, from the interval which has been suffered to pass between the closing of the Letters and the period of publication. In accounting for this it

PREFACE.

is neceffary to remark, that a confiderable portion of the Letters had been transferred to private hands for the fecurity of conveyance, at the time of the author's proceeding upon his expedition into Auftria; and that the non-arrival of thefe at the period expected very confiderably delayed the compilation. The publication of Mr. Grey's tour at nearly the fame period was alfo a ground of difcouragement. If to this be added the obftruction occafioned to the procefs of printing by the author's diftance from the metropolis and the prefs, the hiftory of this delay will have been completely given. The reafons for fpecifying thefe caufes with fo much minutenefs, will be fufficiently obvious to thofe who are acquainted with the bufy infinuations of calumny and malice. Events of
later

late occurrence have split society into so many factions, that jealousies are now excited, against which too much precaution cannot be employed. The author expects to hear it insinuated, as it has been already candidly rumoured, that the publication was delayed for the convenience of adapting it to the humour of the times. If the circumstances already enumerated had not sufficiently done away this imputation, the very difficulty itself of effecting such a task, in the varying circumstances of the present period, would discover the folly of the charge. To these, however—if these should yet be insufficient—the author is ready to annex his most serious declaration; that in no instance, the most trivial particulars alone excepted, has he shaped or accommodated the original spirit and

PREFACE. ix

and train of the journal; and that a confiderable number of the Letters have been printed, with no other alteration, than that of a literal or verbal correction.

A third objection may poffibly arife in the minds of fome, from the internal character of the Letters themfelves, the circumftances of which they treat, and the unreferved freedom with which thefe circumftances are treated. To this it may be replied, that the author has availed himfelf, in travelling and in writing, of that liberty which has in fuch cafes ever been deemed admiffible: and that as he travelled to fee and report, he conceives that he could only do juftice to himfelf, the public, and his fubject, by depicting, as he has done, manners and fentiments in their natural

tural colours; and expressing, on just occasions, the undissembled feelings of his own mind. If the reader maintains a strict attention—in adjudging these Letters—to the particular periods in which they were written; if he considers the circumstances of the times and the state of public opinion; the author is convinced that his enthusiasm will be pronounced to have been of a venial, if not of a commendable character. But events of such variety, and in many particulars of such importance, have taken place during the lapse of the three last years, that the mind will not, without some difficulty, acquire that temper with which it ought to peruse the reports of a preceding period. Labouring under the influence of some recent impressions, the reader will probably

be

be led to confound thofe dates which ought to be kept religiously diſtinct; and thus condemn, by a reference to fubfequent tranfactions, what in the *then* circumſtances he might have been forward to approve. It muſt not be diſſembled, that the largeſt portion of the author's anxiety for the fate of his work is founded in an apprehenſion of this dangerous, yet almoſt inevitable, confuſion in the public mind of dates and feelings. For his own part, he is free to confefs, that though his mind has been affected with the moſt fenfible emotion at the horrors which have deformed the name of *Liberty*, he yet can fee no reafon for reverſing all the maxims of the wifeſt men and the beſt times; he ſtill can contemplate it—in its genuine characters of benignity and order—as the

friend

friend of man, and the happiest cement of civil society. Not all the disorders which have deluged Europe since the æra of the French revolution have induced him to depart from the *principles*\* which supported his original admiration of this extraordinary event. The downfal of limited monarchy, the irruption of Jacobinism, Briſſotinism, and all the modifications of republican tyranny, have cruelly inverted the original picture; but the very hostility which *these* declared against the *first* reformers, and which themselves have experienced from the present less outrageous and democratic rulers, is an argument in favour of the first legiſlative aſſembly, which cannot be defeated by any species of regular and ingenuous reaſoning.

\* Vide Preface to Retrospect.

foning. The evils which have been ingrafted upon this convenient flock, the factions of diforder and equalization, are indifputably leffons of inftructive caution againft hafty enthufiafm and rafh experiment. A torrent of political licentioufnefs has certainly poured in upon the peaceful and prudent inftitutions of fociety; and thofe who occupy refponfible fituations are loudly called upon to fupport the tottering pillars of civil fubordination. In the difcharge, however, of this duty, no compromife ought to be made of truth and juftice; nor fhould zeal tranfport us to criminate, what prudence may have forbidden us to admire. So much it feemed expedient to fay for the publication of fentiments, whofe bearings upon prefent opinion might elfe be expofed to mifconftruction.

construction. The author is aware that expressions may have been curforily employed, which the faftidious fcruples of fome might wifh amended or expunged. But he cannot difcover any fentiment, with which a candid mind *can*, or a Britifh mind *ought*, to be offended. His opinions on the leading political changes are already before the public; and thefe will afford a fufficient clue for unravelling and reconciling what might elfe appear myfterious and inconfiftent.

After fo much faid by way of anticipation, it may now be neceffary to fay fomething of the execution. The Letters are fhort, for the commodioufnefs of detached reading; and as they were in moft inftances difpofed in packets containing a number, they were originally conftructed upon this
concife

concife model, in order to fupport the analogy of chapters in a regular journal. Dates are for the moft part fuperfcribed; but where this is omitted, the Letter is to be confidered as forming a part of a packet, and referred to the date of the preceding. As they are intended for the amufement of the *domeftic* traveller, they are not charged with any fyftematic calculations of diftance or coin, or any critical adjuftment of names and hiftories. Charts and Itineraries are beft fuited to the minutenefs of the firft, and profeffed difquifitions to the gravity of the laft. The ftyle, it is hoped, will be found not wholly unfuiting the familiarity of the occafions; and the errors and redundancies—if fuch fhould appear—will probably be viewed with fome portion of indulgence,

when

when it is confidered, that the Letters were written in the warmth of youthful impetuofity—and that it would have been a breach of tacit faith to introduce any further emendations, than thofe which are juftified by ufage and acknowledged licence. That the volumes have appeared at all, and that they have not appeared in a lefs correct ftate, are owing to the flattering encouragement and the critical fervices of W. Belfham Efq. to whom thefe Letters were originally addreffed, and whofe judicious revifion they had the good fortune to receive. In revealing this circumftance, the author is but difcharging a debt of gratitude to a man, of whofe character—while the public may reafonably differ—his friends can entertain but one opinion. The foundnefs of his judgment, and

the

## PREFACE.

the accuracy of his taste, were a security to the author for the justness of his corrections; and a friendship of long and strict familiarity, undisturbed by the divisions of politics and theology, have afforded him occasions of general improvement, which it is equally his duty and his pride to acknowledge.

In taking leave of the reader the author has only to request, that a candid distinction may be made in perusing his volumes, between the cast of his mind at the period of his travels, and that which he now professes to have received. The demands of a situation the most grave and important have now engaged him in duties and concerns, which necessarily occupy and solemnize his thoughts; and to the faithful discharge of which,

With thefe preliminaries, the author is content to meet the public eye. Convinced that the fentence of the world, when fairly collected, is rarely unjuft, he has endeavoured to furnifh in the remarks premifed, the means of eftablifhing an equitable judgment.

> Speak of me as I am—nothing extenuate,
> Or fet down ought in malice—

Such is the rule, by which, as he fhould judge of others, he wifhes himfelf to be judged.

January 7, 1796.

# CONTENTS.

## VOLUME THE FIRST.

### LETTER I.

*O*BJECT *and plan of correspondence stated
—Variety a species of originality.* Page 1

### LETTER II.

*First sensation of a traveller—French coast—
Evils of the antient system—Prospect of
final good from the present disorders—
Eulogium on the new laws.*    4

### LETTER III.

*Ostend—Ghent—Particulars respecting the
Gantois—Aspect of the place—Churches
—St.*

—*St. Gedule—Criticism and nature not always agreed—Digression on Belgic politics.* - - - Page 8

## LETTER IV.

*Brussels—Gloomy aspect in Holy Week—Strength of devotion—Religious card-party—Prospect of concluding penance—Consecration of days.* - - 15

## LETTER V.

*Description of a religious ceremony—Devout character of common people—Catholic penance transferable property.* - 20

## LETTER VI.

*Penance concluded—Consequent changes—Theatre—Societies—Comtesse de Choiseul—Chivalry not extinct at Brussels—" Ladies Club."* - - 24

## LETTER VII.

*Politeness exemplified.* - 28

## LETTER VIII.

*Philosophy of the heart—Instanced in French Noblesse—Their conduct described—Character of a Frenchman traced in his language—Conclusion in favour of philosophy.* - - - - Page 30

## LETTER IX.

*National varieties source of travellers pleasure—Law of etiquette—*Fourth *law of morals—Defined—Example to the rule—Relation of trifling occurrences defended.* 35

## LETTER X.

*Park—Palace of the arch-duchess—Pillage of the revolutionists—Compared with military law.* - - - 39

## LETTER XI.

*Intention of quitting Brussels—Character of Flemings—Anecdote—Conclusion against them.* - - - 43

## LETTER XII.

*Entrance upon Antwerp—Church of Notre Dame—General state of Antwerp—Amusements—Remains of revolutionary spirit—Political conjectures.* Page 47

## LETTER XIII.

*Vicissitudes in the history of Antwerp—Siege in 1585—Treaty of Munster—No change in the spirit of fanaticism—Portrait of Van Eupen—his machinations, defeat, and flight.* - - - 52

## LETTER XIV.

*From Antwerp to Breda—Country described—Contrast between Dutch and Austrian Brabant—Breda described—Rendezvous of the late revolutionists—Sketch of some particulars previous to the capture of Brussels—Apology for alluding to Belgic affairs—Different views of Prussia and Holland.* - - - 57

## LETTER XV.

*Convenience of travelling through Holland—Entrance of a vessel for Rotterdam—Abrupt separation—Agrémens of land travelling—Passage of the Biesbock—Embarrassed route by land.* - Page 64

## LETTER XVI.

*Dutch Cabaret—Hollanders industrious—Route to Rotterdam—Rotterdam described—Statue of Erasmus—Prudent management of literary honours.* - 72

## LETTER XVII.

*Peculiar character of Rotterdam—Trade the predominant concern—Precipitate departure.* - - - 77

## LETTER XVIII.

*Delft—Its rarities—The Hague—Promenade to Scheveling—Village, &c.—Houses—Palace of the Stadtholder—Churches, Preachers,*

*Preachers,* &c.—*The fair*—*Drefs of Dutch girls*—*Singular hats*—*Apology for severity.* - - Page 80

LETTER XIX.

*Paffage to Amfterdam*—*Mode of travelling*—*Manners of Paffengers*—*Leyden and Haerlem*—*Banks of Canals*—*Firft coup d'œil of Amfterdam*—*Paufe from narration.* - - - 86

LETTER XX.

*City of Amfterdam*—*Eulogium on its commercial character*—*Compared with its quondam rival Antwerp*—*Activity of the city*—*Streets*—*Stadthoufe*—*Churches*—*Carriages*—*Bridge*—*Propofed account of a contrafted fcene.* - - 90

LETTER XXI.

*Trip to Broek*—*View of Amfterdam from Buykfloodt*—*Approach to Broek*—*Broek defcribed*—*Elegant neatnefs of the houfes*—
*Grotefque*

CONTENTS.

*Grotesque forms of the gardens*, &c.—*Interior of the houses—Singular customs—Difficulty of accounting for this neatness—Return to Amsterdam.* - Page 96

LETTER XXII.

*Passage to Utrecht—The city described—Glance at its history—Anecdote from Duclos—Route to Bommel—Bois-le-duc—Country described—Preparation for advancing.* - - - 103

LETTER XXIII.

*Neatness of Hollanders considered—Principally resolvable into necessity—No great personal neatness — Hollanders reputed knavish—Accounted for—Different character of towns and villages—Vindication of the last—Religious anecdotes—Conclusion in favour of their moral virtues.* 109

## LETTER XXIV.

*Singular situation of Holland considered—Goldsmith referred to—Sameness in the aspect of its towns—Gardens criticised—Uncouthness in these consistent with their general habits.* - Page 115

## LETTER XXV.

*Reflections on the national policy of Holland—Orange cockade universal—Attempt to account for this submission—Political disaffection of Hollanders—Spirit of Hollanders unforgiving—Anecdote in proof.* 122

## LETTER XXVI.

*Route from Bois-le-duc described—Maestricht, its lively aspect—Liege, the picture reversed—Spa, its situation—Salubrity of its springs not its only attraction—Dearness of living—Water not the only beverage at Spa.* - - 129

## LETTER XXVII.

*Necessity becoming a virtue—Illustrated in the dress of the female Hollander—Rule applied to salubrious springs—Advantage of the union between amusement and regimen—Its greater disadvantage—Conclusion against Spa.* - Page 134

## LETTER XXVIII.

*Singular grant of indulgence—Departure for Aix—Disgusting effect of invalids—Cathedral, devotion of its worshippers—Same observed at Juliers—Arrival at Dusseldorf.* - - - 138

## LETTER XXIX.

*Works of art best viewed in company—Gallery of the Elector—Chamber of Rubens—Of Vander-Werf—Italian—" La lumière " vraiment soufflée."—The wise and foolish virgins—Holy family—Moral reflection.*
142

## CONTENTS.

### LETTER XXX.
Cologne *described*—Bonn, *palace*, &c.—
*Picturesque route to Remangen*—*Improvement of country to Andernach*—*Reflection on its ruins.* - Page 147

### LETTER XXXI.
*Position of Coblentz*—*Fair sex*--*dress of men*—*Deception of scenery*—*Two evils which exercise a traveller's fortitude*—*Singular coachman*—*Arrival at Mayence.* 152

### LETTER XXXII.
*Mayence described*—*High mass*—*Table d'Hôte*—*Abbés*—*Comparison of manners at French, Dutch, and German tables*—*Hauteur of Ecclesiastics*—*Worms*—*Entrance into Manheim*—*Rendezvous of emigrants*—*Reflections on their fate.* - 156

### LETTER XXXIII.
*Discipline of Manheim*—*Entrance upon Alsace*—*Good effects of the revolution*—*Gaiety*

*of*

*of the people—Route to Strasbourg—Vestige of corruption—Religious procession—Apology for defective descriptions.* Page 162

### LETTER XXXIV.

*The revolution considered—Its effects on language—Changes in Strasbourg—Contrast between revolutionists and emigrants—Political aspect of the place—Contrast of antient and modern decrees—Moore no prophet.* - - 167

### LETTER XXXV.

*Want of specie at Strasbourg—Dread of paper-payment—Orderly state of inhabitants—National emolument—Religious worship protected—Rencontre at Mulhausen—Dialogue.* - - 172

### LETTER XXXVI.

*Advance of clock at Basle—Three kings—Beauty of the Rhine—Character of Basle—Simple*

—*Simple manners of inhabitants—Best species of poetry.* - - Page 178

## LETTER XXXVII.

*Dress of women—Eulogium on Basle—Route to Berne—Mountainous varieties—Singular position of Biestal—Soleure—Arrival at Berne.* - - 183

## LETTER XXXVIII.

*Goût for amusements instanced in an emigrant—Position of Berne—Political discussion—Inquisitive character—Route to Geneva.*
188

## LETTER XXXIX.

*Position of Geneva—Lake—Its banks—Mountains—Grand Saleve—Petit—Mole—Glaciers—Aiguilles—Mont Blanc—Rhone and Arve.* - 194

## LETTER XL.

*Effect of King's flight on police of Geneva—on the people—Commotion upon his arrest—Effect*

CONTENTS. xxxiii

*Effect upon Lausanne—Promenades—Po-
liticians—" La belle democrate"—Love—
Language.* - Page 199

LETTER XLI.

*Dress,* &c.—*Goûté—Genevese dinner—Divisions of Sunday evening—Political state
of Geneva.* - - 204

LETTER XLII.

*Federation celebrated at Ferney—Introduction to company—Speech of Commandant—
English toasted—Compliment returned—
Effects—Good order of the whole—Voltaire's house.* - - 209

LETTER XLIII.

*Lausanne—Environs—Swell of lake—Character of Lausanne—Gibbon—First view
of Glaciers—Project of tour.* 217

LETTER XLIV.

*Route to Chamouni—Bonneville—Singular
inscription—Cascade at Salenche—Chat-*

VOL. I. c *à-bancs*

CONTENTS.

à-bancs—Cascade of Chede—Gaieties of St. Gervais. - Page 221

LETTER XLV.

Glacier de Boissons—Its beauty—Dangers of its vicinity—Ascent of Montanvert—Mer-de-glace—Environs. - 226

LETTER XLVI.

Blair's Cabin—Character of guides—Mont Blanc—Descent from Montanvert—Source of the Arveron—Discontents of Savoyards—Division of lands. - 231

LETTER XLVII.

Evening contemplation—Passage of Col-de-Balme—Valley of Trent—Village. 238

LETTER XLVIII.

Passage of Forclay—St. Blanchier—Valley of Entremont—Inscriptions on houses—Position of Liddes—Pilgrim. 242

## LETTER XLIX.

*St. Pierre—Flesh of animals—Ascent to St. Bernard—Mule good instructor—Barbarous route—Meal at the convent.* Page 247

## LETTER L.

*Environs of convent—Language of the brothers—Lake—Passage of Hannibal—Institution of the convent—Members.* 253

## LETTER LI.

*Employment of the brothers—Their utility questioned—Storm—Descent from St. Bernard's—Mulish resistance.* - 258

## LETTER LII.

*Position of St. Blanchier—St. Martigny—Butterfly-catcher — Eloquent landlord — Goitrous and Cretins—Saussure's hypothesis.* - - - 263

## LETTER LIII.

*Cascade of Pissevache—Entrance on territories of Berne—Bex—Salines—Passage through the mountain.* - 268

## LETTER LIV.

*Appearance upon issuing from the Salines—Bex described—Church dispute—Route to Vevai—Chateau de Chillon—Arrival at Lausanne—Reflection on the tour.* Page 273

## LETTER LV.

*Beauties of the country—Rocks of Millerai Character of the Swiss—Marquis de Langle—Chevalier Mehegan—Balance of opinion.* - - 278

## LETTER LVI.

*Political disturbances—Their origin—Strong measures of the Bernois—Reality of the plot doubted—Alledged grievances considered.* - - 283

## LETTER LVII.

*Vineyards—Climate—Prohibition of French language—Severity of government.* 289

## LETTER LVIII.
*Decline of society—and natural beauty—Preparation for Italian tour.* Page 293

## LETTER LIX.
*Departure from Lausanne—Rencontre at Rolle—Geneva—Judgment against theatres.* - - - 296

## LETTER LX.
*Entrance upon Savoy—Aix les Bains—Chamberri—Aigue-belle route described.* 300

## LETTER LXI.
*Inhabitants of Valley—Village triumph—Lannesbourg—Dislocation of carriages,* &c. - - - 304

## LETTER LXII.
*Ascent of Mont Cenis—Appearance of summit—Descent in sledge—Comparison of antient and modern travellers—Novaleze—Particulars of Suze,* &c. 307

## LETTER LXIII.

*Approach to Turin—Dress of inhabitants—His Sardinian Majesty's palace—Equestrian statue—Four seasons, &c.—Chef d'œuvre of Gerard Dow.* - Page 314

## LETTER LXIV.

*University—Museo del Re—Venus, Tripod, &c.—Isiac table, &c.—General hypothesis—Industria.* - - 318

## LETTER LXV.

*Italian opera—Serious best in England—Buffo in Italy—Theatre de Carignano—Italians excell in humorous song—Dancing, vicious taste.* - - 322

## LETTER LXVI.

*Churches—Places, promenades, &c.—Po—Its poetical history not strictly intelligible—Trade of Turin—Reflection on commerce of Britain.* - - 325

## LETTER LXVII.

*Departure from Turin—Trial of pride—Description of route— Late arrival at Villa Nuova—Padrone defined—Village consequence—Italian accommodations—Counsel to travellers.* - Page 329

## LETTER LXVIII.

*Aleffandria—Tortona—Italian fupper—Nafidienus—Garlick.* - 333

## LETTER LXIX.

*Italian Signora—Charms of a red coat—No part of Italy uninterefting—Caftel San Giovanni—Cathedral—Contraft of temple and worfhippers—Reflection on fuperftition.*
336

## LETTER LXX.

*Piacenza—Piazza Publico—Statues, &c. Cathedral—Dial—Madonna—Altar of St. Anthony—Church of San Agoftino— Wealth of Auguftines—Route to Parma.*
340

## LETTER LXXI.

*Parma—Cathedral—Church San Giovanni —Academy—Chef d'œuvre of Correggio— Its character—Defect of the art—Wooden theatre—Amletto—Italian tragedy—Obstacles to travelling.* - Page 343

## LETTER LXXII.

*Æmilian way—Modena—Taffoni—Cathedral—Singular guide—Chapel San Geminiano—Religious creeping—Secchia— Groundless wars.* - 349

## LETTER LXXIII.

*Bologna—Madonna di San Luca—Portico —Virtues of the image—History of its transfer—Moral of the fable.* 354

## LETTER LXXIV.

*View from Saint Luke—Decollation of St. Paul—L'Instituto—Palace Sampieri— Abraham and Hagar—Christ and the Pharisee*

*Pharisee—St. Paul and St. Peter—Its effects described—Best object of pilgrimage.*
Page 360

LETTER LXXV.

*Churches—Giovanni in Monte, Cecilia of Raphael—Dominican, Massacre of Innocents, Tomb of Dominique, Death of Virgin —Agnes, Martyrdom—Petronius, Meridian, &c.—Musicals—Route from Bologna—Pietra Mala, &c.* - 366

LETTER LXXVI.

*Florence—Gallery—Liberality of Grand Duke —Tribune—Venus de Medicis—Progress of artist imagined—Arrotino—Different hypotheses—Conclusion.* - 369

LETTER LXXVII.

*Wrestlers—Dancing faun—Cabinets of minerals, portraits, &c.—Bust of Alexander —Different opinions—Bust of Brutus— Why unfinished—Conjecture.* - 373

LETTER LXXVIII.

*Streets—Entrance of city—Palace Pitti, Ceilings, Madonna—Ricardi, Evangelists, &c.—General character of place and people.* - - Page 378

LETTER LXXIX.

*Cathedral—San Lorenzo, tombs of Michael Angelo, Chapel di Medicis—Santa Annuntiata, bas reliefs, Madonna, &c.—Dominicans—San Spirito—Santa Croce, Monument of Michael Angelo, Galileo—Reflection on the last.* - - 381

LETTER LXXX.

*Reluctant departure—Peruggia—San Francesco—Resurrection—Raphael indebted to Pietro Perugino—Assumption of Virgin—Analogy of painting and music—Palace Della Penna—Salvator Rosa—General character of Peruggia.* - 385

# CONTENTS.

## LETTER LXXXI.

*Foligno — Village politics — Madonna of Raphael—Delicious route to Spoletto— Gothic aqueduct—Importance of Spoletto.*
Page 390

## LETTER LXXXII.

*Cascade of Terni—River Velino—History— Piano del Marmore—Track from village —Points of view—Mode of descent— Height—General effect.* - 394

## LETTER LXXXIII.

*Highest point of Appennine—Birth place of Tacitus—Route to Narni—Nera-bridge— Otriculum—Flexions of Tiber—Città Castellana—Decrease of natural beauty—Entrance of Rome.* - - 397

## VOLUME THE SECOND.

### LETTER LXXXIV.

*Delectable embarrassment—Roman capitol—Reflection—Museum—Confined space of capitol—Campo Vaccino—Vestiges of antient structures—Contrast of antient and modern Forum.* - Page 1

### LETTER LXXXV.

*Temple of Peace—Imperial Palace—Arch of Titus—Present state—Jewish delicacy—Sonnet of Baldi—Translation.* 6

### LETTER LXXXVI.

*Temple of Antoninus and Faustina—Peter's miracle—Amphitheatre of Vespasian—Extent, strength, and remains—Miraculous anecdote—Arch of Constantine—Magnificent view—Reflection.* - 10

## LETTER LXXXVII.

*Prelude to Christmas—Ceremonies of Nativity—Character of his Holiness—General effect—Papal power on the decline.* Page 17

## LETTER LXXXVIII.

*Multitude of antient monuments—Baths, Dioclesian, Titus—Circuses—Pantheon—Theatre of Marcellus—Aqueducts and baths best testimonies of antient grandeur.* 20

## LETTER LXXXIX.

*Roman burials—Sepulchre of Bibulus—Tombs—Vault of the Scipios—Capo di Bove—Pyramid of C. Cestius—Moles Adriani—Mausoleum of Augustus—Real character of that prince.* - 24

## LETTER XC.

*Fountain of Egeria—Temple of Minerva, Medica—Miscellaneous temples, &c.—Column of Trajan and Antoninus—Roots of bridges*

*bridges — Cleansing of Tiber — Colour — Diminished reputation.*  Page 28

### LETTER XCI.

*Effect of French revolution upon the Pope — Religious precautions — Devotion of city — Procession — Its effect — Religion and traffic of Rome — Rules for calculating the population.* - - 33

### LETTER XCII.

*Conduct of the Pope upon escape of Louis XVI. — Extract from brief — Spirit of the demand.* - - - 37

### LETTER XCIII.

*Barberini Palace — Four Evangelists, sick satyr, sleeping faun — Spada — Statue of Pompey — Ruspigliosi, Aurora — Villa Albani, Medicis, Borghese — Curtius — Slinging David — Fighting Gladiator — Effect upon the mind.* - - 42

## LETTER XCIV.

*St. Peter's—Street conducting to—Area before—Façade—Ornaments of interior—Ascent to Cross—Vatican—Museum—Additions of Pius—Superiority of antient to modern Rome—Apollo—Laocoon, &c.* Page 46

## LETTER XCV.

*St. John Lateran, relics, &c.—Baptistery—Triclinium, instrument of Pope's authority—Scala Santa—Climbing devotion—Miraculous image—Religious grants.* 51

## LETTER XCVI.

*Santa Maria Maggiore, ornaments, Culla Sacra, &c.—San Paolo, its magnificence, speaking crucifix, &c.—Memorable altars on Ostian way—Santa Maria della Croce—Catacombs of Sebastian, &c.—San Pietro in Carcere, Peter's prison—In Montorio, Transfiguration—In Vinculis, miraculous union of chains, &c.—Miscellaneous miracles.* - - 55

## LETTER XCVII.

*Coffee-houses—General subsistence—Fondness for theatricals—Serious opera—Description of comic—*Roman *more than* Italian.
Page 61

## LETTER XCVIII.

*Benediction of horses—Strictly regarded—Romance of scourge—Funeral processions—Efficacy of candles—Existence of miracles.* - - 64

## LETTER XCIX.

*Excursion to Tivoli—Solfaterra, &c.—Cardinal d'Este—Lucan Bridge—Sybils Temple—Villas of Mæcenas, Horace, &c.—Latter disputed—Temple of Tossa—Fall of Anio—Elegant points—Gardens of Este—Adrian's Villa—Village comedy.* 68

## LETTER C.

*Roman jurisprudence—Punishment of the chord—Stiletto—Roman temper vindictive—Anecdote*

CONTENTS.

—*Anecdote—Street aſſaſſination—Roman feelings illuſtrated.* - Page 74

LETTER CI.

*Amuſement of evening—Mildneſs of winter —Roman cloak—Sacred days—Pleaſures of higher and lower ranks—Celebrated emigrants—Academia—Engliſh and Roman dance—Defective education of ladies—Reaſon aſſigned—Morals—Darkneſs of ſtreets.* - 80

LETTER CII.

*Carnival—Promenade of maſks—Interchange of dreſſes between the ſexes—Races—Project of retiring—Ultimate effect of carnival on the mind.* - - 86

LETTER CIII.

*Change in travelling ſince Horace—Velletri —Humours of place—Tre-ponti—Improvement of Pontine Marſh by reigning Pope—Approach to Terracina—Characteriſtic of Terracina—Monte Circello—*

VOL. I. d *Route*

CONTENTS.

Route from Terracina—Beauties of Fondi—Sinuessa—Gaeta—Modern Capua—Reflection on its change.   -   Page 89

LETTER CIV.
Morals of Naples—Close of carnival—Masquerade—Singular mask—Language of natives corrupt—Great use of term mo—Objection to its study.   -   95

LETTER CV.
Bay—Prospect from hotel—Promenades—Beauties of country—Corruption of manners—Accountable in lower orders—Lazzaronis—Their character and use—Assassination—Royal decision.   -   99

LETTER CVI.
Profligacy of higher orders not easily accountable—Opera—Academia—Display of apartments—Music no object of meeting.   103

LETTER CVII.
Visit to Vesuvius—Ascent—View from base—Lava—Cicerone—Caccia del Re—Pain de Sucre

CONTENTS.

*Sucre—Difficult ascent to Crater—Its appearance—Descent to Hermitage—Inhabitants—Dangers reconciled—Power of habit.* - - Page 166

LETTER CVIII.

*Pompeia—Perfect street—Plan of houses and shops, &c.—Subterraneous vaults—Slow progress of clearing — Reasons—Anecdote of King of Naples.* 112

LETTER CIX.

*Changes upon coast—Pozzuolo, Temple of Serapis, &c.—Baiæ, Temple of Venus, Mercury, &c.—Bauli—Piscina Mirabile—Elysian Fields—Live only in description—Grotto del Cane—Phenomenon yet unaccounted for—Baths of Nero—Pisciarella—Soil generally impregnated with heat.*
118

LETTER CX.

*Musæum at Portici—Court-yard—Repository of antiques—Different cabinets—*
d 2 *Ruins*

CONTENTS.

Ruins of Herculaneum — Entrance of lava into houses, &c. — Insensibility of natives — Provision of nature — Uncertainty of soil — Climate, &c. - Page 124

LETTER CXI.

Farnese Bull — Hercules — Tomb of Virgil — Happy tradition — Cicerones — Their character — Case of conscience decided — Honorable credentials. - 129

LETTER CXII.

Eruption of Vesuvius — Ascent of the mountain — Appearance — Flow of Lava — Crater, &c. described — View upon mountain — Nature of the discharge — Departure. 133

LETTER CXIII.

Re-entrance of Rome — Difference of impression — Little attraction in Roman society — Excellence of Roman accent — Oaths — Reverse of Cardinal de Bernis — Royal aunts — Abbé Mauri — Decline of papal power — Political

—*Political precautions—Emigrants distinguished.* Page 138

### LETTER CXIV.

*Route to Sienna—Highest point of Appennine—Sienna, cathedral—Itinerant preacher—Religious policy.* - 144

### LETTER CXV.

*Contrast of Campagna and Tuscany—Attempt to account for evils of the former—Severe impost—Magnitude of farms, &c.—Means of reformation—Obstacle to experiment.* - - 148

### LETTER CXVI.

*Leghorn described—Political rumours—No effect on commercial cities—Contrast of objects at Leghorn and Rome—Corruption of Romish church—Probable mischiefs of its overthrow.* - - 152

CONTENTS.

## LETTER CXVII.
*Voyage to Genoa—Felucca described—Passengers—Their character—Subject of Lotto—French revolution—Sailor's judgment—Virtuoso's amendment.* - Page 156

## LETTER CXVIII.
*Carrara—Its marbles—Port of Lerici—Entertainment, &c.—Spezia—English navy—*CAPITANO *Cook—English prodigies—Passion for stones, best attachment—Successful* virtu*—Piedmontese education—Prince of Carignano and English prince.*
160

## LETTER CXIX.
*Coast from Lerici—Land route—Robbers—Francesconi—Port of Camucci—Genoese orator—French and English character contrasted—Virtuoso discouraged—Entrance into harbour of Genoa.* 166

## LETTER CXX.

*Approach to Genoa described—Structure of houses, &c.—Streets, &c.—Ponte di Carignano—Industry and public spirit.*

Page 170

## LETTER CXXI.

*Palaces—Francesco Balbi—Palazzo Rosso—Head of Holofernes—Ornaments of interior, &c.—Durazzo—Anecdote of possessor.* - - - 174

## LETTER CXXII.

*Albergo de Poveri—Its good administration and uses—Paupers Church, &c.—Procession of children—Extent of building—Hospital—Sala de Feriti—Church of Carignano—Statues, &c.—Sedan—Doge—General effect of city.* - 178

## LETTER CXXIII.

*Departure from Genoa—Sailor's devotion—Lerici—Rencontre—Company—Crisis—*

*Contrary wind—Land expedition—Arrangement.* - Page 184

LETTER CXXIV.

*Exchange of Sarzana and Leghorn—Carriages described—Order of procession—Day-light—German gutturals—Arrival.*
188

LETTER CXXV.

*Pisa—Cathedral, &c.—Torre Pendente—Mechanics no defence against* fear*—Baths, &c.—Route to Florence—Dress of females.* - - 191

LETTER CXXVI.

*Rigours of Quaresima,* &c.*—Second view—Ponte della Trinità—Police—Fair sex—Morals.* - - 195

LETTER CXXVII.

*Appennine—Pietra Mala—Aspect of ground, &c.—Cicerone—Loiano—Sanctity of Good Friday*

Friday—Advantages of mechanical devotion. - - Page 198

## LETTER CXXVIII.

*Functions at Bologna—Sepulture of Christ—Italian oratory—Musical solemnity—San Michaele in Bosco—Pleasures of its vicinity—Revisit to Sampieri—Painting reconsidered, &c.* - 203

## LETTER CXXIX.

*Easter-Eve—Pilgrims, processions, &c.—Easter-Day, Cardinal Legate, Gonfalonier, &c.—Wealth, &c. of city—Defeated by superstition—Papal yoke—Probability of its decline.* - - 207

## LETTER CXXX.

*Route to Ferrara—Altered aspect of town—State of superstition—Humours of Rovigo—Delicious village—Communicative landlord—Mountain of the seven churches—Relics of Saints—Terrace—Religious curiosities.* 212

CONTENTS.

LETTER CXXXI.
*Change of miracle—Defcent of Brenta— Banks of canals, &c.—Approach to Venice—Tour of city—Place of St. Mark— Columns, caffe's, &c.—Rendezvous—Cafinos, &c.—Church of St. Mark, relics, &c.*
Page 218

LETTER CXXXII.
*Church of San Zacharia, Angel and violin— San Giovanni e Paolo, Saviour and the Levite—St. Roche—Santa Maria della Salute—Scalzi—Frari—Precious depofit —Titian's tomb—Reflection.* - 223

LETTER CXXXIII.
*Palace Pifani, Family of Darius—San Georgio Maggiore, Marriage of Cana— Luxuries of the convent—Grand Canal— Ponte di Rialto—Prices of gondolas—Population—Paths and gondolas.* 228

## LETTER CXXXIV.

*Origin of Venice—Advancement—State of Defence—Person of Venetians—Dress—Masking—Amusements—Gondola described—Gondoliers—Political restraints.*

Page 232

## LETTER CXXXV.

*Police defective—Use of the knife—Skirmishes of Sclavonians—Licentiousness tolerated—Reason assigned—Departure from Venice—Village gratitude.* - 237

## LETTER CXXXVI.

*Padua — Sarcophagus, Antenor — Church, St. Antony—Santa Justina—Prato della Valle, Livy, &c.—University town—Vicenza—Olympic Theatre, interior described—Madonna del Monte Berrico—Inhabitants—Courtesy.* - 241

## LETTER CXXXVII.

*Route to Verona—Amphitheatre, interior described—Churches, &c.—Reflections on leaving Italy—Route to Trent—Bolzano, loquacious landlord—Route to Brixen—Change of country—Passing to Inspruck—Dress and manners of Tyrolians.* Page 246

## LETTER CXXXVIII.

*German tragedy—State of Inspruck, &c.—Change of costume—Review of route through Tyrol—Objects of superstition—Different in Italy and Tyrol—Catholic church-yard—Alliance of Catholic to poetic rite.* - - 253

## LETTER CXXXIX.

*Augsbourg, state of country, &c.—Gold and silver head-dress—Political events—Route to Lindau—Boden See—Circuit of lake—Rosbach, &c.—Constance—Emigrant rendezvous—Power of adversity.* 259

LETTER CXL.

*Sympathy—Emigrant sufferings—Surviving Politesse—Polonese princess—State of Constance—Environs, &c.—Route to Schaffhouse—Encounter.* - Page 264

LETTER CXLI.

*Equilibrium restored—Fall of Rhine—Level, rocks, &c.—Points of view—Imagination indulged—Minute beauties—Sole defect—Bridge of wood—Safety against speculation—Route to Zurich—Eglisau—Diverting landlord.* - 269

LETTER CXLII.

*Mind's caprice—Zurich described—Fair sex—Government severe—Effects of politics on Geneva—Only objects not changed.* 274

LETTER CXLIII.

*Villa at Lausanne—Its beauty—Change of possessor—Reasons—Bad effects of defeated opposition*

*opposition—New law respecting travellers—Its operation—Gibbon—Changes felt in society—Not felt by lower orders.*

Page 279

LETTER CXLIV.

*Amusements discover nature—Flask and valz—Sunday diversions—Jeu de l'Epingle—Questions et reponses—Ariosto quoted—Intellectual character of the Swiss—Pleasant repartee.* - - 283

LETTER CXLV.

*Rustic enthusiasm—Heloise—Forcible address to passions—Corrupt tendency—Merits considered—Character of writer—Epitaph on Rousseau—Id. on Voltaire.* 288

LETTER CXLVI.

*Polish princess—Political character—Vivacity, &c.—Bon-mot of Stanislaus—Forced marriage—Italian law—Anecdote—Ariosto wrote from other models—English manners contrasted.* - - - 292

## LETTER CXLVII.

*Swiss mourning for massacre of 10th of August—New plans of travel—Project to Egypt defeated—Courteous adieu of emigrants—Advantage of difficulties.*

Page 297

## LETTER CXLVIII.

*Second tour to Glaciers—Review on route—Jura, Geneva, &c.—Track to Bonneville, environs, &c.—Picturesque approach to Cluse—Valley of Maglan—Cascade—New hotel at Salenche—Cascade of Chede, lake, &c. — Boissons — Montainvert—Guides, Cachat—His atchievements—Saussure, &c.—Unsuccessful expedition to Mont Blanc—Aiguille de Dru—Source of Arveron changed—Arrival at Geneva—Prospect of change of scene.* - 302

## LETTER CXLIX.

*Excursion to Lyons—Addition of company—Patriotic adieu—French boundary—Colonges*

*longes—Village tactics—National troops—Cerdon—Expensive privilege—Montluel—Female politician—Entrance of Lyons—Place Bellecourt—Hotel,* &c.   Page 313

## LETTER CL.
*Table a' Hôte—Discussion—City described—Low population—Indignities of statue of Louis XIV.—Gala procession.*   318

## LETTER CLI.
*Burning of royal portraits, and books,* &c. *—Order of proceeding—Setting fire to pile—Ashes of Louis XIV.—Temper of populace—Dialogue—Farther introduction—Bourgeois guard—Finale of fête.*   323

## LETTER CLII.
*Picture inverted—Prediction—Theatre—Paysan Magistrat—Marseillois march—Symptoms of disorder—Confirmation—Insurrection—Massacre—First victim—Consequences—Procession of mob—New victims —Disco-*

very — Calm — Morning deliberation — Passports—Retreat projected. Page 328

## LETTER CLIII.

Plan of mob—Unfortunate officer—Origin of mob—Conduct of Municipality—Affiches—Counter advertisements—Orderly defence—Carriage engaged—Manners brutalized—Escape anticipated. 336

## LETTER CLIV.

Return to Geneva—Second address of Mayor—Issue from Lyons—Montleuil—Fugitive priests—Nantua—Patriotic volunteers—Guard—Priests undisguisable—Rencontre—English character respected—Arrival—Reflection upon events, &c. 342

## LETTER CLV.

Tour into Germany projected—Attack upon Savoy rumoured—Effect upon Geneva—Arrival at Berne—Deserter—Generous patriot—Embarras—Dulness of Berne. 349

## LETTER CLVI.

*Military festivities—Swiss officers—Precis Historique—Aaraw—Broug—Dilemma.*

Page 354

## LETTER CLVII.

*Route from Broug—Postilion vanquished—Postilion victor—Cascade of Schaffhause reviewed—Table d'Hôte—Swiss politics—Religious œconomy.* - 359

## LETTER CLVIII.

*Swiss towns, their character—German language.—Little analogy with other languages—Plan of tour—Decision—French travellers—Swiss phlegm—English impatience.* - 365

## LETTER CLIX.

*Departure from Schaffhause—German waggon—Company—German character—Accident—Embarrassment.* 370

## LETTER CLX.

*Simile—Embarrassment renewed—Route continued — Post-house — Eclaircissement — Dinner—Journey resumed.* Page 375

## LETTER CLXI.

*Society—Further difficulties in German language—Riedlingen—Pleasant discovery—Journey to Ulm continued—Ulm described, &c.* - - - 381

## LETTER CLXII.

*Embarking for Vienna—Frenchmen obnoxious—Passengers, &c.—Landing—French character in youth and age—Inquisitiveness—Table d'Hôte when agreeable.* 387

## LETTER CLXIII.

*Departure from Gunsburg—Mode of passing the day—Character of passengers—Basle merchant—Hungarian teacher—Madame Vogel—Darmstadt lieutenant—Swiss—Issue from barge.* - 392

## CONTENTS.

### LETTER CLXIV.

*Battle of Blenheim—Scene depicted—Marquisate of Baden—Donavert—Neuberg—Bavarian troops—Adventure—Passing under bridge.* - - Page 397

### LETTER CLXV.

*Forcible current—Ingolstadt—Errors in German character corrected—Diversions of evening—Arrangement of day's voyage—Amusements.* - - 402

### LETTER CLXVI.

*Majestic course of Danube—Military sensibility—Ratisbon—Jealousy of French—Reflection—Comedy of dogs—Departure.* 408

### LETTER CLXVII.

*Village misery—Delicate arrangement—Viltzhofen—Apology for trivial details—Chance of greater adventures.* - 413

### LETTER CLXVIII.

*View of Passau—Nature undescribable——Dresses of females—Scrutiny—Engelhartzel—Austrian officer—Inscription.* 417

## LETTER CLXIX.

*Course to Lintz—Lintz—Interesting scenes—
Strudels — Enchanting picture — Pilgrimage of Morbach — Religious salute —
Crems—Vienna.* - Page 422

## LETTER CLXX.

*Entrance upon Vienna*—Caernerthore *theatre described*—Wiedner *theatre, its species of amusement—Remark on German serious song—Theatre in Josephstadt.* 428

## LETTER CLXXI.

*The Emperor described — Hetz, or combat of wild beasts—Departure of the Hessian.*
433

## LETTER CLXXII.

*Change of residence—German hauteur exhibited in language-masters—Manner of living at Vienna—Diverting embarrassment.* - - - 438

## LETTER CLXXIII.

*Knowledge of life how obtained—Italians at Vienna—Independence maintained by a reformation in dress—By avoiding three sorts of characters—Adventurers, good sort of people, Englishmen—Rule illustrated.* - - Page 444

## LETTER CLXXIV.

*Contrast of Sunday in England and in Vienna —Summer rendezvous—Prater—Augarten—Dancing—Humours of a Tanzsaal described.* - - 450

## LETTER CLXXV.

*Streets of Vienna—Squares—Platz Graben —Platz of the Hof—Reception of the Emperor and Empress at the Opera—General freedom of manners in this city.* 457

## LETTER CLXXVI.

*Pleasure of unobserved speculation—Dining-houses, &c. described—Music—Debate—Political orator.* - - 463

## LETTER CLXXVII.

*Situation of Vienna—Extent—Promenades—
Climate—Use of ofens—State of streets—
Houses—Lights—Hackney coaches—Order of city—Police of Berne reprobated.*
Page 469

## LETTER CLXXVIII.

*Singular rencontre—Discovery of Madame
V———Reflection upon the character of
the Hessian,* - - 475

## LETTER CLXXIX.

*Public buildings—Court—University—Academy—Lombard—Liberal institutions—
Churches—Cathedral—St. Peter's—Hof,
or Court Church—Tomb of Mareschal
Laudohn—Reflections upon sepulchral trophies.* - - 479

## LETTER CLXXX.

*Church of the Reformed—Curious epitaph—
Intention of departure—Custom of* Angedencken—*Proposed route.* - 484

CONTENTS.

### LETTER CLXXXI.

*Pride of office—Entrance upon Bohemia—Particulars respecting the country—Bohemian beauty—Grievances of Wagen-travelling.* - - Page 488

### LETTER CLXXXII.

*Travelling philosophy, what—Vexatious début—Prague described—Reflections on its history—Alliance of cruelty and religion.*
492

### LETTER CLXXXIII.

*Character of the inhabitants—French politics—Language of Bohemia—Union with Prussian in scheme of travel.* 495

### LETTER CLXXXIV.

*Departure from Prague—Carriage described—Price of travelling—Dangers of the night—Arrival at Peterswalda.* 498

### LETTER CLXXXV.

*Village post-house—Route to Dresden—Dresden described—Gallery—Theatre—Appearance*

CONTENTS. lxxiii

*pearance of the Elector at the theatre compared with that of the Emperor — Fair sex—Political landlord.* Page 504

LETTER CLXXXVI.

*Route to Leipsig—Leipsig described—Population—University—Church—Promenade —Character of the inhabitants.* 509

LETTER CLXXXVII.

*Free discussion at Leipsig—Departure for Berlin—Adventure—Injury repaired— Arrival at Potzdam.* - 512

LETTER CLXXXVIII.

*Advance of posting progressive—Visit to Sans-Souci—Parade at Potzdam—Prussian sensibility.* - - 517

LETTER CLXXXIX.

*Journalière—The search—Berlin described —Houses contrasted with the inhabitants —Opera, &c.—Absence of the King, its effect—Probable change in system.* 522

## LETTER CXC.

*Landlord, &c.—Attendants on stranger—Living costly—Mode of life amongst the natives—Caff's—School of speculation.*

Page 526

## LETTER CXCI.

*Society—Language—Accent of Berlin and Vienna contrasted—Eulogium on the language—Libraries—Manners of people—Humours of a dance—English rule of fashion—Pipes—Question of trade.* 530

## LETTER CXCII.

*Severity of climate—Schloss—Prussian Count—Assimilation of German and English character—Study of government neglected.*

536

## LETTER CXCIII.

*Diversions—Theatre—Rotunda—Thiiregarten—Charlottenburg—Fashionable ball—Splendor—Project of departure—Morals of city—German acuteness.* - 539

## LETTER CXCIV.

*Courage defined—Retreat from Berlin accounted for—Entrance of Poſt-wagen—Wagen deſcribed—Inconveniences of route—Conductors—Arrival at Hamburg—Table d'Hôte.* - Page 543

## LETTER CXCV.

*Society defined—Members of Table d'Hôte deſcribed—Miniſter—Heſſian officer—Lubecker—Hamburg officer—Violent Antigallicaniſm of Heſſian—Baron Trenck—Anecdotes of Joſeph II. and laſt Frederic—Heſſian Royaliſm.* - 548

## LETTER CXCVI.

*Pleaſures of a commercial town—Storms—Route projected—Poſition, &c. of city—Mode of life—Military—Burleſque diſtich—Fête of Chriſtmas—Anxiety for French and Engliſh intelligence.* 554

## LETTER CXCVII.

*Sequel of adventures—Travelling flock—Paſſage of Elbe—Haarburg—Waggon, &c.*

&c.—*Luxuries of Bremen—Journey resumed—Rencontre—English pilot—The contract.* - - Page 559

## LETTER CXCVIII.

*Route to Leer—Pilot's harangue—Scrutiny—Varieties on way to Neueskans—Gala—Panic in Friesland—Passage to Gröningen—Country described—Costume—Landlord and pilot—Strobusch—Lemmer—Passage of Zuÿder See—Residue of stock.*
564

## LETTER CXCIX.

*Sensations on prospect of port—Calculations—Dialogue—Compact—Result—Political aspect of country—Route to Rotterdam—Event at entrance—Finances strengthened—Adventures on route to Helvoet—Embarkation—View of Harwich—Apostrophe of emigrant—Landing—Exit pilot—Arrival at metropolis—Change of costume—Final reflection.* - - 570

# LETTER I.

Bruſſels, April 21, 1791.

MY engagement with you on leaving England ſtands full in my recollection. The delay, be aſſured, has not ariſen from any change of inclination or purpoſe, but ſolely from circumſtances of accidental embarraſſment. The channel is now opened, and you ſhall have no reaſon to charge me with a want of punctuality.

That your expectations may not however be unreaſonably elevated, I will juſt ſtate the ſort of entertainment I undertake to furniſh. The track of Europe, which we are to purſue, is already explored: all that could create wonder or afford

## LETTER I.

afford delight, has been so often and so fully displayed in the volumes of ancient and modern travel, that curiosity seems nearly exhausted. What in ages past were marvels, are now *bagatelles;* and if astonishment yet remains to be excited, Mandeville and Munchausen have written in vain.

I undertake not to unlock the cabinets of princes, or to disentangle the intrigues of courts: transient observation must ill succeed in developing the mysteries of political systems. Mine will neither be the voyage of the connoisseur, nor the journal of the naturalist: I can neither pretend to throw light upon the schools of painting, nor the science of physics. If I climb the mountain, it will not be to gauge the atmosphere, to analise the soil, or to class the pebbles: if I range among the vallies, it will not be to gather the lilies, or catch the butterflies. But to human nature in all her varieties, to the

## LETTER I.

manners of men and the temper of the times, to the habits of life and the state of opinions, my attention will be directed; and my observations will be delivered, with only so much of order or ornament as may happen to suggest itself at the moment of impression.

Apprized therefore of my plan, you will not, if I depart from the strict line of gravity or criticism, censure me as volatile, nor condemn me as superficial. I appeal from your judgment, to your candour; from the critic, to the friend: and if, after all, the merit of *originality* be wholly wanting; you may at least derive a sort of pleasure from that *variety*, under which the most exhausted subjects rarely want success. Fashions the most obsolete are daily advanced by some new colourings; and an old play seldom wants attractions, when revived with new scenes and dresses.

# LETTER II.

THERE is something very peculiar in the first sensations of a man who finds himself transferred to a foreign clime, whose aspect exhibits a groupe of novel images. This sensation is perhaps felt with additional force by the inhabitant of an island who has been accustomed to regard himself as " penitus toto divisus orbe." The country he leaves, seems explored in every recess, though he may not have traversed half its provinces: all before him forms a mighty vista, which he contemplates with eager anxiety.

I confess the first sight of the French coast operated upon me like enchantment. With it seemed associated all the images which bore relation to the history of this wide extended empire—the magnificence of its kings, and the lustre of its heroes; its celebrity

celebrity in arts, in letters, and in arms. When I considered that this gallant nation, once the admiration and the dread of Europe, was become the seat of internal distraction and the theatre of political experiment, I sighed over the recollection of its departed grandeur. But when I traced with deeper reflection the foundation of these divisions, and the objects of this experiment—when I viewed in impartial retrospect, the ambition and perfidy which so remarkably characterized the government of that nation; how incompatible its wars with the principles of reason or humanity, how formidable a rival it had ever proved to the power, how determined an enemy to the repose, of Britain—when I reflected how the cabals of this court had perpetuated dissension in the kingdoms of Europe, to gratify the passions and aggrandize the power of its princes; and in how many instances the blood of nations had been sacrificed to the caprice of a mistress,

## LETTER II.

a miſtreſs, or the intrigues of a confeſſor, I could not but exult in the changes effected by the united energies of philoſophy and patriotiſm.

The diſorders which accompany every revolution of political moment, are the indiſpenſable terms upon which ſuch felicity is to be obtained; torrents of blood have been deemed not wantonly ſpent, to procure a leſs good: and I could not but anticipate the coming æra, when the laſt touches ſhall be put to a revolution, which has aſtoniſhed, and may inſtruct mankind: —when out of the ruins of tyranny and ſervitude, ſhall ariſe a government, flouriſhing in all the luſtre of reaſonable authority and juſt ſubordination; a government whoſe *internal* policy ſhall exhibit a king ruling by law, and a people obeying by choice; whoſe *external* policy ſhall diſplay the happy effects of an unambitious and equitable ſyſtem of conduct, in the permanent tranquillity of Europe.

The

## LETTER II.

The ancient prejudices of this nation acknowledged no heroism but that of the sword, and applauded no atchievements but those of conquest. It was reserved for a later æra, and a more enlightened legislature, to establish the dominion of reason on the ruins of prejudice; to annex to the life of each individual, an importance hitherto unfelt; to convert the laurels of war into civic wreaths; and decree those triumphs to the defenders of liberty, which had been prescriptively appropriated to the desolators of their country, and the destroyers of mankind.

## LETTER III.

We landed at Ostend, and took the route by Ghent to Brussels. This gave us an opportunity of seeing a town, which has occupied an important place in the history of Europe. Ghent, or Gand, possessed in ancient times a population far superior to its present numbers; and was of such extent as to occasion a humorous boast of Charles V., that he could put all Paris in his glove, " dans son Gand." This town, the capital of Austrian Flanders, was long the seat of commerce in time of peace, and the bulwark of defence in time of war; no place has acquired more military fame, nor been witness to more heroic acts.

The early records of its history report the spirit and intrepidity of the Gantois.

## LETTER III.

The pacification of Ghent forms a great epoch in their hiftory. This was formed in 1576, by a union of the eſtates for the eſtabliſhment of their religious and civil privileges, and ratified by Philip II. Famed for revolt and fedition of old, it became again the feat of tumult in 1787. Ghent had till that moment taken no decided part, but the entrance of the Brabanters in military force, joined to the infolence of the Auſtrian foldiery, drew the citizens to the party of the infurgents, and the Auſtrian army quitted the place with difgrace. If we may credit the accounts given of this defeat, it redounds infinitely to the difcredit of the Auſtrians, who, to the amount of feveral thouſand difciplined troops, abandoned the town, citadel, and magazine, to the depredations of three or four hundred vagabonds, " flying," as a writer expreſſes it, " devant quelques malheureux de la po-" pulace, fans chefs, fans armes, and fans " culottes."

The

## LETTER III.

The issue of these revolutional tumults had cast a gloom over the place. It wore the aspect of war, though in a state of actual tranquillity. The majority of its inhabitants seem composed of soldiers and ecclesiastics; and promenades, streets, and avenues were thronged with hussars, priests, and beggars.

The churches are the grand ornament of Ghent, as of every country under the influence of superstition. These sacred edifices are adorned with all that art and riches can contribute to constitute splendour; but what renders them most the object of a traveller's attention is, that they are the grand repositories of the chefs d'œuvres of the Flemish school.

The cathedral of St. Gedule is a magnificent building, and crowded with paintings of the Flemish masters. Though it was passion week, and the priests were constantly upon duty, the altars were not as usual thronged with devotees. The population of a Catholic town may be easily inferred

## LETTER III.

inferred from the aspect of its churches at this sacred season. Some few miserable wretches only were to be found engaged in their devotions, and bowing round the deserted shrines. I shall not enter into a detail of the works of the admirable artists which embellish this place, nor attempt to describe the sensations created by them. I suffered my sensibilities to be spontaneously excited, and probably often felt emotions at variance with academical law. Criticism may decree what *ought* to please; but in painting, as in poetry, an appeal will not fail to be made from the understanding to the heart. Shakespeare has charmed, not only *without*, but even *against* rule: and yet the English nation would rather sacrifice the laws that control, and the critics that censure, than yield to oblivion and obscurity one drama of the immortal bard.

A town in the circumstances of Ghent, could not long find amusement for a traveller; the ferocious aspect of the military, whose

## LETTER III.

whofe numbers and difcipline are fcarcely fufficient to retain in fubjection the turbulent malcontents, added to the gloom of evacuated houfes and a deferted theatre, induced us to quit Ghent on the following day, and purfue our route to Bruffels. I could not leave the town without lamenting the evils which have defaced and depopulated a place, that once poffeffed fuch ftrength, fplendour, and opulence. The miferies of unfuccefsful revolt are here accumulated upon the head of the laborious and peaceful citizen.

Political grievances when extended to an enormous height demand political reform; and this can, in certain cafes, only be effected by popular oppofition. That there exifted circumftances fufficiently aggravating, and fufficiently oppreffive, to warrant the remonftrances preferred by the Brabanters, cannot be difputed. The cabals of his minifters and agents, rather than the difpofition of the Emperor, prevented the
equitable

equitable arrangements at firſt required; till the ſpirits of either party became heated, and ineffectual remonſtrance was ſucceeded by outrageous revolt. The knavery and miſconduct of thoſe who headed the refractory Belgians, were the cauſes of thoſe diſtreſſes and diſtractions which afterwards attended them.

The conceſſions of Leopold are a demonſtrative proof of the injuſtice of Joſeph. Had Belgiojaſo poſſeſſed the conciliating talents of Merci d'Argenteau, the ſword probably had never been drawn; and had there been prudence and patriotiſm in the leaders of the revolt, had the poſts of Vandernoot and Van Eupen been ſupplied by a Mirabeau and a Fayette, the ſword had not been ſheathed till Belgic independence had been eſtabliſhed.

I have ever commiſerated the lot of a country, which by conqueſt or ceſſion has become the appendage of a great empire. An arbitrary monarch may poſſeſs in ſome happy moments the feelings of a man, and all that lies within the compafs of his own adminiftration comes more or lefs under his own infpection; but a government by agent, fuffragan, or viceroy, is furely a government moft formidable to the liberties of a people. How are they to prefs through that phalanx of minifters, penfioners, and courtiers, which fill up all the avenues of appeal? The diftance from the fountain of authority extinguifhes hope of redrefs, and urges them to remedies the moft violent and defperate.

# LETTER IV.

WE find Bruffels invefted with the fame military terrors, and deformed by the fame melancholy rites, as Ghent. That part of the town in which the people of fafhion refide, is of modern date; the houfes are built of ftone, the apartments fpacious, and the general afpect of the place is magnificent. The gloomy ceremonies of the holy week have thrown a veil over the ufual gaieties of this capital, and interrupt for the prefent the tide of amufement. Even active occupation is in great part fufpended; and the church has fupplanted the theatre, the ball-room, and the exchange. The avenues of the cathedral are crowded from morning to night. All ranks and conditions feem unanimous in the celebration of the facred feafon.

The

The carnival, which I understand was uncommonly brilliant, has left behind it the memory of some irregularities; but if the most assiduous and uninterrupted attendance upon the ceremonies of the church can avail, there will not remain a folly to blush for, or a crime to repent of. It is really amusing to see the multitudes that throng around the sacred porticoes, and the ardour of the devotional penance which they discover. Not content with worshipping at one shrine, and making interest with one saint, they fly from altar to altar, seek an interest in every sacrifice, and mingle their devotions with the incense of every order. In England, it is deemed unnecessary for the great to interfere in the services of religion; fashion and convenience are there paramount to reason and duty; but here the greatest blend with the meanest in all the services which are called religious, however jealous of rank and superiority in civil and social life.

A card-

## LETTER IV.

A card-party was formed on Friday evening, being the Vendredi Saint, the singular object of which induces me to mention it. It was held at the apartments of the Comtesse de Choiseul, and attended by most of the fashionable people. Agreeably to the law of the assembly, the gains of the evening were to be disposed of, at the discretion of the lady of the house, in purposes of charity. This is a custom of ancient establishment.

An assembly of this nature, where pleasure and religion are combined, must give birth to many singular impressions. No day in the calendar can wear a more gloomy face, or excite more devotional sentiments in the breast of a catholic, than the day of the crucifixion. Every means are employed to excite superstitious horror, and recal to the mind the memory of that darkness which enveloped the face of the earth. All that breathes the air of dissipation must be entirely banished, and amusement so qualified by motive, and so chastised by austerity, as to receive the serious cast of religious exercise. To-morrow is, I understand, the concluding day of this severe penance: consolation will then be administered to the consciences of the devotees, who will emerge, fully acquitted of all past guilt, and at liberty to commence a fresh account. The streets, parade, and promenades will resume their brilliancy: at present, they exhibit a striking picture of spiritual indolence. Superstition has long since consecrated this week to purposes which are deemed incompatible with secular occupation. The days being too sacred for labour, and too long for devotion, a great part of time is yawned away in listless *ennui*.

The consecration of days\* is a custom of barbarous origin; and the pious enthusiasm of the first christians gave it the sanction of their own observance. The church of Eng-

---

\* This is only to be understood in reference to days consecrated to *particular persons*.

land,

land, which has had the merit of restoring to society the days and weeks hallowed by bigotry, still retains some few, which she refuses to secularize, and which serve, like the ancient hangings in a modernized mansion, to mark the date of the edifice, and perpetuate the taste of those who undertook its reform. It is plain, the contract between priest and people in those regions of superstition, is very much in favour of the former, though equally to the satisfaction of each. The latter surrender without reluctance the fruits of their labour to the use of the former, who only engage for an undefined retribution—a bright reversion in the sky—at some future and distant period.

# LETTER V.

Bruffels, April 24, 1791.

I AM juft returned from affifting at a ceremony, in which I appeared to myfelf to make no very refpectable figure. A proclamation, pofted in a public fpot near the Hotel de Ville, announced the return of a celebrity, in which all pious catholics take great intereft, and from which, agreeably to the tenor of the advertifement, every devout chriftian might derive great advantage. It was the celebration of an event moft important to the caufe of religion, in the prefervation of the Image of the Virgin Mary, from the anti-catholic zeal of the reformers of Scotland. The attachment of her friends induced them to hazard much for her fafety. They fled beyond fea with her, and after a thoufand thousand miracles, and experiencing numerous vicissitudes, " per varios fluctus et " tot discrimina rerum," they auspiciously reached Brussels. Many honours were paid her upon her arrival on the Continent, and particularly at the ceremony of her solemn reception among the Augustine monks. Successive popes concurred in granting plenary pardons to all who would commemorate the anniversary of her happy deliverance. The Image was placed in the centre of the church, and illuminated with numberless tapers. High mass was sung, to which succeeded a variety of religious *divertisements*, intended to represent the *hair-breadth escapes* the Virgin had experienced, and the efficacy which this wonderful Image still possessed. All seemed eager to croud around her, and some never quitted her feet. A splendid procession concluded the service: and the holy fathers chaunted their lays, preceded by all kinds of mysterious insignia, from their own to the church of St. Gedule.

## LETTER V.

As I was not so deeply interested in the ceremonies as the rest of the congregation, I had more leisure to comment on the drama. The devotion of the people was unquestionably sincere. They bowed, and prostrated themselves, with an energy and fervour, which indicated the most unsuspicious faith in her more than magnetical virtue. I observed several walking round the shrine, and bowing with the utmost inconvenience to themselves, lest they should accidentally turn their backs upon her. As I had disposed myself in the middle of the aisle, the procession passed me, and gave me an opportunity of admiring the happy influence of a religious life upon these holy fathers, who seemed to have profited much from the residence of the Virgin among them. Countenances more expressive of pleasure and festivity could not be found, even in the paradise of Mahomet. It was not a little surprising to see so great a multitude assisting at those services, considering the recent

recent penance performed in the holy week.

It should seem that the people of Brussels must be desperate sinners, or exemplary saints. The quantum of holiness, including all the beads that are counted, and the *Ave-Marias* that are said, bears certainly, if any allowance be made for human frailty, more than a just proportion to the ordinary *quantum* of sin. But here mankind are persuaded that none of those pious duties will be lost. When sufficient has been done to cancel their own crimes, all supernumerary acts become a sort of clear gain, which rests entirely at their own disposal. The canons of the church allow the transfer of this, with the same ease as any other species of alienable property. If a man die intestate, it naturally reverts to the church, and becomes a part of the ecclesiastical fund. This commerce, in past ages so productive to the proprietors, has suffered considerably in its revenues. A great part of Europe, however, continues pioufly attached to the old traffic, and multitudes yet facrifice folid poffeffions for this imaginary property; convinced, it fhould feem, that the exchange is decidedly in their favour.

## LETTER VI.

Bruffels, April 27, 1791.

THE gloom is diffipated, the curtain is drawn up, and the gay orgies of pleafure fucceed to the melancholy folemnities of penance. The theatre is opened, the artificers refume their occupations, and the circles of the fafhionable world their amufements. If I read aright the countenances of thofe who are emerged from religious aufterity to pleafurable relaxation, they are not a little gratified by the change. The torrent of feftivity, which is now opened,

appears

## LETTER VI.

appears to infinuate, that religious aufterity has had its effect; that its devout fubjects have amply cancelled all paft guilt, and made, as it were, Heaven their creditor for future fins.

The theatre is under very bad management. The edifice itfelf is fufficiently large and commodious, but the fcenery and the performers are much below mediocrity; though the enormous price paid for the boxes, which are engaged by particular perfons, brings in a revenue fully adequate to its fupport. The fociety here is numerous and brilliant; regular evenings are appropriated to thofe ladies who lead the *ton*.

In addition to thofe which are eftablifhed, and of ordinary recurrence, concerts and dances are occafionally given. An introduction once effected, and the regular ceremonies of etiquette performed, the whole field of amufement is opened, and wherever you hear mention of feftivities, you are at liberty to participate them. The

## LETTER VI.

Comteſſe de Choiſeul is at the head of theſe parties; at a very advanced period of life, ſhe poſſeſſes ſound health and hilarity of ſpirits. The duties and the pleaſures of life occupy the whole of her attention, and her time is divided between amuſement and devotion. The dignity of her age and ſtation, and the courteouſneſs of her manners, give her the higheſt importance in the faſhionable aſſemblies.

The modern champion of chivalry has expreſſed in terms of brilliant lamentation, his ſorrow for the extinction of the ancient gallantry of France. But this I aſſure you, that, however expatriated, and rooted from its native ſoil, gallantry flouriſhes here with increaſing vigour: and in no part of Europe, perhaps, is the empire of the fair ſex ſo firmly eſtabliſhed. All who would move in the ſphere of polite life, muſt paſs the ordeal of female ſcrutiny.

The " Ladies club," is by far the moſt brilliant ſociety here, and this club diſpoſes

of

of the fates of every stranger, who solicits a part in the amusements of the place. The ladies who compose it have their regular times of meeting, and of settling business. The stranger who sues for initiation must in due form be proposed; and, under the direction of the lady president, the club proceeds to a ballot. Nor is this always an ineffective form.

The club gave a ball lately at the hotel " Prince de Galles." Each female member has the privilege of introducing a gentleman for the evening, and it was in virtue of this privilege that I obtained admittance. The company were numerous, and exhibited a splendid show of beauty and rank. The greater part was formed by the fugitive noblesse of France. Here were rallied the scattered members of the dis-embodied phalanx; and, in defiance of decrees and spoliations, gave brilliancy and hilarity to the assembly.

# LETTER VII.

Bruffels, May 1, 1791.

POLITENESS is a term with all mankind of familiar and continual ufe; all fuppofe they underftand it; and to requeft a definition, would be to offer an affront. I had an opportunity a few evenings paft, of feeing it exemplified, at leaft in a manner very entertaining, by the Marquis de ———, who has lately purchafed an eftate in the vicinity of Bruffels, upon the excellence of which, he was enlarging to fome Englifh ladies—the convenience of his houfe, and the elegance of his gardens, in which he had exactly copied the Engiifh ftile. He had ftored his cellars with excellent wine, and nothing was wanting to his felicity, but the honour of their opinion upon the tafte and execution

execution of the whole. The ladies gave him to underſtand, that his deſcription had ſo faſcinated them, that they would certainly not loſe ſo fair an opportunity of being amuſed.

This was what the Marquis neither intended nor expected, yet the embarraſſment cauſed no viſible interruption of his converſation. Nothing could indeed charm him more than the honour the ladies intended him, but he muſt not at the ſame time neglect to inform them that his houſe had ſuffered conſiderably in the late tumults—his ground had been ravaged—his plantations deſtroyed—his cellars robbed—and, in a word, ſuch diſorders committed, that the preſent ſituation of his villa would not recompenſe the ladies for the trouble they would be at in viſiting him; and, concluding with a turn of pleaſantry and a handſome bow, left the room with an air " *par* " *faitement bien.*"

I was

I was forcibly ſtruck by the *addreſſe* with which the Marquis extricated himſelf from this delicate diſtreſs, without any ſymptom of alarm, or violation of gallantry. His advance and retreat were equally finiſhed in their kind; and we were compelled to acknowledge, that no man could make an offer with more politeneſs, than a Frenchman; and no man could relieve himſelf from the pain of fulfilling it, with a better grace.

## LETTER VIII.

Bruſſels, April 29, 1791.

THERE is a philoſophy which can triumph over the accidents of life, which can ſmile in the face of the moſt calamitous events, and blunt the ſhafts of the moſt adverſe fortune. It is the philoſophy of the heart, and has no connection with the fabricated ſyſtems of the ſchools. No nation upon earth exempliſy ſo ſtrongly the truth

truth of this maxim, nor give such evidence of the operation of its principle, as the French. Expelled a country which gave them birth—divested of all that gave them importance—stript of their hereditary honours and patrimonial fortunes, they retain what gold or titles could never give, and what no decree can take away, " *la* " *gaieté de cœur.*" Brussels, at this moment, proves an asylum to almost all the expatriated noblesse of France. Every hour announces some new arrival, and hotels and promenades are thronged to excess.

The accumulated evils which pursue these splendid fugitives, the fatal dislodgment they have experienced from the seats which their ancestors had occupied for ages, and which the sanction of government, the prescription of time, and the temper of their vassals, seemed to augur eternal, would be sufficient to depress a people less insensible of calamity. The morning is however occupied in councils, the evening in cards; the presfing exigencies of bufinefs have not weakened in them the thirft of pleafure; though plots, affaffinations, and all the horrid machinations of defeated ariftocracy fill the hours of cabal, they find no place in the circles of fociety. Counter revolutions fall before " *La bagatelle.*" No plots are agitated beyond intrigue; and no affaffinations meditated but of time and fpleen.

No man who mixes with the evening parties would imagine that the countenances he beholds on thofe occafions, are worn by men who are bankrupts in fortune and in title. The charms of fong, the movements of the dance, and the evolutions of Faro equally intereft the whole: the fame gefture, the fame volubility, the fame enchanting vivacity animate the affemblies, that prevailed in days of better fortune.

The moft vigilant obferver would not difcover a moment in which the memory of annihilated grandeur induces a tranfient gloom. If reports tranfpire of any new patriotic

patriotic ravages, an involuntary figh efcapes, which is inftantly replaced by returning gaiety; and neither air nor feature are fuffered to betray the moft diftant fymptoms of dejection or defpair. An Englifhman in fimilar circumftances would fly for refuge to folitude, perhaps to fuicide.

The character of a Frenchman is to be found in his language. A *moderate* man can fcarcely fatisfy himfelf with the terms fuited to the temper of his mind. All is exaggerated and exceffive. If you attempt to be natural, you will yet be figurative; and can fcarcely make yourfelf comprehended, without a metaphor.

Such is the tone of this language, that praife and blame, pleafure and pain, joy and forrow, admit of no mediums. *Charmant* and *fuperbe* is the leaft you can fay of what is recommended to your approbation: if you fay lefs than *vilaine* of what you diflike, you will be deemed phlegmatic;—if you are pleafed, you muft be *ravi*;—if you are vexed,

vexed, you muſt be *deſolé*;—if you are not in extacies, you muſt be *au deſeſpoir*. All theſe you may heighten by a thouſand arts, and you will do the language very little juſtice without theſe augmentatives. If *charmant* is not ſufficient, repeat it, and you will talk more like a Frenchman. There are a million little prefixes which you may employ to great advantage, *très*, *fort*, *infiniment*, &c. which ſerve to colour your ſenſations, and raiſe your expreſſions as far beyond nature as imagination extends.

The genius of the people accords exactly with their language. The moſt lively ſorrow or rapturous joy is excited by the moſt trivial incident: but lively ſenſations, like vivid colours, are not made for permanence. Thus the man endued with this temper of mind, will triumph over all the efforts of malice or misfortune. He is poſſeſſed of reſources, which will illumine the darkeſt ſcenes of miſery. He will combat with undiminiſhed confidence, though thouſands fall; and continue to hope, where all others would deſpair.

# LETTER IX.

Bruffels, April 30, 1791.

NATIONAL varieties form the grand fource of entertainment to a traveller: nor is it of confequence to him, whether the manners and cuftoms of the people he vifits, claim any manifeft fuperiority over thofe of his own country; it is fufficient for the purpofes of his curiofity that they *differ*. Novelty is the charm which commends them to his attention, and the merit of the difference is a fubject of fubfequent reflection.

A celebrated moral philofopher has affigned three laws for the government of man, and as the rules of human conduct— the law of honour, the law of the land, and the divine law. Thefe are certainly very competent to the decifion of any queftion in morals, but had he chosen to have been more universal, he might have added a fourth law—I mean, the law of etiquette; for the law of honour, in which some might suppose it included, only prohibits the perpetration of any act which would degrade the gentleman, or interrupt the offices of social harmony. This, therefore, applies only to the more prominent parts of conduct, and those actions which border upon morality. The law of etiquette confines itself wholly to those minutiæ of deportment, which have as little connection with morals as with physics. A word, a look, or a motion, contrary to etiquette, fixes upon you the stain of culpability. And then, though you had observed the other three with the spirit of a man, the fidelity of a citizen, and the virtue of a saint; you would stand no fairer chance of maintaining your rank in polished society, than a Hottentot. And so various are the character and sentiments of the people of different countries, that a man

might

## LETTER IX.

might as well attempt to find the reasonings of Newton in the system of Des Cartes, and deduce the doctrines of the Koran from the writings of Voltaire, as to determine from the general principles of politesse the maxims of national etiquette.

I was led to these reflections by a circumstance which took place the evening of the ball given by the ladies club. An English gentleman, who had been introduced as a stranger, and whose ignorance of French etiquette might seem to plead his excuse, was actually observed holding conversation with his partner when the dance was ended. Had she been a married lady, this would have attracted no notice. The circumstance would have been imputed to gallantry, or intrigue, in either of which cases, the lady is subject to no authority, and the gentleman responsible to no tribunal—but that of her husband. *He* is in all probability engaged in too many similar intrigues, to find leisure for so irksome a business. Thus a *tête-a-tête* of this nature would neither have been

deemed

deemed criminal nor dangerous. But the lady was *unmarried*, and the extraordinary conduct of the gentleman was referred to the fudden influence of a foft attachment. The eyes of the company were upon him. " Le pauvre homme! il eft amoureux," was circulated in whifpers. This fudden paffion filled up the chafm of converfation in the morning circles; and my friend, who had hitherto continued unfufpicious, was furprifed the following evening, by finding the eyes of the company pointedly fixed upon him. He received with aftonifh- ment the congratulations of fome, the con- dolences of others, and the affurances of all—that he was really in love. It was in vain that he denied the charge, and perfifted againft the exiftence of the paffion; it was in vain that he urged the fhortnefs of the con- verfation, and the innocence of its object; all were unanimous in deciding againft him: and it was refolved *nem. con.* that when a gentleman holds converfation with an un-

- married

married lady, love muſt be either the cauſe or the conſequence.

I ſhould perhaps intreat your indulgence, when I record thoſe trivial details. But though the bold and prominent lines of character are to be found in acts of higher importance; though heroiſm is moſt ſuccefsfully traced in the field, and ſagacity in the cabinet; manners are only to be deciphered in the leſſer incidents of ſocial intercourſe. It is the zephyr and the ſhower which diſcloſe the foliage of the roſe or the myrtle, though ſtorms and tempeſts may be neceſſary to prove the ſtrength of the oak or the cedar.

## LETTER X.

THE park at Bruſſels is a very charming promenade. The walks are indeed for the moſt part ſtraight, cutting each other at right angles, and ornamented with ſtatues. There are, however, ſome varieties in thoſe walks, not uſual in continental gardens.

The buildings which face the park on each side, appear very magnificent from the different avenues. In addition to the amusement of walking, you may retire into some rooms, which are to be found in the recesses of the gardens, to drink *coffee*, *liqueurs*, &c. and read the papers of the day. The fashionable people are to be seen upon the walks usually from twelve to one, and mixed ranks of people in great numbers promenade here in the evening.

I have been to visit a place in the environs of Brussels, which is esteemed one of the most striking beauties of the vicinity; it is the palace of the arch-duchess, and built of a beautiful stone. It merits well the eulogium that has been passed upon it. The apartments are large and well finished, and the situation commands a very charming and extensive prospect. The grounds are, agreeable to the reigning fashion on the continent, laid out à l'Angloise, and difcover

## LETTER X.

cover some taste. The furniture of the Palace, which is said to be uncommonly elegant, was removed, in consequence of the outrages committed during the late troubles. It is now about to be replaced, and the arch-duchess is daily expected to resume her court at Brussels.

All the accounts I have received here, respecting the *dernier coup* of the revolutionists, are filled with the tragical horrors experienced by the inhabitants of Brussels and its environs. Public men and public measures were at first the sole objects of the popular indignation; but upon the ill success of the Brabanters, and the triumphs of the Austrians, the face of affairs changed, and private property fell a sacrifice to the madness of the multitude. Abandoned by their leaders and pursued by their enemies, these unhappy wretches formed the desperate resolution of restoring their ruined hopes and fortunes by a general pillage. The ravages committed on this occasion

were

were unparalleled in number and enormity. Not bounding their infolence to the public roads and ftreets, they entered private houfes, and committed all the outrageous acts of an unprincipled banditti. The entrance of the Auftrian troops terminated thofe depredations, and reftored to the difordered town the appearance of tranquillity.—I fay, *the appearance*, for I cannot reconcile myfelf to the afpect of a place in the fituation of Bruffels at this moment. The ftern countenances of the huzzars, who are ftationed in all poffible avenues—who eye all our motions with the moft favage jealoufy—and who are authorized to fire upon us at their difcretion, ftrike me with a horror which I fhould fcarcely have felt in the tumults which preceded their entrance.

The diforders of a mob are hideous, yet if property is to be fecured at the expence of liberty, and perfonal fafety to be bartered for general protection, I cannot conceive

the

the fituation greatly meliorated. For my own part, I can as eafily imagine mifery to prevail in a free government, as enjoyment to exift under the control of military law.

## LETTER XI.

*Bruffels, May 2, 1791.*

OUR refolution is formed for quitting Bruffels to-morrow, and entering upon the tour of Holland. I leave with regret this court of amufement, though the objects which lie before me moft warmly intereft my curiofity. A traveller fhould not long reft at one place. He may refide with fafety the period neceffary for obfervation; but if he pafs that limit, curiofity ripens into attachment: he ftrikes his roots into the foil, and is not torn away without reluctance. A longer refidence at Bruffels might produce this effect.

If

## LETTER XI.

If I have framed juft fentiments of the character of a modern Fleming, this people have fuffered confiderable degeneracy. In the higher ranks of life, the intercourfe of nations has very much affimilated the external characters of men, and the genuine traits of nature are only to be developed, where neither force nor fafhion have been employed to new-model or refine.

The opinions which I have eftablifhed, from my beft inveftigation, are very difadvantageous to the prefent race. The moft prominent features in their character are ignorance, dulnefs, and obftinacy. A more provoking trio of evil properties cannot be imagined. It was our misfortune, in more than one inftance, to be the victims of them. In the high road between Ghent and Bruffels, we efcaped by a miracle, from the accidental fracture of the fhaft of the carriage, the confequences of an overthrow. The alarm occafioned by this cataftrophe foon brought around us

the

the boors of the adjoining village, who, with folded arms and vacant countenances, encircled the chaife, offering no affiftance, and talking, as if each were emulous to outcroak his fellow in their horrid guttural jargon. At length the arrival of the poftmafter was announced. Scraps of cordage were immediately employed, and this expert veteran, having ended his job, bade the poftilion lead forward. " Allez," faid he, and turning to me, " Soyez tranquilles " meffieurs—tout ira bien, vous ne rifquerez " rien; J'en reponds." Thefe words were fcarcely uttered, when every knot gave up its hold, with an explofion which induced us to difmount with all convenient fpeed; the carriage was then dragged to the neareft town, and put into the hands of a profeffed artificer. It was difficult, among the multitude of workmen, to diftinguifh who was principal, not fewer than fifteen or twenty being employed in this paltry bufinefs. We foon perceived that this Herculean tafk furpaffed their talents, and urged to them the inefficiency of their contrivances; but our advice and directions were treated with equal contempt, and the confequence was, that the fhaft broke from its hold before we had loft fight of the town.

The inhabitants of the Belgic provinces were always a brave and a hardy people, but never famed for quicknefs or penetration. The pillars of their fame are monuments rather of induftry than of genius. They have acquired the praife of agricultural fkill, for the patient labour which they beftowed upon the improvement of their marfhy lands. Their tapeftries were the admiration of Europe, before the reign of good tafte commenced; and if their fchool of painters be excepted, they have, I believe, little elfe to boaft. As to their moral qualities, they rank, if poffible, ftill lower than their intellectual. Impofition and extortion circumvent you on all fides—no vigilance of your own will avail you;

you; and no magistrate will attend to your complaint. Against fraud and dishonesty there are no laws, or the laws have no energy. You even frequently become the victim of rapacity to the very organ of justice; and the man whom you would punish, is the judge to whom you must appeal.

## LETTER XII.

*Spa, May 17, 1791.*

THE scenes which have intervened since my last, are so numerous, and their succession so rapid, that I seem to have made a visionary journey. In thirteen days we have described a course which might well have occupied thrice the number. Our route lay by Antwerp, where we passed the first day after quitting Brussels. No town has been more celebrated for its splendour and its importance than Antwerp.

Antwerp. Entering it with expectations raised to no common height, my disappointment was proportionably severe. Its buildings are, indeed, formed upon a bold model, and exhibit fine speciments of ancient architecture.

The church of Nôtre Dame is a cabinet of rare workmanship and exquisite paintings. It has not the polished elegance of St. Bavon at Ghent, but it is in my opinion more majestic and venerable. The grand altar piece by Rubens, however, made me regard all other objects with comparative indifference. This celebrated painting is a descent from the cross, and possesses an energy, a beauty, and an expression, which entitle it to rank with the first productions of this master. I believe it is generally allowed of this painting, that it has the united excellencies of design and colouring in a very eminent degree, and connoisseurs give it a place in the highest class of crucifixion pieces.

The

## LETTER XII.

The churches and convents are so numerous at Antwerp, that no one but an amateur of the fine arts, of the moſt exhauſtleſs patience, could attend to a particular inveſtigation of the whole. For my own part, I could ſcarcely reſolve upon undertaking the routine, ſuch a melancholy aſpect clouded the face of every thing—the ſtreets appeared depopulated—the beſt houſes cleared of the inhabitants—neither the buſtle of trade, nor the rattle of amuſement, were to be heard. The channel of commerce has been diverted, and pleaſure flown to other climes: ſix thouſand Auſtrian troops were in poſſeſſion of this town, the fanaticiſm and violence of which made ſo conſpicuous a figure in the late Belgic revolution. Though Leopold's clemency paſſed an act of amneſty and oblivion, numbers refuſed to return, either from obſtinacy or diſtruſt.

We went to the theatre in the evening, which exhibited a melancholy picture of deſertion.

## LETTER XII.

defertion. The only amufement which attracts at prefent, is derived from the evolutions of the parade, which are performed in the Place de Mer. Here you may obferve a motley affemblage, of which Abbés compofe the greater part, ranged on the feveral fides, and with folded arms feeking fome occupation for the heavy hours. Scarcely any provifions are to be purchafed in the town, and the fmall market which has furvived holds up a price beyond the capacities of all but the rich.

The ftorm, though hufhed, is not diffipated. Many unquiet fpirits remain, whom neither force nor favour have yet fubdued. Secret combinations ftill exift; the cap of liberty is occafionally exhibited, and the name of VANDERNOODT devoutly invoked. A convivial meeting had, fome few evenings paft, expanded the hearts of fome old rebels; and the orgies of Bacchus having rekindled the flames of freedom, this fally of intemperance was not terminated
without

without the intervention of the military. Dangers more serious may be apprehended from the ambition of the Prussian court, which will doubtless lose no opportunity of re-animating the Belgic discontents; nor is it quite clear that the House of Orange will hold itself bound by the faith of the last treaty to continue neuter.

The manœuvres of the House of Brandenburg are generally known in the late revolution, and the negotiations of Vandernoodt with the House of Orange have not lost their impression. The fate of Belgia is not yet decided, and Leopold holds on a very unsure tenure this part of his dominions.

The general temper of the people may be inferred from the general aspect of the country, in which nothing is to be read but dejection or discontent. Were the overtures of the Emperor cordially embraced, cheerfulness would have relumined the countenance; industry and amusement would have been prosecuted as usual, and

every

every thing ere now have recovered its tone. But, when all stagnates—when trade has no vigour, and pleasure no attraction—a just foundation exists for suspicion, that the wound is not yet healed;—that though quelled by terror, the spirit of sedition yet rages in secret; and only wants a favourable moment for breaking forth with aggravated fury.

## LETTER XIII.

ANTWERP is one among those numerous cities which have experienced the vicissitudes of fortune. For near two centuries it astonished Europe by the magnitude of its riches, and the extent of its commerce. Equally celebrated for the arts of war and peace, it sustained with firmness the attacks of its enemies. The obstinate resistance made by this city to the Duke of Parma, and the ten months siege

## LETTER XIII.

it sustained in 1585, form a very honourable part of its history. In common with the other Belgic towns, it has repeatedly changed its masters, and been repeatedly the subject of war and pillage. Rubens and Vandyke, Cramage, Plantin, and Muretus, are among the number of those who have distinguished Antwerp as a mother of the fine arts, and a nurse of literature.

Weakened by successive assaults from its neighbours, and its tyrants, Antwerp experienced its last and most decisive blow from the Hollanders, by the treaty of Munster. This treaty, consigning to Holland the exclusive navigation of the Scheld, cut off the resources of commercial wealth, and precipitated the declining grandeur of this ancient city, the gloomy and deserted edifices of which still remain the monuments of its past splendour. One *trait* which ever distinguished this city, is still to be found in its decayed and fallen state. Fanaticism has suffered no diminution, nor have any of those rude assaults which subverted its wealth and its commerce, weakened or impaired its rooted attachment to the Catholic faith.

No place in Europe is so immediately under the influence of every religious absurdity. All the long series of monkish iniquities has not convinced these people of the possibility of error in ecclesiastics; and their consciences, their faith, and their purses, are still at the disposal of priests and prelates. The late revolution owed much of its energy to the religious prejudices of this deluded people; and Antwerp and Malines discovered the genuine fury of fanaticism. The notorious Van Eupen, who acted so principal a part in that political drama, was originally a canon of this place; and if we may credit the intelligence received in those parts, and the universal tone of the writings of that time, his history is not greatly to the credit of ecclesiastical purity. In the capacity of Grand Peniten-

## LETTER XIII.

Penitentiary, to which he was exalted by the liberal patronage of the Bishop of Antwerp, his province comprehended all spiritual jurisdiction over the numerous inhabitants of this great see. All cases of conscience, doubts of faith, and religious embarrassments, came under his review, and were determined by his decisions. The duties of his office introduced him into the closets of all, and the illapses of the spirit were sometimes made subservient to the impulses of the flesh. * * * * *

Such was the man who moved the principal springs in those tumults, which so lately shook the Belgic states. Vandernoodt, though foremost in name, was but the organ of this arch-politician; who, expatriated by crimes which insult heaven and earth, had no hope of recovering his forfeited fortunes, but by entering his country sword in hand. To compass his re-establishment, he practised all the arts of political hypocrisy. He is naturally cool, subtle, and enterprising—

under

under the garb of fanctity, he has a heart capable of any crime. Patriotifm was the lure he held out, and by his addrefs he contrived to obtain credit, till he was detected in embroiling, by infidious artifices, the feveral parties of the ftate; afperfing by his emiffaries the intentions of thofe, who from principle efpoufed the caufe of the Belgians—covering with the mantle of religion the machinations of rebellion;—and labouring to eftablifh the empire of the church and the nobleffe, upon the blended ruins of imperial authority and democratic freedom. The conciliatory meafures of Leopold were very ill calculated to ferve the ends of this arch-hypocrite. He therefore employed every finifter engine to prevent a union. The reconciliation which took place between the contending parties defeated his defigns of perfonal aggrandizement, and compelled him to fly from juftice into fome diftant clime, where his hypocrify may hereafter play a more fuccefsful game upon the credulity of mankind.

# LETTER XIV.

WE took the route by Breda into Holland, and for a few leagues rolled along a good *pavée*, and then entered upon a road, which, had we not actually paſſed it, might very fairly have been deemed impaſſable. A deep ſand formed the ſoil, elevated into mounds on one ſide, ſunk into hollow pits on the other, and in many places completely buried in water of confiderable extent; every ſtep the horſes took required great exertion, and their utmoſt efforts could never accelerate them beyond a foot-pace. It was near ten o'clock when we entered Breda, and it was fortunate for us that the gates do not finally cloſe before that time.

All the country between Antwerp and Breda, for many miles, exhibits a melancholy

choly scene—vast wilds and deserts which seem to defy the hand of culture, and upon which the most laborious industry would operate in vain. The lateness of the evening concealed from our view the change of country which takes place as you approach Breda, which is a neat and well fortified town.

We experienced a very striking change in every object around us; the houses and streets had neither the awkwardness nor the filthiness of the Brabant towns. An air of ease, vivacity, and content pervaded the countenances of all—the soldiers wore a less hostile aspect—neither folded arms nor sauntering paces were to be seen; activity, vigour, and industry seemed to prevail; and each appeared emulous to perform the duties of his occupation.

Breda may claim no inconsiderable merit from the public places which adorn it. The palace of the Prince of Orange is delightfully situated, and the gardens which surround

round it are a great ornament to the town. The church of the Proteſtants is a very noble edifice—it is hung with eſcutcheons, which diffuſe a gloom around the ſacred walls, and are but an indifferent ſuccedaneum to the maſterly paintings which fill the Romiſh churches. The monuments which are raiſed againſt the walls in the Engliſh churches oftener deface than adorn the buildings; but the numerous eſcutcheons which inveſt the walls of the beſt churches in Holland give them more the air of mauſoleums, than of places of worſhip. There is a very ancient tomb of marble in one of the receſſes, now crumbling into ruins. What remains is however a curious monument of early taſte and primitive ſculpture.

Breda was diſtinguiſhed as the headquarters of the late revolutionary intrigues. It was here that the firſt committee was formed under the joint conduct of Vandernoodt

noodt and Van Eupen. This committee, at which the factious nobles of Brabant attended, declared Vander-Merfch general of the troops which they refolved to raife; and publifhed a manifefto, dated at Hoogftraten, in the name of the people of Brabant. This manifefto was, by a decree of the Auftrian government, deftroyed at Bruffels, and feveral members of the fecret committee taken into cuftody. Three thoufand infurgents upon this attacked and captured the forts of Lillo and Liefhenfhoek. This was the firft blow ftruck by them, and the government diftracted by internal divifions now loft all energy. The defeat of Chroeder at Turnhout foon followed, which gave fpirit to the revolutionifts, and excited the higheft alarm at the court of Bruffels. The entry of the rebels into Ghent, and the difhonourable retreat of D'Arbers with his four thoufand troops, gave to the revolution a force and a

refpecta-

refpectability, which profelyted thofe who, averfe to its principle, would yet profit from its fuccefs.

The impolitic meafure of concluding an armiftice at Tirlemont by D'Alton, at the head of an army fully competent to annihilate the rebels, was the finifhing ftroke of this ill-judging infatuated miniftry. The armiftice opened a channel for communication between the regular troops and the vagrant rebels; and the glow of patriotifm being thus diffeminated, not lefs than 500 men deferted at once—filling the air with the moft outrageous fhouts of liberty and revolution. Thefe were of the regiment of Murray; their example operated upon others---defertions took place from all quarters, and every part of Bruffels refounded with the popular cry of " Vivent " les Patriotes! Au Diable les Royaliftes!" This was fhortly after fucceeded by the departure of the Auftrian troops from Bruffels, which Vandernoodt on the 18th December

cember 1789 entered with all the triumphal honours of a proud victor; was hailed with the loudest acclamations as the subverter of tyranny, and the author of Belgic independence.

I must entreat your pardon for the frequent reflections with which I trouble you on the Belgic affairs. Every part of Brabant bears the vestiges of the late commotions, and interests by its melancholy aspect our pity and indignation. The court of Berlin had doubtless some objects of profound policy to compass in fomenting the discontents of the Belgians against the Austrian government. The transfer of the Belgic provinces to the Prussian sovereignty would have furnished that power with a vast ascendant, and enabled it to assume a tone with the Emperor very much to the advantage of its authority. Holland, ever attentive to the main point, contemplated with a feeling beyond indifference the apprehended disunion of the Belgic states from the Austrian government---

ment—regardless who sways the sceptre, provided they occupy the market, these prudent speculators promised themselves an augmentation of their commercial advantages. This is the notorious object of Dutch intrigue, and their neighbours, who experience its effects, were not at a loss to account for the secret fuel added to the flames of rebellion. " Le seul avantage " qu'ils en veulent tirer," said the Brabanters; " c'est de vendre aux Belges " de mauvaises munitions a très-haut " prix."

# LETTER XV.

HOLLAND is certainly a very convenient country to travel through, provided a man will make up his mind to difpenfe with the fplendour of equipage. All the roads which communicate with its environs are intolerably bad, but a carriage of the country will roll over them without difficulty, yet not always without alarm to the traveller. Had we availed ourfelves of the precaution given before we quitted Bruffels, of leaving our carriage at Antwerp, we fhould have experienced lefs difficulty in paffing the moor between that place and Breda. The grand advantage in making the tour of Holland arifes from the canals which pierce the country, and form a ̀ ̀eeable mode of communication between the feveral places.

We

## LETTER XV.

We had been led into an error by the inſtructions furniſhed us at Breda, and had entered a veſſel for Rotterdam, which we ſoon found ill-adapted for the conveyance of paſſengers. Our ſituation in it became irkſome—the veſſel was dirty—the cabin filled with children. The air without was extremely cold, and the Captain could only reply to our complaints in a language we did not underſtand. Theſe diſagreeables, added to the apprehenſions of a long paſſage, the wind blowing hard and contrary, induced us to form a reſolution of abandoning the veſſel the firſt opportunity, and trying our fortune by land.

Shortly after our forming this determination the veſſel came to a mooring in the vicinity of ſome few houſes, from which we promiſed ourſelves information reſpecting the route to Rotterdam by land. We diſembarked, to reconnoitre; and after many fruitleſs experiments, had the good fortune to diſcover a ſchool-maſter, who underſtanding French, acquainted us with the particulars which we wifhed to learn.

Inftructed by him that we could procure a cabriolet in the adjacent village, we returned to the veffel, in order to fettle with our Captain. It was a work of no fmall difficulty to make him comprehend our intentions. We endeavoured, by figns, to teftify that we were completely *ennuied* of this mode of travelling. Every motion we made embarraffed him, till paying him the whole fare of our paffage, we threw our luggage over our fhoulders, and left him to meditate on the fingularity of our conduct, at which he had little reafon to repine. By the good offices of the village fchool-mafter we obtained a carriage, and traverfed upon a wretched road, through the moft wild, fwampy, and defert country, for more than a league and a half. In our driver we had the firft picture of a real Dutchman. In his figure he was fhort, with broad hips, and fpherical fhoulders: his features were fharp, yet

yet steady—a two-inch pipe issued from his mouth, and completed his profile.

One of the *agrémens* of travelling in these cabriolets, which are the only carriages that can run over the heavy roads, is, that if the wind should set against you, it always comes strongly impregnated with tobacco. It was our fate, whenever we travelled in those carriages, to receive the incense which those amateurs of the pipe are constantly offering to those who sit behind them. Our situation reminded me of the inhabitants of the upper regions, who are usually represented as riding in cabriolets, invested with circumambient clouds.

By eight o'clock in the evening, we arrived at the extreme limit of our journey by land. Mynheer transferred us to the *commissaire*, who was to answer for our conveyance over the Biesbock, usually stiled the Moerdyke. There are no harlequins in Holland. There may be such a thing as *dispatch*, in the warehouses and manufactures; but I question if the language contains an expreſſion ſynonimous to the English word *haſte*.

All I mean by this, is, that though the evening was ſo far advanced, and we had ſo much water to croſs, theſe ſteady-pacing wights would not accelerate their movements in arranging the few preliminaries neceſſary to embarkation. At length we entered the boat, and caught a breeze, which continued in our favour but a ſhort time; then veered and blew a head, and in the third and laſt place ſunk into a dead calm. Night had now thrown a gloomy veil over heaven and earth—a pale and ill-formed moon afforded a few faint glimmerings, which opened our eyes to the tracks which ſurrounded us. A mighty waſte of water, whoſe boundaries were only to be diſcerned on one ſide, preſented a moſt chilling ſcene; and the deſolate ſwamps, which ſurrounded it, ſcarcely wore a leſs melancholy aſpect. A man and a boy were all who compoſed the crew of the veſſel conveying us over this melan-

melancholy lake. We were barbarians to each other: we could neither animate them to activity, nor question them of our danger. How often have I deplored in my tour through this country, the fatal ambition of those proud architects, who, by their rash designs upon heaven, provoked the division of tongues, and the annihilation of universal language.

Not to aggravate our perils by water, I shall remark that all was perfectly calm—that, if you except the extreme cold that prevailed, the little prospect of coming to an anchor in any reasonable time, the apprehension natural to a situation of the most dreary description, at the mercy, and under the direction of two strangers, whom we could neither soften by promises, nor alarm by threats; if you except these, and some trifling concomitant inconveniences, we encountered no evil of moment. But I must tell you, that our perils, which appeared at their zenith on the water, were considerably augmented

augmented when we gained the land; for, wearied with their exertions, our conductors brought us to a mooring, which suited their convenience, but was very little to our accommodation. No vestige of a house, or habitable spot, appeared. Our guides pointed to us that we were to use our feet; and one preceding, and one bringing up the rear, we traversed a region of the most doleful appearance. Like the fiend that bewilders the lorn traveller, our pilot carried us over marshes and fens, where we could with difficulty find ground sufficiently firm to bear our feet.

The facility with which our leader surmounted those embarrassments, was an aggravation of our distress. It was important to our safety that we kept close: we could not check him, because we could not explain; and some part of the track over which he hurried us, was piled into heaps of swashy clay, and, at numerous intervals, divided by streams that broke from the adjoining

## LETTER XV.

joining canal. At length a gleam of light darted upon us, and preffing with anxious exertion we arrived at a *cabaret*, where it was deftined we fhould pafs the remainder of the night.

If you tell me that I have drawn a melancholy picture of thefe pigmy perils, I affure you that they appeared to us in gigantic forms. Though I guarded you againft the expectation of prodigious events, I did not intend to encounter danger, or combat terrors, without making you a party in our adventures. If it fuit the mournful temper of your foul, you may commiferate our painful fenfations. If, on the contrary, this finds you in the moment of gaiety, you are welcome to laugh at our embarraffments, provided you triumph in our fuccefs.

# LETTER XVI.

THE Dutch are reprefented as very trickifh and impofing. This character applies in the great towns, but I have a better opinion of the villagers. They have all the marks of honefty, and certainly all the *agrémens* of cleanlinefs. An old woman opened the door to us, after having fatisfied herfelf by queftions to our guides of our good intentions. She conducted us into a chamber, which, from its fituation, I fhould rather ftyle a cellar. We were thoroughly wetted by, what an Hibernian alone would call, our land expedition; and a very few figns made the old matron comprehend that we wifhed for a fire, which, by her induftrious attentions, foon blazed before us.

She

## LETTER XVI.

She then opened, what appeared to us, a cupboard-door, full three feet from the ground;—when a voice from within addreſſed us in French. We held a ſhort dialogue, in which the inviſible perſon engaged to furniſh us a carriage in the morning, when, wiſhing us a good night, the old woman cloſed the door upon him.

The Dutch are very induſtrious, and riſe very early—men of all ranks drink coffee in great abundance. The labourers ſip their coffee before they go out to their toils, and appear to eat very little. This may, in all probability, be owing to the quantities of ſpirits which they are accuſtomed to ſwallow. I have repeatedly ſeen the moſt robuſt men taking their morning's meal, previous to the fatigues of the field, and this has confiſted in two or three cups of weak coffee, a glaſs or two of Hollands—then the pipe is kindled, and with *one*, ſcarcely ſquare inch of bread, theſe laborious hinds are equipped for the moſt ſturdy ſervices. Our old hoſteſs had
kindled

## LETTER XVI.

kindled a fire, and boiled our coffee by five o'clock; and notwithstanding the late hour at which we entered, all were up and active, and by six o'clock we were seated in a cabriolet, and took leave of this curious company.

A great change of scenery takes place as you proceed to Rotterdam. The country is still open, but less deformed with wild wastes, or marshy grounds. The roads also improve, and you have an agreeable variety of villages and rivers. The Old Maese, which we first passed, exhibited a noble view. This is navigable for vessels of considerable burden. Numbers of these were lying in the river, and gave a very commercial appearance to the country. Our route after this lay through some villages, whose extreme neatness attracted our particular attention. Nothing can equal the purity of these cottages. The excessive labour they bestow on every article of the most minute importance, leaves nothing to offend the

eye,

## LETTER XVI.

eye, and gives the humbleſt cot that air of elegant ſimplicity which palaces do not always poſſeſs.

Rotterdam is a fine object for many miles before you reach it. The country is quite open, and the road purſues a very ſerpentine courſe, which gives you ſufficient time to meditate on the ſingular beauties of that celebrated city. Rotterdam will ſtrike the traveller with wonder; perhaps no town in Europe poſſeſſes objects ſo expreſſive of commercial importance. The canals are numerous and large; crouded with veſſels in all parts, and covered with numerous draw-bridges, they exhibit a magnificent ſcene. All theſe canals are bordered with trees and *promenades*. Wherever the eye turns, objects of commercial grandeur ſtrike it with aſtoniſhment. The public buildings are all conſecrated to the ſame purpoſes. The churches are heavy and taſteleſs. There are cabinets of paintings in the poſſeſſion of ſome private individuals; but the only public

## LETTER XVI.

lic monument of letters and the fine arts, is a statue to the memory of Erasmus, who was a native of this place, and among the few luminaries of science which this country has produced. The artist has inspired the countenance with wonderfully fine intelligence.

The different degrees of zeal with which the memory of Erasmus was cherished, bespoke in past times a growing taste for literature. The statue first raised in honour of this great scholar, A. D. 1540, was of wood. Seventeen years refined their feelings, and blushing for the little respect they had shewn to the memory of the man who had immortalized their city, the statue of *wood* was exchanged for a statue of *stone*. A succeeding age, emulous of its predecessors, gave to the Apotheosis of Erasmus the last touch, and raised this statue of *bronze*. Doubtless this œconomical people had at the first well calculated the extent of the future expenditure, if literary characters should

should abound in the republic; but finding this swampy soil unpropitious to genius, and productive only of dull commentators and sombrous logicians, they converted the image of *wood* into a statue of *stone*, without risquing, in consequence of this precedent, any material diminution of the public revenue. In the sixty-five years which succeeded, no rival Erasmuses yet appearing, the utmost extravagance of civic honours was exhausted upon him, and a statue of *bronze* erected, all apprehension of future claim being at length entirely dissipated.

## LETTER XVII.

WHAT Rome is to the antiquary, and Florence to the connoisseur, that is Rotterdam to the merchant. The manœuvres of a Prussian army are grand and striking; but the strength there displayed excites reflections,

reflections, at which the heart revolts. When the olive is exchanged for the laurel, though the eye may be dazzled with military splendor, the heart sickens with grief. Commerce is the only art of national aggrandizement which reason sanctions, and humanity approves. This increases the strength, and extends the limits of an empire, without abridging the liberties, or shedding the blood of mankind.

Regarded in this view Rotterdam claims a distinguished rank among the objects of curiosity. Streets, markets, and quays, are crouded with the sons of active industry. Every coffee-house is a *bourse*, and all the society that is there cultivated, refers to bargains, transfers, and contracts. Here are no theatres, but warehouses; no routs, but on the Change; no amusements, but counting of gains. They have little deference for a stranger, particularly if he appears to take no interest in their commercial transactions. You may dine in company

## LETTER XVII.

company with them, yet fcarcely obtain the interchange of a minute's converfation: this being with them ufually taken up by topics of infinitely higher moment, than thofe which the vague curiofity of a traveller would ftart. Their language, it muft be owned, feems formed for them, and they for their language. Rude, harfh, and guttural—it never was intended for the polite intercourfe of fociety, nor the foft effufions of an amorous paffion. But gallantry and politenefs are playthings to tare and trett; and all the courtly graces of language are baubles, compared with thofe finewy terms that tie and untie with effect the knots of trade.

We foon fatisfied ourfelves with the rarities of Rotterdam, and as we did not enter feelingly into the fublime fpeculations of thefe, we could not help regretting the dearth of public entertainments. The objects which ftruck us at firft, foon loft their energy. Familiarized in a few hours to

their

their canals and their warehouses, we panted to find some new scene; and parting from this mart of traffic, this depositary of commercial wealth, we entered a passage-boat at the close of the Saturday evening, and made the best of our way to the Hague.

## LETTER XVIII.

THE lateness of the evening obliged us to pass between Rotterdam and the Hague, more rapidly than we wished. On our way we scarcely stopped at Delft, which is a pretty town of no great extent, but distinguished by two churches, in one of which is the monument raised to the memory of the famous Admiral Van Tromp. The china manufacture has been long celebrated throughout Europe, and still preserves its vigor and reputation. The town is charmingly situated, and the canal runs by it.

We

## LETTER XVIII.

We quitted the barge at Delft, and took carriage, in order to reach the Hague before the gates should shut. Here a new scene opened upon us. The Hague exhibits a striking contrast to Rotterdam. It is a town built in a stile of uncommon elegance, with all the air of fashionable residence. It has not the bustle, the population, nor the crouded objects of Rotterdam, yet it has the aspect of cheerfulness, and combines the vivacity of trade with the polish of pleasure. The *promenade* towards Scheveling is one of the finest things in Holland, and perhaps in Europe. It extends more than two English miles in length, and is kept in the most delightful order. The village at Scheveling, which terminates it, forms a very agreeable boundary, and the ocean rising above the land closes the vista, and gives to the whole a wonderful sublimity. Scheveling is a fishing town, and is situated on a fine sand—the view of the sea from this sand is beautiful and extensive. As to the gardens of Count Bentinck and other *maisons de plaisance*, they are certainly curiosities in Holland, where the moſt uncouth diſtribution of grounds prevails, but merit little the attention of an Engliſh traveller, who will have ſeen in his own country more taſte diſplayed in the green which ſurrounds the cottage, than in the moſt admired villas * of Holland.

When I remarked that the houſes were built in a ſtile of elegance and grandeur, I did not mean to applaud the taſte of the architects, as many of them wear a heavy and ſombrous aſpect; but the general effect is ſtriking. The palace of the Stadtholder is more celebrated for the paintings and cabinets which adorn it within, than the face it exhibits without. The churches are ſpacious, but not numerous: the whole town poſſeſſes but *three;* of which one is the church of the reformed,

* Mr. Hope's manſion at Haerlem is a known exception to this general character.

the second the Lutheran, and the third Romish. The first is the handsomest, and was, at the time I saw it, filled with a splendid audience. The preachers here preserve those immense wigs, which in England ornament only the heads of the judges. Thus accoutred, and with only a small bible before them, they wear a very oratorical appearance—resort to an action by no means ungraceful, and appear animated and energetic. The still silence which prevailed throughout the hallowed edifice, convinced me that the impressive ardor of the preacher was not without its desired effect.

We were fortunate in being at the Hague during the fair. This began on the Sunday afternoon, agreeable to the practice in these countries, which, if it does not enjoin Sunday as the beginning, usually includes it within the number. This fair may possibly have given us a more cheerful idea of this place, than it would ordinarily excite. Theatres, reviews, public breakfasts, and every species of amusement, took place; all the public roads were filled with carriages, paffing and repaffing, and the ftreets were crouded with puppet-fhews, mountebanks, and wild beafts. What amufed me beyond other novelties, was the fingular drefs of the Dutch girls. Any one would have imagined, that the figures which appeared on thefe occafions were mafques, or defigned as caricatures; but the numbers which crouded all the public ways, and the winning airs they affected, convinced me, that nothing but my want of tafte refifted the influence of fuch fingular attractions. Imagine a fhort figure, with more breadth than goes to the proportion of elegance, and with very little alteration in the width downwards to the waift, the petticoats defcending half way only below the knee.— Imagine further, a round face, ufually fmall, covered with a hat of near three feet in diameter, perfectly circular, and applied to the head in a part contiguous to the circumference.

cumference. You will readily perceive, that the hat, thus difpofed, will project before the face, nearly the fpace of the whole diameter, touching the head, agreeably to the property of fpheres, only in one point. Now you have nothing to do but to conceive a number of thefe figures in motion, brandifhing their horizontal hats, rolling their diminutive eyes, and affecting a thoufand ridiculous graces, under cover of this extenfive canopy. The *tout enfemble* brought to my recollection thofe fculptural vagaries, in which a human figure is often made the prop of a cathedral feat, the fupport of a wainfcot pulpit, or the ftand of a mahogany table. If you deem my obfervations fomewhat fatirical, I muft, in my own vindication, fay, that this is a country in which few objects are to be found for panegyric or applaufe. The fingularity of its fituation, and the extent of its commerce, are almoft the only topics on which curiofity would dwell, without terminating in cenfure: and our daily obfervation evinces, that a nation, great in the arts of commerce, and poffeffed of all the refources of fplendor and affluence, may yet be ignorant of the arts of refinement, and yield to nations lefs important, and lefs opulent, in the more fafcinating attainments of elegance and good tafte.

## LETTER XIX.

THE paffage by water from the Hague to Amfterdam exhibits fome pleafant fcenery, and the boats are under fo dextrous management, that you never travel flower than four miles an hour. They will pretend to greater fpeed, but I never found the motion exceed this. People are ufually counfelled to engage the *ruffle*, which is the name diftinguifhing the beft cabbin; and for thofe who are averfe to mixing with a promifcuous fociety, and have a decided antipathy to fmoke, it is certainly a very wife precau-

precaution. Motives of curiosity always determined us to prefer the opposite measure; and we had many opportunities, by this means, of commenting upon the manners of this singular people.

Every man who enters the boat, whatever be his condition, either brings a pipe in his mouth or his hand. A slight touch of the hat, upon entering the cabbin, franks him for the whole time of his stay; and the laws of etiquette allow him to smoke in silence to the end of the passage. We see, as at a meeting of quakers, fixed features and changeless postures; the whole visage mysterious, and solemn, but betraying, it must be confessed, more of absence than intelligence. Hours will pass, and no mouth expand, but to whiff the smoke: nor any limb be put in motion, except to rekindle the pipe. The *coutume* of those societies, in the liberal use of the *crachoir*, does not preserve that attention to delicacy which some constitutions would require.

## LETTER XIX.

On our way to Amſterdam we had an opportunity of taking a tranſient view of Leyden, and of Haerlem. The Dutch towns have ſo cloſe a reſemblance to each other, in their canals, their bridges, and their buildings, that a traveller's curioſity is ſoon ſatiated. The univerſity of Leyden owes its celebrity more to the talents of its profeſſors, than the ſplendor or magnitude of its edifices. The oil painting by Jean de Leyde, is the only attraction which the Hotel-de-Ville poſſeſſes. Haerlem boaſts Laurentius Coſter, one of the inventors of printing, as a native. The great church, and the ſuperb organ which it contains, are known throughout Europe.

A ſhort time ſuffices to examine all the objects of curioſity in thoſe towns, which are a perpetual repetition of the firſt impreſſion. The banks of the canals are ornamented with various gardens and pleaſure grounds, which the maſters of the veſſels are induſtrious to diſplay. I ſhall ſuſpend my

## LETTER XIX.

my obfervations upon this clafs of curiofities till a future occafion. The firft coup-d'œil, as we approched Amfterdam, was fingular. I counted between 70 and 80 windmills, as we were coming down the canal. A grander object foon prefented itfelf—the harbour crouded with veffels, and exhibiting all the apparatus of commercial opulence.

We entered this city at the clofe of the evening, and took up our quarters at Young's Hotel, which is ufually efteemed the beft, but for fituation and convenience does little credit to a city of fuch magnitude.

I fhall indulge you with the privilege of recreating your fpirits, and recovering from the *ennui* which this uninterefting recital muft have occafioned, before I venture my remarks upon Amfterdam. If the paffage has appeared dull and heavy in the relation, I affure you it was not lefs fo in the performance. The equable motion of the

barge,

barge, the uniform folemnity of our fociety, and the unvaried face of the country, gave birth to a fombrous depreffion, diffipated only by the change of fcene, which took place in the great and populous town of Amfterdam. We quickly perceived, that Amfterdam had few attractions for *delicate* curiofity. Amufement, however, we could not fail to derive from the novel fcenes it inclofed, though they were ufually deformed by fome offenfive appendages: fatisfaction was, in moft inftances, lowered by difguft, and one fenfe generally gratified at the expence of another.

## LETTER XX.

THE city of Amfterdam is renowned throughout Europe for its population, its traffic, and its opulence. Nothing can equal the grandeur of its port, which is

thronged

thronged with veffels of all magnitudes. Wherever the eye ranges, mafts and fails appear, covering the whole fphere of vifion, and exhibiting the proud triumphs of commercial enterprize. It is contended of this harbour, that it wants depth; and that veffels of great burden, which enter the Texel, are reduced to numerous inconveniences: yet the toiling induftry, and the perfevering talents of this laborious people, have baffled all the oppofition, and furmounted all the difficulties of nature and fituation. They have ftripped the furrounding nations of their refources, and concentrated the rays of commerce in their own republic. Not content with barricadoeing their realms againft the rude affaults of Neptune, carrying off his waves by artificial channels, and preferving, by daily efforts, their empire from diluvian deftruction—they have fought a good beyond the narrow pittance which their chill and cheerlefs foil produces, have emulated the greateft powers in navigating the ocean,

and

## LETTER XX.

and in importing from diſtant parts of the globe the luxuries of happier climes.

While I viewed this harbour, and ruminated on the ſucceſſive advances of this people to the higheſt pinnacle of national proſperity [*], I turned my eye to that city which once diſputed the palm of commerce with this republic, and which, by the growing importance of this neighbouring power, had been reduced to inſignificance. The treaty of Weſtphalia raiſed the grandeur of Holland upon the ruins of Antwerp. The forts of Lillo and Liefenſhock determined the fate of that unfortunate city, and the antient majeſty of the Scheld now bows to the uſurped authority and furtive honours of the Texel.

The ardour, the activity, the croud, and the buſtle, which prevail in all quarters of the

---

[*] The trade of Amſterdam has of late years been very much on the decline, and now conſiſts chiefly in the negociation of bills of exchange. The real imports and exports do not probably much exceed one half of what they were ſome years paſt.

port,

LETTER XX.

port, are inconceivable. Bells are founding, and veffels parting, at all hours. Piles of merchandize, and throngs of paffengers, fill all the avenues. It appears the mart of exhauftlefs plenty, and the grand depofitary of Europe. The ftreets of Amfterdam are narrow and filthy—the whole city pierced by an infinity of canals, which cut each other in every poffible direction. The Bourfe is convenient, and not inelegant. The Maifon de Ville, or Stadthoufe, is fpacious and magnificent—encumbered neverthelefs with fanciful ornaments, and ill-proportioned in its feveral parts; but the fcale on which it is built is immenfe, and the general effect ftupendous. The churches are raifed after no very fuperior model, and can boaft of few attractive ornaments. I entered three the fecond evening of our ftay, where fervice was performed; numerous congregations hung attentive on the preacher's accents, and zeal on the one part was returned by correfponding emotion on the other.

It

It requires no small perseverance to run over the objects most deserving attention at Amsterdam. The uniformity of the streets, and the uncleanness incident to a crouded population, offend the eye, while the action of the sun upon the stagnant waters increases in a high degree the difficulties of being pleased.

Nothing can wear a more aukward appearance than the carriages, the bodies of which are placed on low sledges, and drawn by one horse. The driver is on foot; and in addition to the concern of the horse, he is obliged to watch every movement of the sledge, that the carriage may not be overset. The origin of this custom is well known to be founded in the apprehension of danger to the houses by the violence of wheel-carriages, and all the *fiacres* are therefore, by authority of the government, constructed upon sledges. Some few years past, no four-wheel carriages were to be seen. Later refinements have at length introduced

troduced them, and this inelegant and inexpeditious mode of vifiting and airing is abandoned to perfons, whofe fortune or frugality admit not a more coftly equipage.

The bridge over the Amftel is confidered as a choice *morceau* of antient architecture, and is a great ornament to the river, which rolls beneath its arches.

I faw nothing beyond thefe, which merits a moment's difcuffion; and I haften from thofe fcenes of uncleanly afpect, this compound of villanous fmells, as Falftaff would call it, to one of the moft charming vifions that ever feafted my eyes—where all that prefented itfelf gave birth to oppofite fenfations, and banifhed for a moment every obnoxious image this city had excited. But I muft referve this account for a fubfequent letter. Your nerves might fuffer by too fudden a tranfition, and fome interval may be neceffary to purify the channel of thofe ideas which have fo long dwelt upon polluted

luted objects. The scenes to which I shall conduct you, will repay the penance of a short delay. They are curious, on the score of singularity, if not upon the principle of taste. They boast a neatness unexampled in courts or palaces, and in a certain mode of ornament have no parallel in Europe.

## LETTER XXI.

In my last I engaged to furnish you with a relation of a little excursion made into North Holland, for the purpose of visiting the village of Broek. It was early in the morning, that, curious to examine a place of which report had spoken so loudly, we entered a vessel for Buyk-floodt. This passage took up an hour, and gave us a very gratifying view of the scenes which most adorn Amsterdam.—Parting from the port, we turned our eyes to contemplate the mighty

mart

mart of commerce we had quitted—the objects were crouded, and the groupe sublime.

The city appeared invested with numerous flotas, which reared their towering masts, like forest-trees, into the air. All that offends the eye, and deforms the aspect of this celebrated city, was obscured and concealed by the more prominent objects which form its grandeur. The opening scenes of North Holland presented a beautiful contrast to the country behind. All was soft, still, and flourishing—the houses exhibited the appearance of ease, affluence, and neatness: the lands, highly cultured, displayed the marks of laborious industry, and growing fertility.

From Buyksloodt, which is charmingly, situated, at an equal distance from Amsterdam and Broek, we entered a second boat, which was to convey us to the latter—the canal ran along a most pleasing country—the banks were occasionally crowned by some neat villa of private residence, or some beautiful rendezvous of public resort.

We were gradually prepared by the different cottages on the banks of this canal, for the scenes to which our ardent curiosity tended. Broek at length caught our eye. It is a village of no great extent, situate on the western side of the canal, and forming the most ravishing landscape. As we eyed it from the boat, it resembled a finished picture, and appeared to exist only in imagination, or upon canvas. We landed with anxious curiosity, and pursued some winding-paths, in order to examine, with more minute attention, this enchanting vision. Placed within the bosom of these surrounding beauties, I fancied myself in that Elysium, which poets have described, where all that meets the senses is creative of pleasurable tranquillity. The houses were painted with the most vivid and varied colours. The windows were transparent as chrystal; and the tiles which roofed these pure abodes, adorned

## LETTER XXI.

adorned with varnished surfaces, reflected a thousand hues from the rays of a meridian sun. The gardens were framed with singular art and ingenuity, and were distributed into the most fanciful divisions. Each several department exhibited a groupe of fantastic forms. The shrubs, which had shot their roots deep into the soil, were sculptured into all the forms of real and imaginary nature. Birds, beasts, and reptiles of every description, were here congregated in peaceful union, as in the ark of old: all wore the same livery, and derived their nutriment from the same elements. The church, however, was excepted from the law of universal decoration. The only ornaments of this sacred building were finished simplicity, and spotless purity—happy emblems of those sacrifices which alone adorn the altar of religious adoration. Wherever the eye could penetrate, or the feet could stray, throughout this fascinating village, all was completely correspondent.

The

## LETTER XXI.

The areas which surrounded the houses—the winding walks, alleys, and avenues, were equally correct.

Nor is it alone exterior elegance to which these people aspire—the insides of many houses are richly decorated, and finished with the most costly ornaments. We obtained admittance into one, and were astonished at the polished surfaces which every article of the most minute description possessed. One apartment, which we entered, was paved with small square tiles, put together without any cement, and presenting the most pleasing aspect. The furniture of a chamber in the same house was very sumptuous, composed of silken ornaments, richly embroidered. This is, agreeably to antient prescription, bequeathed from father to son, and preserved as an offering to Hymen—such is the custom of these Arcadian villagers—from generation to generation. There is also a practice prevailing here, common, I believe, to all the natives of North Holland:

LETTER XXI.

land: To every house, of whatever quality, there is an artificial door, elevated near three feet above the level of the ground, and never opened but upon two occasions. When any part of the family marries, the bride and bridegroom enter the house by this door; and when either of the parties die, the corpse is carried out by the same door. Immediately after the due ceremonies are performed in either of those cases, this door is fastened up, never to turn on its hinges again, till some new event of a similar nature demand its services. The extraordinary neatness which prevails throughout the whole is a prodigy.

On a visit which the late Emperor Joseph made to this village, he is said to have experienced the rigour of those injunctions, which are laid upon all who view the Orphan House; and before he was admitted to tread the sacred floor, he conformed to the ceremony of taking off his shoes. That care and attention may preserve the
several

several apartments in a state of internal neatness, is readily conceivable; but that the outsides of their houses, roofs, and fronts,—their gravelled grounds, and open paths, should exhibit no marks of occasional violence, should betray no symptoms injurious to their systematic correctness, is a mystery for which I cannot account. The natural action of the elements—the blowing storm, and the driving shower, might well be deemed, too strong opponents of art and nature: yet, exposed to all the vicissitudes of the seasons, not a vestige of injury could be traced. How patient must be that assiduity, which watches those accidents, which imperceptibly repairs their ravages, and gives to those unexampled productions of industry, uniformity and permanence.

I quitted this singular spot with reluctance. As the barge moved slowly along, my eyes feasted upon the parting fairy landscape. I could not govern my sensations.

tions.—Did ever poet image aught so fair?

> Dreaming in whispering groves, by the hoarse brook,
> Or prophet, to whose vision heaven descends!

The picture gradually disappeared, as the colours faded, and was at length ravished from my sight. The vulgar scenes of Amsterdam reduced my ideas to a less rapturous standard. Were I to measure existence with the antediluvian antients, I should never be able to erase those scenes from my mind, nor entirely convince myself, that the whole was not a delightful illusion of the fancy.

## LETTER XXII.

I WAS so extremely delighted with the little I saw of North Holland, that I could, with great pleasure, have penetrated farther; but our time did not admit of any extension of the tour. At a very short distance from Broek lies Saardam, a village in many refpects fimilar to that we vifited, but more particularly celebrated for the temporary refidence of the Czar Peter the Great, who fpent a confiderable time here; and *Peterfhoff*, or Peter's houfe, is fhewn to the prefent day. We contented ourfelves with viewing it as we paffed, and quitted Amfterdam the following day. We continued to travel by water, and the paffage between Amfterdam and Utrecht difplayed a greater variety of fcenery, than we had yet met with in any part of Holland. The country wore a more fertile afpect, and the banks of the canal were covered with gardens.

Utrecht is built very much upon the model of the towns we had before feen. Its public buildings poffefs no particular beauty. Its univerfity owes none of its celebrity to the magnificence of its ftructures. The great tower of St. Martin is indeed a very noble remnant of antient art. The view from

## LETTER XXII.

from the summit of this tower is very extensive. Near twenty cities may be discovered by the eye, within a very bounded space. I ascended the tower with great eagerness, and was impatient to reach the point of observation. But, when arrived at a certain height I took a survey of the country—my situation was not perfectly to my satisfaction: the stone, mouldered by the finger of time, and apparently loosened by decay, wore a tremendous aspect. Having climbed within a few paces of the summit, I descended, with a sober determination to take in future my views from some less aspiring eminence, where, if I saw objects to less advantage, I should also see them with less trepidation. I took little pains to examine the town. It wore a very dull appearance, and was animated only by the images it revived, of its political importance. This city was distinguished in 1572, for the union of the provinces, which was there formed. And the celebrated Congress of
1712,

1712, has interwoven the name of Utrecht, with the hiſtory of the greateſt ſtates in Europe. Duclos's Hiſtorical Records of thoſe Times, have ſome particulars of a very intereſting nature, reſpecting the conduct of the Dutch in this Congreſs. One anecdote related by him, I will tranſcribe. Villars, you recollect, had gained an important victory over the allies at Denain. The Dutch miniſters ſtill however preſumed, notwithſtanding this diſaſter, and the armiſtice concluded between England and France, to talk in a ſtyle of great haughtineſs, But the Cardinal de Polignac aroſe and ſilenced them, by declaring in a firm and deciſive manner, that the period for haughty and imperious language was paſt. " Meſſrs." ſaid he, " les circonſtances " ſont changées—il faut changer du ton. " Nous traiterons chez vous, de vous, & " ſans vous."

From Utrecht we took cabriolets for Bois-le-duc, or, as the Dutch call it, Hertzogenboſche.

bofche. This occupied a night, and part of the following day. The route we purfued is not very frequently travelled. It gave us however an opportunity of feeing another part of the country. It was between ten and eleven o'clock when we reached the banks of the Leck, and the latenefs of the hour was pleaded as an excufe for not paffing the river; fo we flept in our clothes till morning, and paffed the river at fun-rife. We then proceeded to Bommel, crofling that arm of the Rhine which bears the name of the Waal.

From Bommel to Bois-le-duc, we had to encounter a road worfe than any yet feen, and which admonifhed us momentarily to prepare for the chance of an overthrow. The country around was wretched, barren, and fwampy. After crofling the Maefe, we arrived fafe in the middle of the day at Bois-le-duc, where the carriage waited for us. It had been our plan, previous to commencing the expedition, to take this courfe,

and

and issue by Bois-le-duc, which formed a more extensive tour than is usually made. The customary track is to quit Holland by way of Gorcum and Breda, on which side the country is more fertile, and the roads infinitely better, than by the route we took; and I know of no advantages which can be mentioned, to counterbalance those inconveniences, except that of traversing more extensively the country, and making ourselves acquainted with some of its worst parts.

Bois-le-duc had nothing to attract us; but for the purposes of refreshment, we determined to continue there the day. We had travelled very hard for a week past, and had seldom rested night or day. The inn at which we were lodged, offered us comfortable quarters, had we resolved to spend a longer time; but, impatient to enter upon the pressing parts of our tour, we settled every preliminary for our journey to Maestricht, and held ourselves in readiness for an early departure.

## LETTER XXIII.

THE Dutch are univerfally celebrated for their attention to cleanlinefs; and *artifice* is not more proverbial of this nation, than *neatnefs*. I have before remarked, how well this obfervation is founded with refpect to the villages: here, indeed, it prevails in every poffible fhape, and pervades all ranks. No labour is fpared to give ornaments and luftre to the meaneft cottage, nor is it in the power of the painter to do more than juftice to thofe polifhed fcenes. But this extraordinary attention to neatnefs has a nearer connection with neceffity than choice. The moift exhalations which arife from the fwampy foil they inhabit, would be an over-match for inferior induftry; and without thofe repeated exertions, their health and their property muft be defolated by by their invariable foes, Damp and Mildew. What was firſt their irkſome duty, is now become their pleaſure and their pride.

In many houſes the beſt chambers are kept conſtantly cloſed. Suites of apartments are in many inſtances reſerved for the ſingle purpoſe of oſtentatious neatneſs, while the rich poſſeſſor himſelf inhabits a garret, or a cellar. A Dutchman is not remarkable for perſonal cleanlineſs, and the crachoir, of which they make ſo general a uſe, demonſtrates that they have at leaſt a ſet of feelings not ſtrictly in uniſon with delicacy.

It is univerſally remarked of this people, that they are knaviſh and extortionate—their trading avarice would ſeem to render this charge not wholly undeſerving of credit. The extreme paſſion for wealth which actuates them, and the credit attached to extended poſſeſſions, are not very favourable to the cultivation of uncorrupt integrity. The mind abſorbed in the adoration of such an idol, is often found slipping: the darling pursuit will not suffer check from slight obstacles, and the progress from one stage of avarice to another, is imperceptibly rapid. The tender feelings of honour and honesty once repulsed, become less obtrusive in their monitions, till at length the most essential principles of morality are regarded as shadowy distinctions.

That such reasonings are strictly applicable to the Hollanders, I shall neither pretend to affirm or deny.—Such is at least the turn of general opinion; but I think, however, that justice has not always been done to those laborious people. The character they may have merited in the great towns, and the most notorious places of resort, is ill-applied to the hardy inhabitants of the humble cot: and a numerous class undoubtedly exists, who, secluded from the crouded mart, have not yet become tinctured with the national foible. Were I to pronounce upon these, agreeably to the experience I have

had

## LETTER XXIII.

had of some, and the observation I made upon others, I should rank them with the more meritorious part of mankind, over whom honesty, virtue, and content, maintain an equal influence. There was an expression in the countenance of those toiling villagers, which disarmed fear in the most perilous situation.

When we entered the dark abode, after crossing the Biesboch, and found ourselves surrounded with men whose language we could not speak—the solitary and desert situation inspired alarm; but a few moments interview with those uncouth cottagers discovered how groundless had been such terrors. The language of nature spake in their looks the integrity of their hearts, and we passed the evening with less dependence upon the arms we carried, than the unsuspicious honesty we found. The little apartment which we occupied, exhibited a circumstance rarely found in houses appropriated to the purposes of a *cabaret*. In one

## LETTER XXIII.

one corner of the chamber was a book, apparently deftined for general ufe. One of our guides had taken up the volume, and was occupied great part of the night in ftudying its contents. Curious to know the object of his amufement, I intreated his permiffion to view the book, and found that the lad was regaling himfelf with fcripture hiftory, and though nearly exhaufted with the fatigues of the voyage, he fpent great part of the night in reading the Bible.

Our paffage between Leyden and Haerlem gave me an opportunity of remarking another circumftance of fimilar report to their religious character. The mafter of the veffel had prepared his dinner, which confifted of fome potatoes, boiled to a powder over the little fire-pan which kindled the pipes. He had placed his little difh upon a bench—when, taking up his hat, he held it before his eyes for fome moments; and having confecrated by this act of devotion the provifion before him, he devoured it

VOL. I. I without

without apprehenſion or delay. I obſerved his partner, who ſucceeded him, perform the ſame ſacred rite upon beginning his ſimple meal.

Thoſe circumſtances made me decide, that great reſpect was paid to religious obligations, ſince the preſence of ſtrangers did not interrupt the order of duty. An equal curioſity induced me to take up a book which lay open upon a table at the *cabaret* on the banks of the Maeſe, of which I confeſs I could not report ſo favourably. The balance, however, yet ſtands on the better ſide; and if I were to draw any concluſions from my own obſervations in relation to religion and morals, it would certainly contain an encomium upon their virtue, which I am willing to believe the Hollanders deſerve in a higher degree than is confiſtent with general opinion.

## LETTER XXIV.

I KNOW not any thing which ſtrikes a traveller more, in entering upon Holland, than the nature and general face of the country, preſſed by the riſing ocean, whoſe mighty waves are elevated beyond the level of the land. It appears the country of art, wreſted by the induſtry of its natives from the realms of Neptune, and guarded by eternal toils againſt his irruptions. Nothing can equal the impreſſion excited by a view of the diſtant waves, whoſe ſwelling ſurges ſeem ready to ſwallow up lands, cities, and hamlets, in primæval ruin. Goldſmith's accurate picture of this country recurred to my memory, as I meditated upon its miraculous exiſtence:

> To men of other minds my fancy flies,
> Emboſom'd in the deep, where Holland lies:
> Methinks her patient ſons before me ſtand,
> Where the broad ocean leans againſt the land,

## LETTER XXIV.

> And fedulous to ftop the coming tide,
> Lift the tall rampire's artificial pride;
> Onward, methinks, and diligently flow,
> The firm compacted bulwark feems to grow,
> Spreads its long arms amidft the watery roar,
> Scoops out an empire, and ufurps the fhore:
> While the pent ocean, rifing o'er the pile,
> Sees an amphibious world beneath him fmile,
> The flow canal, the yellow-bloffom'd vale,
> The willow tufted bank, the gliding fail,
> The crouded mart, the cultivated plain,
> A new creation—refcued from his reign.

It will naturally be imagined, that a country under fuch circumftances, can boaft little beauty. Flat, fwampy, and open, it exhibits no variety to the eye—the foil appears coarfe, the profpects dreary, and the atmofphere chilled, and impregnated with conftant exhalations.

But if no pleafing varieties exift in the general afpect of the country, a ftill greater uniformity appears in the beft and moft populous towns. Divided and fub-divided by an equal multiplicity of canals—pierced by ftreets, and crouded by buildings in the fame mercantile ftile of taftelefs grandeur, they

## LETTER XXIV.

they afford only a perpetual repetition of the fame impreffion. The water, which ufually contributes to variety, here adds to the uniformity, and is indeed its grand fource, conducted, as it invariably is, in thofe channels which beft fuit the purpofes of commodious navigation. The gardens are only fo far eftimable, as they exhibit at one period of the year a fhow of beautiful flowers, and ferve to convince the traveller that vegetation *actually exifts*, amidft the profufion of water, which overfpreads the face of the country. In all other refpects, the Dutch gardens are proverbially at variance with every principle of tafte and elegance.

I dwelt with rapture on thofe which ornamented the village of Broek, becaufe they pretended to no magnitude or ftile. They were confiftent with every other part of the fyftem, and contributed effentially to the decoration of that artificial fcene. They had a merit in that fituation, which they would

would have wanted in another, where any thing beyond neatness and singularity were attempted. But to examine those mangled grounds which cover the banks of their canals, and which are denominated gardens, is only to see how far depraved taste can extend. Nature is, in those regions, wholly out of repute. From some secret suspicions of her awkwardness, they impose a code of vegetative laws, agreeably to which it should seem she *must* act, and condemn all deviations from it as inelegant luxuriances. Hence the pruning knives, and a thousand instruments, are perpetually in hand to keep her in order. They think that trees ought to grow like animals—like door-posts—like walls—or in short like any thing but what they were intended for. Hence you see what these people call a garden, is often a range of parapets, a string of alleys, or a very menagerie. They seem to have found out the art of effecting what the elder sages thought impracticable, and

weakened

## LETTER XXIV.

weakened my faith in that maxim of Horace, which I before deemed univerſal :—

"Naturam expellas furcâ, tamen uſque recurret."

A more complete victory of art over nature never exiſted. Proſtrate, enchained, expiring, the latter ſeems now to ſubmit without a ſtruggle to the tyranny of the former, reſolving to wage no longer a war upon ſuch unequal terms. Moſt of the gardens, I ſaw, led to thoſe reflections : they were adorned with the trophies of victorious art. Shaped into the fantaſtic forms of dragons, griffins, or dolphins—the deſpairing ſhrubs ſeemed to meditate no further irregularities, but conformed their vigorous ſhoots to thoſe arbitrary laws by which they had been diſciplined. A garden *a l'Angloiſe*, is not without its imitators in Holland, yet almoſt the whole country is ſtill over-run with thoſe Gothic devices. They are ſtill held in ſecret reſpect, and cultivated with unwearied attention. They are esteemed the precious monuments of *antient* art—the invaluable bequests of their industrious ancestors, and the chief ornaments of their country.

There is certainly a consistency in this predilection: it is very much in character with the air, the dress, and the habits of life, which those people cultivate in themselves. Moulded personally on no principle of elegance, they borrow no improvements from their dresses, which are equally at war with convenience and beauty. Nature seems to have hewn them with a rough chisel, and formed them upon a plan of business. All their pursuits bear reference to the same principle: taste is industriously excluded from all their designs, to whatever they apply; and their buildings and gardens are not more grotesque and uncouth, than their habits and manners. Any man, however, who sees the intensenefs with which they pursue their plans of traffic, will cease to wonder that so wealthy a nation should yet

be

# LETTER XXIV.

be so far removed from refinement. The elegancies of life have scarcely a name in their vernacular tongue; the vortex of trade ingulphs all considerations; and wealth is sufficiently respectable, to atone for the absence of every other quality. These maxims, which are here reverenced by all ranks, are sufficient to preclude the introduction of those improvements which adorn society, and give a lustre to states. It would indeed be a novel event in the history of mankind, if any thing great in arts or refinements should arise from a nation, whose sole talent is industry, and whose ruling passion is the love of gain.

## LETTER XXV.

THE kings of Spain, from the time they became masters of the mines of Mexico and Peru, have been considered as the cashiers of Europe; and it was well said by Boccalini, that Spain is to Europe, what the mouth is to the body, " tout y passe,.et rien n'y reste." However Holland may stand in the same predicament in one respect, it certainly differs very widely in the other. The Dutch are at this moment the cashiers of Europe, and the bankers of every state; but with a policy peculiar to themselves, they convert the weaknesses of other nations, into the instruments of their own aggrandizement. Their speculations are usually formed upon solid principles; and though they appear to hazard much, they seldom sustain loss. So completely are they

occupied

## LETTER XXV.

occupied by the predominant concerns of negotiation, that they appear indifferent about their governmeut. Naturally they are bold, steady, and enamoured of liberty. Europe has witnessed their courage when provoked. Few nations have entered the lists of war with more reluctance, or quitted them with more renown. A slight injury will not arouse, nor a slight revenge appease them. Inveigled into treaties by hope or fear, never by choice, they usually relieve themselves from such obligations. They hold them no farther binding, than their interest dictates, and never scruple to traffic with the declared enemies of their allies—provided it can be done with secrecy and safety. Considering themselves rather in the capacity of a commercial association, than a state of Europe, they regard the cabals of cabinets, and the revolutions of empires, with political indifference. Unambitious of those laurels for which monarchs too often interrupt the peace of mankind,

they

they calmly cultivate the arts of induſtry, and ſtudy to fill their coffers; while kingdoms, inflamed by trivial animoſities, are exhauſting their treaſures to equalize dominion, and preſerve the balance of power. The ſame phlegmatic inattention is apparent to the political movements which take place in the boſom of their own country. Conſtitutionally averſe to monarchical authority, and inheriting from their anceſtors a rooted attachment to republican government, they yet ſubmit to forms which ſhadow forth a ſubjection that their forefathers had bluſhed to acknowledge. We were under the neceſſity of wearing the orange cockade, throughout every part of Holland. All ranks of people continue to wear this badge of princely authority. Formerly it marked the diſtinction of parties— at preſent it covers thoſe diviſions, familiarizes theſe tame deſcendants of a hardy race to a yoke at which they ſecretly revolt, and tends to eſtabliſh the authority of a power
whoſe

## LETTER XXV.

whose existence at one moment appeared equivocal.

The reasonings which determine the Hollanders to such passive measures, are not founded on the extinction of antient prejudices, or the forfeiture of original spirit; but the inconveniences which would result to *trade* from an opposition to the victorious power. The grand wheels and springs must be for a period neglected—revolutions would generate confusion, and arrest for a time the tide of commerce: nor can plans of revolt be successfully supported, without great expence of time, labour, and manufactures.

It is evident, that considerations of this nature must influence the Dutch to their present conduct, as they are by no means reconciled to the authority of the Stadtholder. Personal safety was pleaded as the reason for assuming thus universally this badge of servitude, yet discontents are numerous, and the *throne* of the Stadtholder

appears

appears but ill-fecured. The government which exifts at this moment is certainly ill-fuited to the temper and genius of a people whofe reigning prejudice is an averfion to princes. It is a government, whofe parts do not well affimilate, and which never have accorded. The fuperaddition of an hereditary Prince to the pre-eftablifhed authority of the ftate, has counteracted their antient labours—has deftroyed the uniformity, the purity, the correctnefs of their republic, and opened a channel for political interference from the Powers of Europe. Louis the XIV. and XV. by turns, gave them a Stadtholder; and the late commotions, which fhook the Houfe of Orange, were not viewed with political indifference by the Powers of Europe.

What will be the iffue of thofe difcontents, which, through quelled, are not compofed, time can alone decide; but certain it is, that the temper of the Hollander is not the moft placable, nor the moft difpofed to forgivenefs.

## LETTER XXV.

nefs. Princes are, in general, obnoxious to this people, who acknowledge no diftinctions but thofe of property; and if a Hollander has ever imagined the reigning Prince tinctured with principles of tyranny—if he has at any period detected him in defigns to aggrandize his own authority, and contract the public liberties, he will ever regard him with fufpicion, and no after-acts can purge the memory of this delinquency.

Louis XV. experienced in this ftubborn people, the lafting effects of firft impreffions. Mafter of Flanders, and in poffeffion of 35,000 Dutch prifoners, he preffed them to accept a peace, which their fituation would have rendered a more proper requeft on their part; but they obftinately refufed to attend to his offers. Impreffed with the *hauteur* of Louis XIV. in 1672, they could not confider a fucceffor of the fame *name*, as divefted of the fame *qualities*. Deeming that what a prince could offer, a republic fhould not accept, they viewed with a fu-

fpicious

spicious eye all his overtures—referring his most specious declarations to artifice or necessity, and deeming every effort to effect a conciliation, a symptom of weakness, or a snare for their seduction.

Voltaire has remarked this conduct in the Dutch with his usual animation: " L'ir-
" ruption de Louis XIV. & l'année
" 1672, etoient encore dans leurs cœurs,
" et j'ose dire que je me suis apperçu plus
" d'une fois que leur esprit frappé de la
" hauteur de Louis XIV. ne pouvant conce-
" voir la moderation de Louis XV. ils ne
" la crurent jamais sincere. On regardoit
" toutes ses demarches pacifiques, et tous ses
" ménagemens, tantôt comme des preuves
" de faiblesse, tantôt commes dos pieges."

## LETTER XXVI.

THE journey from Bois-le-duc to Maestricht was very laborious for the horses, and very irksome to ourselves. The road continued to exhibit numberless difficulties; it was almost the whole way composed of a sandy soil, ploughed into deep and dangerous furrows; and we had the mortification to be dragged for two days, at a foot pace, over a country which wore the most desolate aspect. The only objects which rose out of this barren soil were some scattered gibbets, which well assorted with the murderous face of the country.

Our first night was, however, passed at a very pretty village, whose name was so guttural, that I could not divine how many consonants went to the formation of it; for you know, both in Dutch and Flemish lore, a few vowels go a great way. I must content myself, therefore, with telling you, that it was about half way between Bois-le-duc and Maeſtricht—was ſurrounded in its immediate precincts by ſome charming village ſcenery, and wore a very picturesque appearance: and this will, I hope, compenſate for the omiſſion of a hoarſe name, " quod verſu dicere non eſt."

Our ſecond day's journey was equally forlorn, and equally diſguſting, till our eyes caught the banks of the Meuſe, and the lofty bulwarks of Maeſtricht. It was fair-time when we entered it. All were dreſſed in their holiday attire—the ſtreets were crowded with old and young, and the air was filled with the ſounds of mirth, interrupted by the diſſonant braying of trumpets. We ſaw nothing in Maeſtricht beyond the ordinary run of towns. Its fortifications are, indeed, poſſeſſed of immenſe ſtrength, and exhibit an impregnable ſyſtem of defence. There is a cave into which the curious ſometimes venture; but the circumſtances accompanying it did not induce us to add to that number.

Our

## LETTER XXVI.

Our next day was taken up in the journey from Maeſtricht to Spa, which gave us an opportunity of ſeeing Liege. I have before remarked, that Amſterdam was the moſt uncleanly town I ever ſaw. I ſhall now except Liege. I never could have imagined a town in ſuch a ſituation deformed by ſo much filth. The ſtreets were paved, the buildings faced, and the houſes lined with dirt of the blackeſt colouring. In addition to this, the whole town was in uproar. Huſſars, with naked ſabres, were ſtationed at regular intervals throughout every avenue of the town; and the ſavage countenances of theſe rude barbarians, were to be encountered at every ſtep. The cathedral is noble, the *bourſe* ſpacious and commodious. We were not a little rejoiced to quit this town in the afternoon, and I think we left behind us the aggregate of every thing that is dark, tremendous, and offenſive.

Our route then lay upon a good *pavée*, with no inconſiderable hills, to Spa, and we entered this ſingular place in the duſk of the evening. The great charm of Spa consists in the blended society, which is there found from various motives. The country is romantic, and the *promenades* pleasant. The places of usual residence are embosomed by hills of no great magnitude, but whose relative situation to the town gives a picturesque air to the spot. The salubrity of the springs first formed the importance of this place: but as mankind are oftener afflicted with *imaginary* than *real* complaints, as the disorders of the spirits are more numerous than the maladies of the body, Spa is less in repute for its medicinal nostrums than its more potent attractions—the ball-rooms, the concerts, and the galas.

If one may judge from the exorbitant charges here made, health is not purchased upon moderate terms; and though the springs gush unbribed from the soil, their waters do not continue to flow with equal liberality. A Spa residence, of the shortest duration, is not made without considerable expence. Were a palace to be converted

into

into a caravanfera, fcarcely would an higher price be fixed upon the apartments than is here demanded. Yet our kind landlords affure us, that the price of our apartments will increafe in, what appears to me, a geometric progreffion with the advancement of the feafon.

One would imagine, that in a place which nature deftined as an afylum for the fick, as a kind of grand hofpital of invalids,—wine would be a fuperfluous article, and fcarcely fetch any price. The contrary is the fact: the afflicted multitude who crowd here, feem to fwallow down—no doubt by the advice of their phyficians—larger potions of this favourite beverage than even of the pure and unadulterated element: by which judicious medical arrangement, this place maintains its reputation, as the grand continental mart, not only of health, but of feftivity and pleafure.

## LETTER XXVII.

Spa, May 20, 1791.

MANKIND have almost uniformly converted necessity into a virtue, and what has been originally submitted to with reluctance has usually terminated in choice. The swampy soil of Holland, and the numerous nervous fevers which arose from this circumstance, gave birth to those black patches upon each temple, which, by the superstition of antient times, were deemed specifics against nervous affections. These are now become a part of the Dutch dress. In vain does " La petite Hollandoise" put on her broad orbicular bonnet, or coiff herself in uncouth lustre; till the large black patches are affixed, she can expect to make no conquest. She may display her rounded shoulder, and exhibit her slip-shod heel; yet will

will her artillery prove ineffectual without the aid of these proud ornaments.

Something similar has taken place in the numerous springs and baths throughout Europe. Accident discovered their salubrious effects in remedying disorders, and restoring shattered constitutions. Amusements are deemed necessary to the dissipation of that languor, which ill health and medicinal regimen are apt to engender. The colours of pleasure are never displayed in vain. The votaries of amusement soon crowded to that standard, where the banners of their goddess were exalted, and the empire thus became divided between the valetudinarian and the voluptuary.

This commerce is not without its advantages. Doubtless the associated supplicants of Esculapius had formed a ghastly band, and might have passed a miserable *sejour* in the society of each other. The pallid face, the leaden eye, the hollow cheek, and the emaciated frame required the introduction of some more cheerful countenances; the commixture of those in whom the tide of blood is not chilled by age, nor tainted by malady, would enliven the scenes thus deformed, and tend to accelerate the salutary effects of the springs. But mankind know no medium; at present the rivulets of health are swallowed up in the torrents of pleasure, the severity of regimen relaxes into the luxury of debauch, and the medicinal potion is supplanted by the Bacchanalian draught. Nor is this all—the harpies of fortune are disposed in every quarter of this Circean Elysium. The young and the incautious are inveigled by the specious appearances of personal splendor and titled consequence. Fortunes are thus committed, not to the mercy of a card, or the chance of a die,—but to the artifice of those, whose sole talent is imposture, and whose sole property is vested in the funds of human weakness.

The anecdotes which are here circulated, and the estimates here formed upon the issue

of

# LETTER XXVII.

of former seasons, render it more than probable, that the vast influx of company in the present, will exhibit various revolutions of fortune in the gaming circle. Charmed, as I am, with the aspect of its hills, and the fame of its waters, I cannot but consider Spa as first amongst those places of general resort, which swell the tide of human corruption. I cannot but believe, that more morals are debauched by the contagion of its vices, than nerves braced by the vigour of its air; and that more fortunes are ruined by the fascination of its amusements, than constitutions restored by the salubrity of its springs.

## LETTER XXVIII.

Duſſeldorf, May 25, 1791.

THE man who travels for higher purpoſes than thoſe of pleaſure, will not make a long reſidence at Spa. We left it after having beſtowed a whole week upon contemplating its deſerted ſprings, and ſtrolling amongſt its ſilent promenades. I glanced on the Sunday over the tablets which decorate the church; and found, that ſuperſtition has *once* enjoyed as great dominion here as pleaſure *now* does. I could not forbear remarking one in particular, which held out a variety of indulgences to the *confrères* of the holy ſacrament. One of thoſe grants purported, that if any one of this fraternity viſit the ſick with the holy ſacrament; or, if indiſpoſed, write " Pater " Noſter," and " Ave Maria," five times, he ſhall be entitled to indulgence for ſixty days next

next enfuing. This appears a very reafonable purchafe, and is, I imagine, the only article at Spa, which has not advanced in price. Aix-la-Chapelle finifhed our journey of Monday. The road paffed for the greater part through a hilly country, and ill-announced, by its vaft inequalities in the neighbourhood of Aix, the entrance to an afylum of invalids.

Aix is, indeed, a grand infirmary; the baths are falubrious and convenient; they are deemed highly reftorative of decayed conftitutions; and are, therefore, frequented by numbers, whofe debaucheries have fcarcely left them the ftrength to complain. That quarter of the town in which the hotels ftand, is alfo the fituation of the baths, and for the moft part, the refidence of the invalids. There is an air of vivacity in the fhops, the porticoes, and the affembly rooms; and the general exterior is not without a pleafant and cheerful effect. But fo many ghaftly figures are perpetually moving

ing before you, wrapped in sedans, or crawling from seat to seat, that cheerfulness is crossed by a thousand painful emotions; and amusement in such a scene would scarcely have upon me a better effect, than a dance in a dungeon, or a concert in a lazaretto.

The cathedral of this town is a very noble monument of antient times, and stands in high repute for the regalia of Charlemagne, and other precious toys, which it is known to contain. The greatest curiosity it had for me, was the groupe of worshippers, which was planted round one of its altars. An old Franciscan was conducting the religious ceremonies; and the people, who were of various qualities and conditions, had thrown themselves for the most part into the attitude resembling a cross. They extended their arms as they knelt, and preserved both these and their countenance immoveably fixed,—notwithstanding the interruption they might be supposed to
experience

experience from the paffing and repaffing of ftrangers. An equal fervor of devotion prefented itfelf at Juliers, to which we paffed in the evening of yefterday. The rain was falling inceffantly; yet this did not deter a number of people from repairing to an altar erected in the open ftreet, facing the window of our hotel, in order to perform their vefpers. For nearly an hour they fucceeded each other in thefe facred fervices,—kneeling upon the naked ftones, without the leaft precaution, in contempt of the frowns of weather, or the fmiles of the rude fpectator.

I confefs I feel rebuked, rather than diverted, by fuch examples; nor can I withhold my refpect from thofe, who, after the way which *we* call fuperftition, fo fervently worfhip the God of their fathers. We left Juliers this morning by fun-rife, and taking a breakfaft with an honeft German, three leagues on our way, obtained from him inftructions for our route; and having croffed

the

the Rhine, in face of Duffeldorf, find ourselves agreeably accommodated by the good offices of Zimmerman, at the Hotel de Deux Ponts.

LETTER XXIX.

May 26, 1791.

I KNOW not how others may feel, but I must confess very little pleasure is by me derivable from the *solitary* contemplation of works of art. When the eye has feasted upon the charming tints of a captivating picture, and is called to gaze upon others in succession,—it appears as though some discussion of the first, and some communication upon its excellencies were indispensable. Such at least was the temper of my mind in viewing the gallery of Duffeldorf; and as we are now housed under the roof of an honest post-master, five leagues on our way to Cologne, I am impatient to disclose to you the impressions I received from the invaluable collection that place contains.

You must not expect *as yet* much science in my descriptions; for I have not yet learnt the technical phraseology. From some motive which has escaped me, I chose to invert the usual order of observation, and intreated to see the chamber of Rubens first. The three principal paintings in this department were the Adoration of the Shepherds, the Death of Seneca, and the Last Judgment. In the first of these the countenance of the Virgin was wonderfully expressive of solemnity and joy—the looks of the shepherds of surprize and congratulation. The Death of Seneca made me shudder. Of the Last Judgment, I *ought* to speak in raptures, but shall refer you to those, whose optics are better qualified to do justice to this vast and sublime groupe.

The second chamber was that of Vander-Werf. The paintings of this master, whose polished pencil defies the strictness of criticism, cifm, prefent little that can move the heart. I gave him but a fhort trial, and haftened to the third, or Italian chamber. Where Raphael formed his gay and youthful idea of St. John the Baptift, I know not,—but I fhould rather have expected to find this great preacher of repentance in the Hermit of Salvator Rofa, which hangs in the fame apartment.

Two admirable productions of Carlo Dolci, of very different characters, fhared my next attention. The firft prefented our Saviour bearing his crofs. I was particularly ftruck with the delicacy of execution in the livid hue, which the burden of a crofs, and the anguifh of a crown of thorns muft naturally induce. The fecond was a St. Agnes the Martyr, in whofe countenance the painter had contrived to introduce fuch touches of fweetnefs, that I could have gazed upon it for ever.

Two paintings of Schalken interefted me greatly. The firft reprefented " la lumiere
" vraiement

## LETTER XXIX.

"vraiement fouflée," or "the candle actually blown out." This is one of the pleasantest things I ever faw. A girl is pictured as holding in her hand a lighted candle, which a boy endeavours to blow out, and fhe— by a counter-action of breath—to recover. The boy's lungs are, however, too ftrong for the girl's refiftance: he gives a fteady blaft, and the candle is feen upon the point of lofing its flame. All thefe circumftances and effects, with the correfponding fluctuations of light and fhade, are rendered with inimitable accuracy.

The fecond of this mafter was of a more ferious defcription, and reprefented "the wife and foolifh virgins." The painter has chofen the moment, when the call is heard of, "Behold the Bridegroom cometh! "Go ye out to meet him."—The wife virgins are defcribed, as obeying with promptitude the fummons; their countenances wear the air of confidence, and fpeak the language of preparation. Their lamps are trimmed,

trimmed, the lights are brilliant, and they appear to have heard the sudden call without fear or surprize. On the other hand, a greater scene of confusion and derangement cannot be imagined, than that in which the foolish virgins are found. Their air is that of persons perplexed and disconcerted: some of their lamps are already out, in others the light is expiring. They are busied in fruitless endeavours to preserve the fading, or rekindle the extinguished flame. The agitation, with which they supplicate a supply of oil from their wiser companions, is extreme. Those latter regard their ill-timed petitions with looks expressive of astonishment at their improvidence, and inability to supply them. This is surely a master-piece of painting for the artful disposition of lights, and the strong delineation of circumstance and character.

The beauteous groupe of the Holy Family, by Raphael, came unfortunately too late to produce its perfect effect. Schalken
had

had full poffeffion of me,—and while diligent to ftudy the chafter lights of that perfect mafter, the flafhes of the Dutchman danced like a meteor before my eyes. Such is the influence of firft impreffions on future habits; and—to indulge a tranfient moral reflection—he has ill ftudied life and nature, who fhall think it indifferent, which of two oppofing principles fhall have been the *firſt* inculcated.

## LETTER XXX.

Coblentz, May 30, 1791.

COLOGNE was the firſt town we entered after leaving the poſt-houſe from which I laſt wrote. It is a very antient and dignified city. The Romans knew it by the diſtinction of Colonia Agrippina; and it has been befieged and plundered as often as its rank and dignity demanded. Would you wiſh for more honours? It is an Hanſe town,

town, possesses an university, boasts an archbishopric, a principality, and a thousand other important appendages. The city is of wide extent; its churches are numerous and splendid, its fortifications strong, and its inhabitants civil and obliging. You will, by this time, assuredly allow, that I have not made a bad use of my time, in learning so much of the history and manners of a town, in which I passed *four hours*.

Before we entered Cologne, we had to pass the Rhine. Ourselves and equipage were embarked in a large ferry-boat, and quickly whirled across. The inn, where we stopped, abounded in German barons and French counts: a peep at the cathedral, and a stroll about the streets, were all the actual observations I had opportunity to make.

We passed the night, and a considerable portion of the following day at Bonn, which, in respect of situation, far surpasses Cologne. The palace of the Elector commands

## LETTER XXX.

mands a very fine landscape of mountainous country, and, at the time I entered the gardens, a groupe of velvet suits—retired from the *ennui* of the drawing-room—were cooling themselves with a *promenade*. I attended the mummery of the cathedral—a mixed emotion of indignation and respect possessed me; and I knew not whether most to despise the absurdity of the worship, or admire the devotion of the worshippers.

The village where we passed last night is called Remangen, between four and five leagues distant from Bonn. The country now begins to wear an interesting appearance, and the road which conducted us from Bonn to Remangen was distinguished by beauties of a peculiar nature—mountains on the one hand clothed with vineyards, the Rhine flowing in silent majesty on the other.

The approach to Remangen was marked with circumstances of singular sublimity. The road passed under a rock, upon whose bosom

bosom were thrown, as it were in rude confusion, houses and vineyards; and from whose shady summit glittered the spire of a church. This mass of rock over-arched the road, which was here very narrow; and the whole appeared to project in formidable magnificence over the Rhine that rolled below. I strolled in the evening over these picturesque scenes; and, seated upon the heights, was charmed with the landscape softened by the last tints of the setting sun, and the harmony of three rustic voices, which sung a *trio* upon the rocks below me—a practice very frequent among the Germans.

We left Remangen the ensuing morning, and passed through a continuation of that scenery I have described, but still improving in beauty. The mountains to our right were of considerable magnitude, and shaped in various forms; yet all appeared in an high state of fertility and culture. Andernach, where we breakfasted, is a curious remnant

## LETTER XXX.

remnant of antient strength. It is surrounded by ramparts mounted with a covert way, by which one can make the tour of the whole place, and view from a sufficient eminence the houses beneath. I know not the history of this place, but judge, from the magnitude of its fortifications, that it has once been of considerable note, and not unfrequently the seat of war. My mind was occupied by serious reflections, when I trod among its ruins, and counted its dilapidated towers. " And such, said I, is hu-
" man grandeur, and such the boasted
" monuments of arms and heroism—" I had continued my reverie, but the crack of the whip announced the moment of departure; and I was dragged in sullen silence to the place from which I now write.

# LETTER XXXI.

Mayence, June 2, 1791.

SITUATED at the confluence of the Rhine and Moselle, and flanked with mountains overspread with shrubs and ruins, Coblentz presents a very charming picture to the traveller's eye. I have kept a tolerable look-out upon the countenances of the fair-sex as I ascended the Rhine, and have found their beauty upon the increase as I advanced into the country.

The dresses of the men are stiff, formal, gothic. It is truly ridiculous to look from the window upon the bag-wigs, swords, and chapeaus-bras that pass. I told you above of mountains and ruins that entered into the scenery of Coblentz; but crossing the Rhine to the opposite vineyards,

## LETTER XXXI.

yards; the fairy vifions faded, the objects grew lefs interefting in proportion as they were more nearly viewed; and my difficulties increafed, when I had flattered myfelf with the idea of conquering them. After encountering much heat and fatigue, I relinquifhed my project, and retired to my old ftation. Thus, like the greater part of human profpects, thefe diftant delights appeared to advantage only in the expectation.

There are two evils in travelling, for which a man muft prepare himfelf with fortitude,—a change of language, and of money. This latter is extremely perplexing in running through the different Electorates and Principalities. Every tranfition of half a dozen leagues has introduced us to a people—not indeed of a different fpeech—but of a different coin; and it would require profound fkill in calculation to pafs without detriment from Duffeldorf to Mayence.

I have

## LETTER XXXI.

I have viewed the town of Coblentz, and read its history; but as the first has furnished me with nothing extraordinary, and the second would present to you nothing interesting—I shall neither amuse you with the measurement of its streets, or the detail of its revolutions; studious to avoid (though not always with success) the foible of those travellers, who, in the hope of giving importance to their temporary journals, forget themselves into historians—while the reader is left to murmur at being introduced to a people, not of modern, but of antient manners.

In the room, then, of erudite intelligence, I shall relate to you two grievous evils, which we experienced at Coblentz,—in the extortion of our landlord, and the desertion of our coachman. The first is an old and uninteresting complaint, the latter has something more of novelty and importance. Our coachman—he, alas! I mean, who once occupied the office—was known at Brussels,

his

his native town, by the name of Antoine: all our intercourse with him discovered but one *fault*, and one *virtue*. His fault was *obstinacy*—his virtue *universal language*. His obstinacy was cool, phlegmatic, and invincible. It shewed itself in a strict adherence to first habits; and, in defiance of advice and remonstrance, he to the last continued to carry his long green whip like a weeping willow bending solemnly over his right shoulder.

But justice must be done to his *virtue*. As an universal linguist, he served us for guide, interpreter, caterer—and in short, in every possible way of mediation. Such were the powers of his tongue, that he would argue with equal volubility in Dutch, Flemish, French, or German. He turned restive at Coblentz, where he seemed to have found a society he approved; and folding his arms, when summoned to his duty, peremptorily refused us the further services of his whip, and his tongue.

Thus

Thus disappointed, we continued our route, not without difficulty, to this place. We were amused, as we passed, with the varying views of a very fine country, visited some hot springs in our way, and arrived without accident before Mayence at the close of yesterday.

## LETTER XXXII.

*Spire, June 4, 1791.*

MAYENCE, or, as it is stiled in German orthography, Mentz, is a very fine town. The approach to it from the bridge of boats here thrown across the Rhine is strikingly beautiful. It possesses a very noble quay, extending along the banks of the river; and is rendered, by its fortifications, capable of a strong defence.

The day after our arrival was the festival of the Ascension, and I attended the celebration of high mass at one of the principal churches.

churches. It was a grand folemnity, accompanied with very excellent mufic, and the audience very crowded. I was particularly ftruck with the beautiful countenances of a long range of children, who attended the performance. But what has furprized and diverted me, at this and fome other towns through which we have lately paffed, is, that boys eight or nine years of age walk the ftreets with queues literally reaching half way down their legs.

The table d'hôte where we dined was attended by a very brilliant circle of officers and Abbés. The latter appeared of more than ordinary confequence, were dreffed in very fhowy fuits, and wore half a dozen ftars, croffes, &c. Their hands were wrapped up in very wide ruffles, and their profeffion was only to be traced in the fhortnefs of their hair.

I have often been led to remark the very ftriking fuperiority in accommodation, which a ftranger finds in a French fociety,
above

above that of every other nation. By whatever name it be called, and from whatever cause it proceed, the attention of a Frenchman to the embarrassment of a stranger is wonderful. I have witnessed on many occasions the exercise of this disposition. At a Dutch table d'hôte, one finds the reverse of this. Business swallows up all. The concerns of the change, the rate of merchandize, the rise and fall of the stocks, are the objects which take place of every consideration; and leave them neither leisure nor inclination to consult the ease, or relieve the embarrassment of a stranger. One is but little bettered at a German table: *themselves* are the parties whom they are anxious to oblige, and their attentions are excited to provide in the best manner for their own entertainment. I shall not draw the comparison between either of these, and what prevails at our public tables in England, lest my national vanity should be humbled by the conclusion.

I was

## LETTER XXXII.

I was not at a loss to account for the *hauteur* of the ecclesiastics in this town, as the chapter is composed of dignified characters; and no man can become a canon, till he has proved himself noble four generations deep. The wines drank here were exceedingly good. The richest vineyards are to be found in the neighbourhood; and Hocheim, which has given name to the Hock, is at no great distance from Mentz.

We employed the close of the day in making a journey of four leagues to Oppenheim, a town no longer of consequence. It stands close upon the Rhine, and is surrounded with scenery of no ordinary beauty. We passed our night here, and advanced the following day through Worms to Manheim. You will not expect me to describe with minuteness a town where I only took a breakfast. I shall content myself, therefore, with saying, that Worms is a pleasant town, situated about five leagues from Mentz. As to its antient history, you will find

find it more celebrated in ecclefiaftical than civil records. Within this town, that intrepid champion of reformation, Martin Luther, made his celebrated defence before the ftates of the empire.

Our entrance into Manheim was obftructed by fome military formalities, and the treatment we received indicated much feverity and vigilance. I was very much ftruck with the beauty of Manheim, whofe appearance eclipfes, indeed, all the towns I have feen upon the Rhine. On entering the ftreets, we could difcover little befides French officers ftrolling arm in arm, bearing the white cockade. We very foon learnt, that this place is the rendezvous of the emigrants; that here they are fuffered to poffefs, not only an afylum againft danger, but a nurfery of vengeance; that here they are indulged with a particular fpecies of protection and countenance; and that hopes the moft fanguine are by them entertained of recovering their forfeited domains,

mains, and humbling in their turn those by whom they have been humbled. All the inns were crouded with those dignified Refugees; and the day after our arrival, great preparations were making to receive the Comte d'Artois.

I could not but reflect, when I saw them assembled on the parade, and considered the impossibility of their return,—how strikingly public justice is executed upon them, as a body, in their proscription. A century past, Germany received into its hospitable bosom, Protestants, exiled by the ancestors of those who are now paying the forfeit of ancient oppressions. So true is it, that the ways of Providence are filled with equity; and the revolutions of empires resolve themselves into so many dispensations of retributive justice.

# LETTER XXXIII.

Strafbourg, June 7, 1791.

I TOLD you in my laft, that the difcipline of Manheim appeared very ftrict; and I found upon enquiry, that regulations of great feverity were enforced. I was cautioned, by the waiter at our inn, when proceeding to walk with my *fword-ftick*, to difarm myfelf before I left the room; as orders the moft rigorous had been iffued on that fubject. I muft refer you, for particulars of this beautiful town, to thofe who have feen more of it; and you will not have any great difficulty in finding defcriptions of its palace, its gallery, its fquares, and its fortifications. I paffed but a day here, and flept at Spire the following evening. There is nothing very remarkable in Spire, excepting.

cepting its remote antiquity. It stands about six leagues from Manheim.

The following morning, we entered the province of Alsace. This was announced to us by an Office of the customs, bearing the inscription of " Bureau National," and superscribed " La Loi et Le Roi." We were commanded to halt, and the Officers inspected all our luggage. We were happy to be informed, that this is the sole inconvenience of this nature we shall experience till we quit the kingdom. This, therefore, is one of those improvements in the police of the country, for which we stand indebted to the wisdom of its Reformers. The recollection of what we experienced in Flanders, and of what was practised in France under the old system, disposed us to wish all possible prosperity to the new Government.

Passing the wood, which conducts to the town of Lauterbourg, we were incommoded with a deep and hot sand, and pursued by flies of an extraordinary magnitude. I was amufed with the very fudden change which I difcovered in the appearance, the drefs, and the air of the inhabitants, in paffing from the head-quarters of Ariftocracy. The people all wear, without exception, the national cockade; and each town has its *Garde Nationale*. I never faw people more at their eafe. They appear not yet to have recovered from thofe paroxyfms of tranfport, into which the Revolution firft threw them; and they are frolicking without apprehenfion, at a time when the exiled nobleffe are plotting fchemes for their deftruction, at the diftance of half a dozen leagues from their frontier.

The town of Lauterbourg was enlivened by the notes of military mufic; and the popular air of " Ca ira" refounded in every ftreet. The wine in this town was delicious, and appeared more abundant than we had yet feen it. We rofe at an early hour, and made a journey of twelve leagues, which brought us to Strafbourg. The heat
continued

continued to persecute us all this day, but we found relief by bathing in the Rhine.

Our entrance into Strasbourg was obstructed for a short time by the demand of a passport. Against this we stood out with some violence, perceiving the object of the officer was to obtain a fee, and were at length victorious. So difficult is it for the wisest and best regulations to defeat, in every instance, the attempts of corruption. The heavings of subdued oppression will occasion some temporary interruption; but truth, justice, and order will finally triumph.

I have, I believe, omitted in its place to mention, that our route from Coblentz was obstructed by a long religious procession. A very large cross was borne at the head of those devotees: priests in surplices succeeded; and a promiscuous throng of men, women, and children brought up the rear. They chaunted—as the procession moved—various services; and produced a very agreeable harmony. We had some difficulty

ficulty to pafs them; and foon encountered a fecond fett, who were defcending the hill to meet them, and chaunting their matins with the fame mufical folemnity. The picturefque fcenes through which we were paffing, received an interefting colouring from thofe ceremonies of fuperftitious devotion.

My mind is, indeed, full of the varied imagery, which a rapid movement through fuch an extent of country has introduced. I have a thoufand pictures continually before me, of lofty mountains and level plains, of craggy rocks and cultured fields; but the fucceffion has been fo quick, that I can hardly review them with diftinctnefs. You will have much to fupply, as you travel with me, from the hiftories of thôfe who have gone before. Such obfervations as circumftances fuggeft, fhall be duly regiftered as I pafs; and fo much fhall be recorded for your entertainment, as the current of thought may at that moment fupply; but I pretend to

answer

answer for no higher amusement than can be found in the imperfect colourings of a rapid pencil—faithful rather to the idea impressed, than to the subject which may give it birth.

## LETTER XXXIV.

Basle, June 10, 1791.

WHAT a stupendous event is this Revolution! The evil which has baffled ages of resistance, and which seemed to know no limits of duration, has in a moment vanished. Surely, it is an interesting sight to contemplate upon the spot, those changes which have taken place upon a people, bound in the chain of immemorial tyranny. There is something so novel in the phraseology now employed, that the very language seems animated by the Revolutionary spirit. Liberty, Law, Constitution, Rights of men, are terms indeed of no new creation; but they had slept for ever in the cabinets of the learned, if the event—now the subject of universal celebration—had not awakened them into life and action.

I told you in my last, that we entered Strasbourg on the evening of the 6th. The following morning I amused myself in examining the different parts of the town. You have heard sufficiently of the Cathedral, its brazen gates, its stupendous tower, its wonderful clock, &c. On those subjects nothing can be added; but the temper of the people has assumed a new feature; and those long conversant with the country, are alone competent to tell,—how great are the changes which have been introduced into the manners, the sentiments, and conversation of the French.

For myself, who have not had that advantage,—I find it tolerably supplied by the intercourse I held with the Emigrants at Brussels, upon whom no change whatever had

had paffed, except a tranfient chagrin, which yielded to the firft occafion of merriment. I find a very ftriking contraft between the manners of the Revolutionifts and the Ariftocrats. The turn of politics which the firft have adopted has confolidated very greatly their natural vivacity, and reduced the buoyancy of their former levities to an agreeable humour.

All is political at Strafbourg. The corner of every ftreet is covered with *Programmas*, and the walls of every church decorated with Proclamations and Decrees. The greater part of the latter, advertife the fale of the national effects. It is very gratifying to fee, how rationally the language of the Preamble is worded; and what juft modifications of expreffion now convey the fanction of royal authority : " Louis XVI. " par la grace de Dieu et la loi conftitu- " tionelle de l'état, Roi de François, falut. " L'Affemblee Nationale a decretée, et nous " voulons et ordonnons," &c.——O Spirit of Louis XIV! what a contraft does this
préfent

present to the ancient form of the Royal decrees; and what a complete reformation of syſtem does it beſpeak, in thoſe who *will*, and thoſe who *obey!*—One ſcarcely walks twenty yards now, without meeting in places of public obſervation—a declaration of civil rights; and all the ſhops of muſic and prints, are hung with national ballads and political caricatures.

The counterpart to this, may be read in an extract from one of the late King's letters to Marechal Richelieu : " Je ne puis " plus differer à faire ſentir à mon parle- " ment, que je ſuis *le maître abſolue*,—et que " ma *puiſſance abſolue* vient de DIEU,—et que " je n'en dois compte qu'à *lui*, le jour où il " me retirera de ce monde." And again, in another letter, he tells him : " Je leur ferai " voir, que je ne tiens mon pouvoir que " de DIEU,—que je n'ai de compte à rendre " qu'à *lui*,—et que perſonne dans mon roy- " aume ne doit s'oppoſer à ma volonté." It forms a very intereſting ſpeculation to

bring

bring together those sentiments of a few years past, and the patriotic declarations of the reigning sovereign. Louis XVI. is said to have expressed on every occasion the greatest readiness to accommodate his conduct to the wishes of the nation. " Je ne veux que " le bien de mon peuple," is a sentiment in which he has frequently indulged.

Moore was certainly no mean student of the French character. Perhaps no man ever caught with more accuracy, or rendered with more felicity, "the living man-" ners" of this nation. But he was not endued with the spirit of prophecy. The *steadiest* sight sees *distant* objects darkly and confusedly. Let him speak for himself: " If any of their kings were to behave in " such an imprudent and outrageous man-" ner as to occasion a revolt, and if the " insurgents actually got the better, I que-" stion if they would think of new-model-" ling the government, and limiting the " power of the crown, as was done in Bri-
" tain

" tain at the Revolution, so as to prevent
" the like abuses for the future. They never
" would think of going farther, I imagine,
" than placing another prince of the Bour-
" bon family upon the throne, with the
" same power that his predecessor had, and
" then quietly laying down their arms,
" satisfied with his royal word, or declara-
" tion, to govern with more equity." *Letter VI. on France.*——Upon such prediction, the events that have since happened are a sufficient commentary.

## LETTER XXXV.

*Basle, June 10, 1791.*

THE general complaint at Strasbourg was want of money. Nothing is to be found in circulation, but paper and copper. " Tout iroit bien," said an old man, " si on avoit de l'argent." At all the shops, the greatest apprehensions are entertained of being paid for their merchandize in paper. This, amongſt each other, they are obliged to admit; but in their intercourſe with ſtrangers, they ſtruggle very hard for ſpecie.

I turned into the ſhop of a *Marchande de modes* to purchaſe ſome articles. The bargain was ſtruck, the ſeveral particulars wrapped up, and I was ſearching in my pocket for the money; when obſerving me draw out ſome paper by accident, ſhe laid immediate hold upon the packet I had purchaſed, and demanded with haſte, " Allez-" vous me payer en papier, Monſieur?" " Si fait," ſaid I. " Eh bien donc," replied ſhe, " je garderai ma marchandiſe." I ſoon relieved her of the anxiety ſhe felt, and brought a glow upon her cheek, by counting out upon the table the ſum agreed. This is indeed the greateſt—I had almoſt ſaid the only—grievance that I have diſcovered among them; and they ſcruple not to predict, that the very favourable ſale of the national domains will raiſe the credit of their

their paper, and give them as much money as they have liberty.

I muſt aſſure you, that I found the ſtate of the people in this part of France very different from what it had been repreſented. At Manheim and Worms, reports prevailed of the moſt ſerious tumults now reigning in France; and we were more than once cautioned againſt truſting ourſelves amongſt a *canaille*, who would hang us up at the lamp-poſt for a word or a look. This ſtatement has ſo little connection with truth, that every thing paſſes with the utmoſt order; and, ſo far as I can judge from obſervation and report, freedom of remark encounters leſs danger here than at the court of Manheim. Nothing could ſurpaſs the ſtrictneſs which prevailed in every quarter where the fugitive nobility are received; and if I might draw concluſions reſpecting the country at large from what I ſee around me, reſtraint of opinion is exiled with thoſe who owed to its exiſtence their guilty pre-eminence.

The

## LETTER XXXV.

The day after our arrival, was rendered festive by a new enrolment of National guards. This was formed out of the citizens over the age of eighteen years, and was effected without the least symptom of disorder. Beside the guard thus regularly embodied, the citizens are seen every evening in different parts of the town, learning, against an emergency, the use of arms. It certainly is animating to read, in a thousand conspicuous places, proclamations setting forth the right of private judgment; allowing to every man the free exercise of his opinion in matters of religion; and establishing to each individual the liberty of adopting that mode of worship he best approves.

This would, however, be nugatory and ridiculous, were the slightest encouragement given to contumacy and disorder. This has been said *out* of the country; but the contrary has appeared wherever I have enquired. I read upon the door of the cathedral

thedral at Strasbourg an advertisement, which stated, "That a young man having behaved improperly in the Cathedral during the performance of divine service; and, after admonition from the centinel, persisted in a conduct *unbecoming the solemnity of the place and occasion*, was, by the officers of the police, sentenced to imprisonment for this *insult offered to religious worship*." This accords but ill with a toleration of disorder.

Before I left Strasbourg, I visited the mausoleum of Marechal Saxe, at the church of St. Thomas; and had an offer of seeing the National armoury, but it came too late to serve me. We reached Colmar in the evening, after a journey of sixteen leagues. Yesterday we made a very fatiguing one of fourteen leagues, and reached Basle in the evening. The heat and the dust were excessively troublesome. It was not without difficulty that we procured a bason of milk at a village where the horses were baited.

Coffee

## LETTER XXXV.

Coffee is in general abundant in these parts of the country; and this is one of the first instances of distress which we have experienced upon the article of breakfast.

At the village of Mulhausen, eight leagues from Colmar, we alighted to dine. The house was ordinary; and four travellers, wrapped in white night-caps, apparently of mean condition, were about to commence their meal. I enquired of the hostess, if we could be also accommodated with a dinner. She told me with an air of great unconcern, that we might dine with those gentlemen; or—if that did not please us—we might take what they left; for that was the whole that her kitchen could produce. We did not long deliberate upon the choice which our landlady had given us. The dinner was indeed better than the company. They were Germans, except one,—who conversed with us in French, and asked me many questions respecting the opinions entertained abroad of their Revolution. I told him,

him, I had seen many Ariſtocrats at Manheim. He aſked me, if they had raiſed any troops? I told him, No; there were none but Officers. " Ah, ma foi, Monſieur," ſaid he, " une armée d'officiers s'avancera " peu." Another, with whom I afterwards converſed, declaimed with ſome violence againſt the propriety of Alſace being continued under the French government: " On nous fait payer," ſaid he, " 80,000 " livres pour être François; et c'eſt payer " aſſez cher, le *privi ege* d'être gouverné par " des *etrangers*."

## LETTER XXXVI.

Baſle, June 11, 1791.

WE entered Baſle at what would elſewhere be called eight, but what is here called nine, o'clock. I have never yet heard a ſatisfactory account of this advance of an hour in the time of the day, or what

were

were the real circumſtances that occaſioned it. An old traveller, who paſſed this way near two hundred years ago, reports of it, that a conſpiracy had been formed to betray the city, and that the falſe ſtriking of the clock diſconcerted the plot. He further ſays, that they preſerved a certain ſtone, called the *Heiſteine*, upon which the heads of the conſuls and other conſpirators were ſtruck off; unluckily adding, however, that people were not agreed upon this piece of hiſtory,—and that ſome referred the advance of the clock to a deſign of haſtening the proceedings of the council. It is, however, a curious circumſtance, to ſee a whole city one complete hour in all their tranſactions before their neighbours; and to a ſtranger, it occaſions ſome embarraſſment, as the ſun will neither riſe nor ſet in conformity to the decrees of Baſle.

The hotel of the Three Kings is that to which all the world goes; and I ſhould ſuppoſe there is not a pleaſanter Inn in Eu-rope.

rope. Situated on the weſtern banks of the Rhine, it commands a delightful view; and the ſaloon appropriated to the table d'hôte is the moſt cheerful apartment I ever was in. The walls are hung with various engravings, repreſenting ſome of the choiceſt ſcenery in Switzerland. The Rhine is here in its greateſt beauty, and fills a wider bed between this place and Straſbourg, than in any other part of its courſe. Nothing can ſurpaſs its colouring. The ſea, in all its azure and ſerenity, can alone furniſh a parallel to the cerulean tranſparency of its waters. It has conſiderable rapidity in its deſcent towards Straſbourg, and the boats which paſs thither are broke up and ſold. The ſame is done upon the Rhone and the Danube, it being impracticable, without infinite labour and coſt, to bring up a veſſel againſt ſo ſtrong a current.

The place and the people preſented to me an appearance particularly gratifying, by the ſtrong characters every where obſervable, of ſimplicity,

## LETTER XXXVI.

simplicity, cleanliness, and industry. Basle has been a place of no small dignity in the earlier periods of its history; though I question if it ever possessed, in the days of its Imperial grandeur, so solid a prosperity as it now derives from its union with the Cantons of Switzerland. Basle counts among its citizens, several men of eminence in arts and literature. Holben and Buxtorf were once, in their several departments, the ornaments of this town; and the great Erasmus is honoured with a monument in the Cathedral, upon the spot that contains his ashes. In addition to those distinctions, it claims the merit of having invented paper in the year 1417.

I took a walk in the evening through the different parts of the town, which are connected by a bridge over the Rhine. The shops appeared abundant in commodities: every one active in his occupation, and content with his condition. It was sun-set when I returned from my walk; and I found the shops shut, and the families seated upon benches at the doors of their houses. Here they enjoy the cool breeze of the evening, and relax from the fatigues of the day in cheerful conversation. I found this the case throughout all quarters of the town; and I seemed to myself passing through a saloon, the company in which was ranged in the highest order on both sides. This favours strongly of ancient and uncorrupt simplicity. Goldsmith has drawn the picture of it in his "Deserted Village." I had the images in my mind before I saw Basle, and was the more gratified in the revival of them, than I should have been by the first impression. Surely the noblest effect of the Muse is to learn to appreciate nature; and that Poetry is of the highest character, which conveys the faithfullest images of unadulterated life. It is on this principle that I consider Thomson and Goldsmith, as the oracles of genuine poetry, and the very best instructors of moral

ral fentiment. What volumes of verfe have been written with ufelefs elaboration!

> " To me more dear, congenial to my heart,
> " One native charm, than all the glofs of art."

## LETTER XXXVII.

*Berne, June 12, 1791.*

THE drefs of the women at Bafle was very fingular. Their hair was combed fmooth back from the forehead—bound at the crown with a fillet—and brought behind into two plaits of confiderable length. Thefe are further lengthened by black ribbons appended to them, which defcend almoft to their heels. Their countenances, without much beauty, were very pleafant and cheerful. They appeared very affable and unreferved. The generality of them drefs in black. This I had at firft fuppofed to be particular to the Black Forefters, but I find it is not confined to them; and that the univerfality of this ufage originates in œconomical reafons. The fhort petticoats—fo much the favourite of the *Hollandoife*—is here worn with much greater advantage; and difcovers a well-fhaped leg, ufually adorned with a fcarlet ftocking, forming—in the opinion of the females of Bafle—a fine contraft to the *fombre* fhades of their accuftomed habit.

I cannot difmifs the article of Bafle, without affuring you, that I was never more pleafed with a place which pretends to fo little. It owes all its beauties to nature and to induftry. Its only ornaments are, the landfcapes which furround it, and the fimple manners of thofe who inhabit it. Men, women, and children, all appeared engaged in the common caufe of enriching its markets, and fupporting its commerce. Here are no paftimes for the gay, no indulgences for the vicious: but the heart which can tafte of purer pleafures, and rejoice in the felicity of the human race, may here receive

## LETTER XXXVII.

no common gratification, in contemplating a virtuous, a united, and a happy people.

We left Baſle in the morning of the 11th, and have arrived at Berne, after a journey of two days. I will endeavour to give you a faint ſketch of the country through which we have paſſed; but eloquent indeed muſt be that pen, and animated that pencil, which can do adequate juſtice to ſuch ſcenes of pre-eminent beauty. As we left Baſle, we gradually entered upon a mountainous country, with the Rhine flowing to the left of us. The road continued tolerable, excepting that in different parts it was ſcattered with looſe and inconvenient fragments of ſtone. The courſe is ſerpentine, for the facility of aſcent; and this gives a greater ſcope for variety in the different landſcapes that preſent themſelves.

At Lieſtal, where we reſted during the heat of the day, the mountains appeared to gather round us. I was induced, by the ſingular appearance of one of theſe, to

make

make an ineffectual attempt at reaching its fummit, by catching at the roots, fhrubs, and maffes of ftone which covered its furface. From Lieftal we entered upon a route which exhibited to our eyes the grandeft pictures imaginable. Mountains piled on mountains feemed to inclofe us on all hands. Thefe were of various forms and complexions. Some rofe in conical beauty; others prefented afpects more rude and majeftic. Some were clothed with verdure; others with dufky umbrage; and others, difplaying their bofoms of naked flint, feemed to fet vegetation and culture at defiance. The road in many parts pierces thefe rocks; among which, as you pafs, you hear the roar of waters—defcending from precipice to precipice; and trace, among the ftupendous fcenery, the hut that protects the peafant from the ftorm. The approach of Bieftal paffes over a mountain, efteemed a league in afcent. The entrance to this place was particularly ftriking. On our

right,

LETTER XXXVII. 189

right, were mountains of uncouth form and prodigious height — on our left, vallies clothed with verdure, and scattered with human habitations. It was dusk when we entered, and the sun had given place to the softer shades of twilight.

This morning we left Bieftal, and passed through Soleure to Berne. The scenery increased in beauty and magnificence as we advanced. Soleure is a town of very pleasant appearance, and the Church is a very elegant building. This place is the capital of the Canton which bears its name; is of the Catholic religion, and the ordinary residence of the French ambassador to the Helvetic Union. It being Sunday, all the villagers and inhabitants of the town were parading in groups, with their short cloaths and their scarlet stockings. At the table d'hôte there were many Emigrants; but no articles of intelligence transpired. Our object was to reach Berne in the evening, which we effected; and the necessity of

some

some repose, must plead my excuse for withdrawing myself thus abruptly from your society.

## LETTER XXXVIII.

Geneva, June 17, 1791.

THE night of our arrival at Berne we supped at the table d'hôte, and met some agreeable company. Among others, was a Frenchman, who appeared a wellbred man. We asked him some questions respecting Berne. He pictured it in most deplorable colours. "Ah mon Dieu! tout "est tranquille ici: il n'y a point de spec- "tacles, ni de caffé, ni de societé." His countenance interpreted very fully the calamitous situation in which he found himself. "Je me mourai!" was his conclusion. He was particularly complimentary upon the English nation as a nation of splendor and

and amusements. "On y trouve tant de "belles choses," said he; and then began enumerating Bath, Vauxhall, &c. I could not help reflecting on this principle, which seems to enter so universally into the character of a Frenchman. This man was, to appearance, a well-educated man—at least upon the system of French Education;—and he was an exile from his country: yet the *gout* for amusements still continued to prevail over every other feeling; and the Revolution of his country, appeared to him only so far inconvenient,—as it had robbed him of his amusements and his rank.

The situation of Berne is extremely fine. The scenery around it is indeed magnificent. The town is almost encircled by the river Aar; the houses are remarkably well built with Arcades; and the utmost neatness is kept up in every quarter. Berne is not entirely without its amusements. These are principally the pleasures of the Promenade; and perhaps no city in Europe can
boast

boaſt a terrace whoſe view commands a more ſublime collection of natural objects. Our table d'hôte was enlivened, the day after our arrival, by a political diſputation upon the intereſts of Europe; and it was warmly contended, *à l'unanime*, that England ſhould unite with Spain, and ſtrike a blow at the Empreſs of Ruſſia.

We encountered at table, in the evening, one of thoſe inquiſitive characters who offer no ſmall annoyance to ſtrangers. He was a man of a certain age, but of a moſt voluble tongue. He attacked us the moment we were ſeated, with a ſucceſſion of interrogatories, of " What place we came " from?—Which way we were going?— " Whether we had made the tour of Swit- " zerland, or whether we intended it?" and then began, unaſked, to give us his advice. He inſiſted upon it, we *muſt* make an excurſion in the neighbourhood of Berne—that we muſt *not* content ourſelves with a direct route to Geneva—and enumerated

merated a variety of objects to which we *ought* to attend. Finding the answers we gave, were not likely to silence him—we began to be more laconic in our replies. This induced a calm of a few minutes; when, turning his head from us, he broke out aloud with, " D'où venez-vous, Monsieur?" to an officer at the further end of the room. A Frenchman makes great allowance for frivolous enquiry—The officer replied with the utmost readiness to this first question, and to those which succeeded; and thus we became perfectly acquainted with his history. " Où allez-vous?—Quand par-
" tez-vous?—Etes-vous marié?—Madame
" doit être malheureuse pendant votre ab-
" sence." Such was the nature of his attack upon the officer.

I feared the arrival of supper would bring our affairs again into play: and it happened just as I had surmised. He took his chair by me, and renewed the charge, with the same persevering curiosity, during the whole of the seſſion. " Eh bien, vous " allez à Geneve. Il faut, cependant, faire " des petites tours; ou bien, il faut revenir " à Berne. Comptez-vous reſter à Geneve? " J'y ſerai en quinze jours-moi. Je ſerai " mortifié de ne pas vous trouver." Such were the perſecutions I experienced during ſupper. Fortunately for me, he recollected that a gentleman, who ſat oppoſite him, had not yet been catechized. He opened the trenches againſt him, and drew out in a few ſeconds the whole of his hiſtory. We took advantage of this diverſion made in our favour, and withdrew ourſelves from his farther importunities. I had Horace full in my recollection, during this adventure; and when he opened his attack upon me, with " Comment vous va- " t-il, mon cher?" I thought I heard, " Quid agis dulciſſime rerum?"

We left Berne the following morning; and dining at the charming town of Morat, paſſed in the evening to Paliere; where we had

## LETTER XXXVIII.

had some difficulty to find accommodations —such were the numbers of French emigrants who are on their way to Worms and Manheim. From Paliere we proceeded early the next day, and arrived by the setting of the sun at Lausanne. It was not our intention to make any stay at Lausanne; and as the journey from Brussels had been long and fatiguing, we hastened to the place of our destination. Reposing therefore the night at Lausanne, we made our last day's journey, in the finest weather and upon such a road as we have not before witnessed, and arrived yesterday evening at Geneva. Here we fix for some time our residence, and such is the general aspect of the country, that I think we may promise ourselves a very agreeable *séjour*.

## LETTER XXXIX.

Geneva, June 28, 1791.

I HAVE now been near a fortnight at Geneva, and have little more to report to you than the state of the weather. Our mode of life is perfectly recluse. The scenery with which we are surrounded is the object of our constant contemplation, and our evenings are invariably passed in sauntering upon the banks of the Lake.

Here let me indulge for a moment in drawing some faint outline of this magnificent country. The Lake, which in magnitude is rivalled only by that of Constance, is situated in a valley between the Alps and the Jura, which runs through Switzerland as the Appenine through Italy. The width of this Lake is well proportioned to the height of those mountains which inclose it; and

and the form of its bed is such as to give scope for all the varieties of scenery. Its waters are deliciously pure, and exhibit—particularly at their issue—the most enchanting transparency.

At the head of this Lake is situated Villeneuve, at the rectilinear distance of fifteen leagues. Along the banks of the Lake, on either side, are scattered towns and villages, whose magnitude is so reduced by the stupendous mountains which tower behind them, that they appear but clusters of diminutive sheds, and scarcely seem to rise out of the waters. The mountains of which I speak, are those which stand on the side of Savoy, and form a part of the Alps. These present a very noble range of bold and majestic objects: their forms, their magnitude, and their aspect, have every variety necessary to the harmony of the scene. The grand Saleve is the first in order, proceeding from Geneva, which it flanks. This is a mountain of no pre-eminent height. Its furface is covered with an agreeable verdure, and fcattered with fome cottages in thofe declivities which approach the town. Its fummit exhibits the form of a wedge whofe angle is rounded off. Next to this ftands the Petit Saleve, which bears a more pointed form, and whofe roots approach more nearly the borders of the Lake. The Mole rifes next— of a very dufky hue, and conical figure, which contrafts well with the long and uniform appearance of the Voifons ftanding beyond it. The real figure of the Mole is faid to be by no means confonant with its apparent form, which is indeed conveyed to the eye in the ftrict character of the cone. Here are the mountains which ftand along the fouthern bank of the Lake, and which form to the imagination the rear-guard of the Alps.

Behind thefe darker maffes are ranged the Glaciers, which exhibit through the interftices of the former their lucid fummits.
This

## LETTER XXXIX.

This chain of icy fubftances prefents to the eye no uniform appearance: in fome of its parts are glaffy promontories difcovered, fhooting their filver points into the clouds. Thefe are known by the name of *Aiguilles*, from the figure they reprefent. In others the blended fnows and ice are fwelled into unequal maffes, and exhibit different configurations of the moft tranfparent materials. Parent of all—the Mont Blanc—ftands clothed in a robe of the pureft white, and appears indeed fovereign of the furrounding fcenes. The fummit of this mountain rifes much above the reft; and, though by no means fo in reality, has the appearance of a conical figure rounded at its point. Such is the outline of thofe objects which form the back-ground of this majeftic picture; and the foftened light which beams at the fetting of the fun, paints them to the eye in all the chafteft colouring which fancy ever imagined.

## LETTER XXXIX.

The Rhone iffues from the Lake at Geneva. This noble river takes its courfe through the town, and its fteep* waters exhibit a colouring of the richeft blue. The Arve, rolling down its torrent from the fnowy Alps, forms its junction with the Rhone in the vicinity of Geneva; and at an angle, which occafions great turbulence to the commixing waters. Our houfe is fituated at fome little diftance from the town, and our communication with it is not likely to be great. It participates, in common with all the ftates of Europe, of that political ferment to which France has given birth; and, though the ariftocratic party adminifter the government at prefent, they are not without apprehenfions from the reftlefs activity of their democratic rivals.

## LETTER XL.

Geneva, July 12, 1791.

SINCE I laſt wrote, very important intelligence has tranſpired. The news of the King's flight was very ſoon conveyed to this place, and every precaution was taken to prevent its operating any miſchief in this little republic. All the avenues were beſet with guards, to prevent a ſtranger's paſſing the territory; and patroles of horſe paraded the whole of the night. I heard ſome private letters from Paris read, which announced the moſt perfect unconcern, on the part of the Pariſians, at the departure of their king. The converſation in the public places of reſort was ſaid to have been, " Le " roi a pris la fuite."—" Eh bien !" ſaid the reſt, " on s'en paſſera."

This event, and the subsequent arrest, were variously received here, and in the *Pais de Vaud*. Many of the Genevese assembled every evening upon the promenades, comparing the separate accounts which each had privately received, as many had sons, cousins, or nephews in the national guard of Paris. " Le roi est parti," said one ;" " Tant mieux," said an old democrat, " on sera moins embarrassé." The evening after the retaking of the king, the promenade was in singular commotion ; and the people were divided by sentiments of joy and sorrow. " On l'a repri," said one—" Tant pis pour eux," said another— " Apparemment on lui tranchera la tête," said a third. Such were the remarks upon the promenades of Geneva at this event.

At Lausanne, I understood, that political sentiment expressed itself in a more public manner. The news of the king's escape occasioned so great joy at this last place, that the aristocrates—who compose by far the majority

## LETTER XL.

majority—indulged themselves in public illuminations. This triumph was however to undergo a mortification: the king was arrested, and the news was not long in making its way to Lausanne. The democrates would not lose so favourable an opportunity of disturbing their antagonists; they illuminated in their turn, and had the advantage of the laugh on their side.

I have mentioned the promenades at Geneva: they merit indeed more than a simple notice, at least those which are within the walls of the town. But as the gates are shut * irrevocably at half past eight o'clock—a time at which one scarcely begins to find the air sufficiently cool for respiration—I am obliged to confine myself to those walks which lie without the gates. These are frequented of an evening by large companies, with whom I am become in some degree familiarized, without the assistance of letters recommendatory. The grand

* The shutting of the gates is regulated by the hour of sunset.

enquiry

enquiry on the subject of politics relates to Paine and *Pierce*—by which they mean Price—a name they cannot pronounce. I told them all that I knew about them, *i. e.* just so much as they knew, and all the world knew before—that they were reputed champions of no mean strength in the field of politics.

Of this groupe is a veteran, less distinguished by his own character than by a very elegant daughter, whose personal charms and brilliant conversation have given her much celebrity. Expert in every subject of general interest, she is more particularly attached to political discussion, and has, by her beauty and her principles, acquired the appellation of " La belle democrate." She is very fond of enquiring into the character of the English ladies, for whom she has the highest respect. She wished to know, what particular system of politics the English women now defended. I told her, the ladies with us seldom interfered in political discussion.

cuffion. She took it for a rebuke—" Ap-
" paramment Monfieur penfe que les dames
" ne doivent pas fe meler de la politique."
" Pardonnez moi," faid I. Madamoifelle
is often attended upon the promenade by
a German, who appears deeply captivated
with her charms, without however being
fortunate enough to excite a reciprocal paffion. " Il ne fait que parler de la meta-
" phyfique," fays fhe—" L'amour ne
" s'ouvre pas ordinairement comme ça."
His accent offends her ear. " The Germans
" murder our language," fhe fays, " more
" than any people in Europe." I obferved to
her, that the Englifh feldom attained to a juft-
nefs of pronunciation. " J'en conviens,"
fays fhe, " mais les Allemands travaillent a
" prononcer notre langue, au lieu que vous
" autres ne vous en embarraffez point; et
" j'aime plutôt celui qui ne la prononce pas,
" que celui qui la prononce mal."

# LETTER XLI.

Geneva, July 15, 1791.

THE dress of the Genevese is fashioned upon a very agreeable model. The generality of females of every condition are far removed from sicklinefs or deformity, and those of the higher classes are pleasing in their persons and their manners. Rousseau has indeed charged them with want of parental tenderness, in sending their infants to be nursed, or rather neglected, by the inhabitants of the mountains: but in this, as in other respects, modern Geneva bears little resemblance to the ancient.

The custom of taking a *gouté*, corresponding to our tea, I have not seen elsewhere; though I understand it is not peculiar to this place. I was invited to one of those repasts

repasts by the old patriot, and was surprized to find such variety of eatables at such an hour; it was five o'clock in the afternoon. The moment the company were seated, baskets of bread were handed about; these were followed by anchovies, and tarts of an extraordinary size. In the mean time, coffee, tea, wine, liqueurs, &c. were put in circulation; in so much that I, who had but just risen from dinner, made a very contemptible figure amongst them. " Il me " semble que les Anglois mangent peu," said one of the company. I replied in the affirmative, to avoid being further solicited. " Ils s'en tiennent beaucoup a leur *rosbeef*," exclaimed another of the party, who had destroyed a host of eatables. At the sound of *rosbeef*, Monsf. A. seemed suddenly struck; and apologizing for not having provided *rosbeef* for my *goûté*, insisted upon my consenting to dine with him at noon on the following Sunday. I waited on him the day appointed, and was much amused with

my

my entertainment. A variety of articles were served up; and I was urged to feast upon soup, dishes of rice, &c. till I had quite lost sight of the grand desideratum. At length, when the desert should have come, enters a piece of roast beef of an immoderate size. It was diverting to see the bustle it created among the company, whose eyes were fixed alternately on *me* and the *beef*; and each appeared to wait with anxious curiosity the havoc my appetite was to make upon this huge mass of flesh. Nothing but the very marked intention of gratifying me, prevented my resisting their intreaties *in toto*: and their disappointment was so great at the very small progress I made, that I question if Monsieur will ever think it worth his while to consult again the palate of an Englishman.

The great festivities here are on the Sunday; and, notwithstanding the strict devotion which prevails during three parts of the day, the evening is celebrated with the most

most cheerful gaieties. The principal amusement is upon the Lake, which is usually covered with pleasure-boats, and affords a very delightful spectacle. Some of these boats are of a very considerable size, and are decorated with very brilliant ornaments. In these they amuse themselves with music, dancing, and playing off fireworks—principally those of a violent explosion. The reverberation of this, from the vast chain of mountains which surround the Lake, resembles very accurately the rolling of thunder, and is listened to with the most eager attention.

This little republic is not without its political ferments. It should seem, from their numerous precautions, that some great danger was apprehended. The orders of the Syndies are unusually strict. The vigilance of the magistrates and the bourgeois-guard is unremitting. For greater security, the gate, which formerly faced the Swiss quarter, has been within these two or three weeks,

weeks, with great labour and expence, turned towards the French territory: whence, it should seem, that hostilities were eventually expected. During the whole affair of the king's flight, every species of caution was employed; and the circumspection which this government thought neceſſary to exercise on that occaſion, convinces me that they conceive much of their own security to depend upon the particular turn of French affairs. Their fortifications are undergoing repair; the inhabitants have lately been inrolled; and all the measures which vigilance can dictate, are now put in practice, with a view to guard againſt the designs of the democratic minority.

LETTER XLII.

Geneva, July 15, 1791.

I RECEIVED yesterday a very high degree of entertainment, and am anxious to report to you the journals of my proceedings. It was, as you will recollect, the commemoration of the French revolution; and, as agreeable to a decree of the National Assembly, the day was to be celebrated throughout France. Ferney, the ancient residence of Voltaire, was among the number of those towns which announced an intention of observing this anniversary. I had for some time past determined upon making a visit to Ferney, in order to view the mansion once occupied by this illustrious man; and my curiosity to witness this extraordinary festival, decided me to put my plan in execution on this day. I knew not the state of the place; nor could foresee, whether my person might be safe among a number of

men,

## LETTER XLII.

men, assembled to celebrate the orgies of Liberty and Bacchus. I was unwilling therefore to be a solitary guest, and an order of council had been issued forbidding any subject of the Republic to be found at Ferney during this festival. I shortly however picked up an Englishman, of whom I had some slight knowledge; and who, though profoundly ignorant of the language, had as much curiosity as was necessary for my purpose. We placed severally a cockade in our hats, and drove to Ferney.

The village wore a very gay appearance: all the inhabitants, and many from the environs, were parading in numerous parties, dressed in all the trappings of their Sunday wardrobes. Having found with some difficulty a stand for our whiskey and horse, we repaired to a part of the town, which from the crowds assembled there seemed to be the place of rendezvous. We passed through many ranks of spectators, and came to a large area, in the centre of which was

elevated

elevated the national standard, and the colours inscribed with—"Vivre libre, ou mou-
"rir," were streaming in the air. This space was not inclosed with any fixed barrier, but preserved for the company by the National guard; who acted alternately as centinels, and kept the line unbroken by the spectators. Within this area were two long tables, very nearly filled with company, and two smaller ones, occupied by select parties. At the head of the *upper* table sat the Commandant; and beside him, the lady president. The rest were for the most part officers of the guard, or, what is the same thing, volunteers; for the duties and the honours are taken in rotation. I understood from some of the attendants, that we should find no difficulty in being admitted to the table. I therefore applied to a very genteel man, who was doing the duty of centinel, for permission to sit at the table. He assured me, it would do them singular honour. We therefore took our seats, and

were served with some refreshment upon paying our quota.

The attention of the company was soon drawn upon us; and those nearest us at the table were solicitous to recommend themselves by drinking our healths. A band of military music regaled us during dinner. This ended, proclamation was made for silence: and the Commandant delivered an address upon the important advantages of the revolution. After commenting with some warmth upon these, and recommending as essential to their continuance, order and obedience to the constituted authorities,--he toasted the magistrates, the national assembly, &c. Every toast was drank with loud acclamations, and accompanied with the music of some popular air. When the Commandant had got through the toasts of office, he demanded silence, and begged leave to drink, " A la santée des Anglois, " nos meilleurs amis." This was received with the loudest bursts of applause. It was echoed

echoed from every quarter, and the music
struck up " ça ira;" which was sung by the
greater part of the company. The nature
of this toast turned the eyes of all upon us;
and as my companion was not linguist
enough to return the compliment, I mounted the bench. " Silence le plus profonde,"
was called for on all hands; and I pro-
claimed aloud, " A la fantée des François,
" fucces à la nouvelle conftitution, fondée
" fur des principes eternelles, comme na-
" turelles." This had its effect: music,
shouts, and songs, expressed their sense of
gratitude: we were immediately handed
by an officer to the upper table,—presented
to the Lady President, who invited us to the
ball. Ten thousand courtesies were now
shewn us. They threw to the ground the
burgundy we had purchased, and gave us
in exchange some of the first quality. They
spoke in terms of the warmest regard of the
English nation, whose example they pretended only to follow; and commended that
generosity,

generosity, which declined to take advantage of their present distractions.

An officer now hurried us away to drink coffee: I was glad of the opportunity of being relieved from the superabundant civilities of the company. He conducted us to a house where liqueurs, &c. were served up, and many patriotic songs were sung by the different Officers. My friend, who was rather warmed by the burgundy and liqueurs, than enlightened by the conversation, desired me to express to these Frenchmen the respect he had for them : I interpreted his intentions, and all shook hands with him—shouting at the same time, " Bravo, le bon Anglois !" The liqueur was forcible, and the vivacity of the songs animating: these had a mechanical effect upon the humours of my companion. He desired me to assure these Frenchmen, that he loved liberty as much as they did, and that he had an estate in England, but that he would willingly sacrifice it all for the sake
of

## LETTER XLII.

of liberty. I again became his interpreter, and his hand was again demanded—with a repetition, in a ftill higher tone, of " Bravo, le bon Anglois!" The afternoon was indeed paffed in the greateft hilarity, and without the leaft infringement of decorum. Never did I fee men whofe air, converfation, and gefture difcovered more happinefs. They harangued, they danced, and omitted no poffible expreffion of gaiety. What particularly ftruck me in the midft of all this enthufiafm was, that not a term of reproach was ufed againft the king; nor a fentiment of revenge breathed againft thofe from whofe yoke they had fo recently efcaped. Their feelings feemed to be engroffed by the fingle confideration of their prefent felicity, and not an evil paffion was fuffered to difturb the ferenity of their pleafures. Upon the whole, no feftival—which had for its object the commemoration of fuch an event,— could have been conducted with greater harmony, propriety, and good order.

We contrived to withdraw ourselves from the company at the approach of evening; and made a visit to Voltaire's house. This was a gratification I could not refuse myself. The situation is fine; in the house itself there is nothing remarkable. We were shewn the apartment in which Voltaire usually passed his time. This is hung round with the portraits of eminent men, and adorned with the urn containing his heart, which he bequeathed, or pretended to bequeath, to this place. The church and theatre are still in existence,—but all around proclaims the master's fall. Upon returning from Voltaire's villa, we found the gaieties of the ball-room were commencing; but, adopting the prudence of the " conviva " satur," we entered our whiskey for Geneva. As we drove through the town, we were received with shouts, and waving of hats. These compliments we returned in the best manner we could; and bade adieu to Ferney,—not a little satisfied with the adventures of the day.

LETTER XLIII.

*Lausanne, July 20, 1791.*

BY a change of system, our residence at Geneva was shortened by two months, and we are now at Lausanne—or rather in the environs, which are delicious beyond compare. The scenery wants indeed that softness and harmony which the Genevese territory possesses; but then it has to boast magnificence, boldness, and variety. The house we inhabit, is in the village of Ouchy, nearly a mile and half from the town. It is small and rustic, situated within a dozen yards of the Lake, and confronted by the mountains of Savoy, and the rocks of Millerie. Since we have been here, the Lake —which is subject to ebb and flow—has been more than once worked into a storm, and risen to a considerable height. This is a phenomenon for the solution of which

many

many hypotheses have been offered. That most approved is Mr. Bertrand's, who supposes, that electric clouds elevate the waters to various degrees of height, in proportion to the quantity of the electric fluid; and that the subsequent fall, or sinking of the waters—particularly in the narrow parts of the Lake, where these *seiches*, as they are called, are most violent—occasions these sudden storms.

Here is a good circulating library, and gazettes of every kind. But Lausanne is now so much frequented by foreigners, and particularly English,—that every thing peculiar and original is extirpated. In compliance with fashion and interest, every thing is *anglicised*; and you may now have the satisfaction of paying as much for the hire of a horse, a carriage, or a house,— as at the most splendid place of English resort.

Gibbon is the *grand monarque* of literature at Lausanne: I have seen, conversed,

and

and dined with him. These are, I think, the three requisites, in order to know something of a man. His conversation is correct and eloquent; his periods are measured, and his manner of delivering them solemn. He appears rather inditing to an amanuensis, than holding conversation with a stranger. But though he talks too oracularly,— he is at his table cheerful, frank, and convivial. His hospitalities are however not strictly *patriotic:* his predilection for the Swiss is notorious; and, as a love of preeminence may not be classed amongst the least of his failings, he seems to have decided well in the choice of his society.

The state of the weather here is remarkably fine, but hot to a degree of suffocation. We purpose taking advantage of this part of the season, and making in a few days a visit to the Glaciers of Chamouni. I have now full in my recollection, the first glimpse I caught of those wonderful regions. It was on my way from Paliere to Lausanne,

and

and within about a league of this latter place. We had alighted from our carriage, while the horses ascended a hill;—and as we approached the summit, one of the most magnificent sights in nature presented itself on a sudden to our astonished eyes: it was a distant view of the Glaciers; and the unusual appearance they made, would not suffer me to suppose that they were of a solider texture than the fleecy and transparent cloud;— till the reports of those better acquainted with the country, rectified the errors of an indistinct vision. It was at the close of the day, and all the lustre of a setting sun was playing upon their spotless summits.—The scenery was at once novel, and sublime. I anticipate a thousand pleasures in visiting these singular regions, where an external conflict is kept up between heat and cold; and mountains of ice experience no sensible diminution from the scorching rays of a solstitial sun.

## LETTER XLIV.

*Lausanne, Aug. 10, 1791.*

I AM now returned from a tour among the Glaciers; and what my recollection, aided by an occasional note made on the way, can supply, shall now be penned down for your amusement. It was on Thursday, July 28, that we left Lausanne on this expedition. We composed together a party of seven, not including servants. The morning of the 29th, we left Geneva, at an early hour; and crossing the brook at Chesne, little more than a mile from the town of Geneva, we entered the territory of Savoy. The road to Bonneville, the town where we first halted, became gradually mountainous, and we at length found ourselves at the foot of the Mole. Of this mountain I have before remarked, that its appearance

appearance from Geneva prefents a conical form; but this vanifhed as we approached: and, agreeable to the teftimony of Mr. Sauffure, fome who have made an expedition to Bonneville in order to examine the Mole, have returned without feeing it—having miftaken for it fome other mountain whofe figure refembled moft nearly the form under which this appears at a diftance. We began, in this part of our journey, to enter the land of fprings, and the heat being immoderate, often regaled ourfelves with draughts from thefe icy waters. We were dreffed in the lighteft clothing, yet fuffered very much from the fcorching rays of the fun, and their reflection from the fides of the mountains. We took fome refrefhment at Bonneville, and found fhelter there for fome hours from the fervors of the day. I ftrolled to the church for amufement, and found it not behind its fellows in faintly dignity. Many cafkets were placed upon the different altars, containing *moft unqueftionable* frag-

ments of ancient worthies. I tranfcribed from one of thefe precious repofitories the following infcription—I leave the Monk who wrote it, to defend the purity of its concords.
" Reliquias Sanctæ Vincentiæ ritè cognitas
" in hoc capfulo inclufas generationi fide-
" lium Bonopolis in facello S$^{ti}$ Petri exponi
" permittuntur."

We left Bonneville after repofing two or three hours, and paffed by a very fingular and romantic route to Salenche. Every poffible diverfity of fcenery is to be found in this latter ftage. Springs and cafcades iffue from the roots of the rocks which inclofe the track, or fcatter their waters down the fhelving fides. The heat raged unabated, till the approach to Salenche gave us a diftant view of the Glaciers, whofe icy fummits afforded—to the imagination at leaft—fome relief. Salenche terminated our journey of the day, and the evening was employed in making the neceffary arrangements for our conveyance to Chamouni, and viewing a

cafcade

cafcade at fome little diftance; I know not its name. The approach to it was over rough and loofe ftones, fome of which lay fo far under the water, that it was problematical whether the feet would alight upon them or not. The cataract gufhed from a hollow rock, and was not without its grotefque ornaments; but when the difficulties of egrefs and regrefs are calculated, the balance of pleafure preponderates but little in its favour.

From a neceffity—to which we were conftrained to fubmit--we were not provided with *char-a-bancs* on the following day till near eleven o'clock. The char-a-banc is a fmall ftrong carriage, in which two or three may ride. Upon this you fit, with your feet near the ground, refting upon a fwinging board, and are drawn fideways. It is furprizing how faft the mules trot with thefe vehicles at their heels, over fome of the rougheft and moft craggy tracks; their feet are at once fure and invulnerable. Our char-a-bancs a-bancs halted at the village of Chede, and we were very greatly entertained with a view of the cafcade. The water appeared to fall from a height of about 150 feet: as it defcends it is very regularly fcattered, till in the lower part of its defcent it is diffipated in the gentleft diftillation. There was much beauty in this fine cafcade, the effect of which is not a little improved by the furrounding fcenery. We had loft the hour at which it is viewed to the greateft advantage,—the guides affuring us that had we arrived fomewhat fooner, we fhould have had the pleafure of feeing a rainbow formed upon this tranfparent fhower.—Reentering our char-a-bancs, we paffed over a rough and broken track, blocked up in fome parts by hideous maffes of rock, intercepted in others by furious torrents that poured from the heights, till we entered upon a charming plain, in which was fituated St. Gervais. Here all was gaudy. The Curé had given an entertainment:

mass was just over, and the villagers had commenced their dance. We partook under a tree of the refreshments of the place, and diverted ourselves with seeing these peasants perform the evolutions of the Valz. Shortly after this we entered the valley of Chamouni, and arrived by five o'clock at the foot of the Glacier de Boisons.

LETTER XLV.

THE Glacier de Boisons is the first to which strangers are generally introduced. It makes scarcely any figure from the valley, standing among many others of much greater magnitude. Being severally furnished with a long stick pointed with iron, we ascended with ease the lower part of the mountain, which was covered with turf and not very steep; but the approach towards the ice was difficult, and the sticks were eminently useful. Previous to our arrival

rival upon the level with the Mer-de-glace, we were stopped by the guides in order to view the magnificent prospect before us. It presented a range of icy pyramids of the purest complexion, and of the boldest forms: we were filled with astonishment at a spectacle which blended so perfectly the grand and the beautiful.

Arrived at the summit of the mountain, we entered upon the Glacier, but found great difficulty in keeping our feet. The sun had glossed the surface, and rendered it almost impossible to tread with any degree of security. In passing amongst these frozen tracts, we came to many wide chasms and gulphs of a formidable depth. We threw down flakes of ice or stones, whose fall returned a tremendous sound. It was curious to observe upon the highest parts many masses of stone ready to precipitate; and upon the mountains in descending we saw some of dreadful bulk, which had at different times been tumbled from the summit of the Glacier.

Pierre Balmat, our principal guide, related to us, that he was witnefs to the fall of one of the largeſt of thefe; and that it was attended with the moſt tremendous circumſtances. Indeed it appears extraordinary that men ſhould be found to inhabit regions, where they are continually expofed to thefe impending dangers. All the way as we deſcended, we obferved the ruins of trees whofe trunks had been ſplit afunder, or their roots torn from the ground, by the violence of thefe *Avalanches*. We had fuffered but little fatigue by the whole of this expedition; the ice afforded us water of the moſt refreſhing coolnefs, and ſtrawberries abounded upon the mountain, over which we paſſed on leaving the ice. Evening was now advancing: we re-entered our char-a-bancs, and ſhortly arrived at the Priory of Chamouni.

Pierre Balmat undertook all the neceſſary arrangements for the bufinefs of Montanvert, which we were next to undertake;

and

## LETTER XLV.

and the following morning, after an early mass, came to announce that all was in readiness. We were but four who resolved on this expedition; and we began to ascend the mountain, having Pierre Balmat at our head, and another guide bringing up the rear, each charged with their portion of luggage, provision, &c. The first league, or hour as it is called, was rugged, but not steep. It is so much of the way as is usually made by the mules. We began from this boundary to experience some difficulties: the track, without being less rugged, became more steep; and we had occasionally to pass along a precipice, which could not be regarded without dizziness, and from which a false step must inevitably have terminated the journey. The prospect before us annihilated all sense of fear or fatigue; and, after an arduous struggle of about three hours, we gained the summit of the Montanvert, and had the glorious Mer-de-glace full in view.

## LETTER XLV.

We had afcended the mountain very lightly clad, and had been much oppreffed by heat. The tranfition was inftantaneous to a chilling cold. The guides admonifhed us to wrap ourfelves up fpeedily, as the air from the Glacier might have a dangerous effect. The Mer-de-glace refembles exactly a billowy expanfe of water frozen while the waves were yet fwelling with the majefty of the ftorm. We defcended by a rugged path to the level of the ice; and by a proper union of courage and caution, afcended and defcended over the vaft columns of ice which covered this furface. Wherever the eye ranged, nothing prefented itfelf but objects of terrible grandeur;—precipices, over which hung the loofening rocks—gulphs, where the projected ftone could fcarcely find a bottom. The whole valley appeared, as ftill heaving with the tempeft. Before I quitted the ice, I caft a parting view at the vaft range of rocky fpires and columns that

inclofed

inclosed it. To the left, I saw the vale of Chamouni far below; and to the right, the Glacier extended more than twenty leagues among regions inacceffible to human difcovery. I felt an enthufiafm, which is revived in the narration—but which the moſt elaborate defcription is ill calculated to communicate.

## LETTER XLVI.

Our repaſt was prepared by the induſtrious guides in a ſhed known by the name of Blair's Cabin. It is principally formed by ſtones, placed without cement upon each other; and the table is of one ſingle ſtone. It was, as Balmat reported, erected by a gentleman of the name of Blair, in confequence of a violent hail-ſtorm—not unufual in thefe regions—from which himfelf and his friends had fuffered. The traveller owes Mr. Blair gratitude for this piece of philanthropy. The interior of this cabin is covered with a regifter of names engraved upon the walls by thofe who have vifited thefe fcenes.

Nothing can furpafs the intrepidity and zeal of the guides of Chamouni. There are no dangers, however formidable, that they will not face. When Mont Blanc was deemed inacceffible—an opinion which prevailed till within a few years—the exertions of the guides were neverthelefs indefatigable. An accident at length unfolded what the labour of years—perhaps of ages—might have explored in vain. The cafual wanderings of Jacques Balmat to a confiderable height opened to him a track, by which he deemed the afcent practicable. This fecret he communicated to Paccard, who had cured him of an illnefs contracted on the mountain. They agreed to make the attempt, in which they perfectly fucceeded Aug. 1786. Upon this M. Sauffure, whofe long refearches in that particular line had led him to offer rewards for any difcoveries of this nature,

repaired

## LETTER XLVI.

repaired to Chamouni the following year; and, with eighteen guides furnished with a tent, provisions, and inftruments of obfervation, afcended, with unparalleled hardihood and extreme danger, Mont Blanc Aug. 1787.

Having finifhed our repaft, and allowed due time for our guides to refrefh themfelves, we began to defcend. The beginning of the defcent was not accompanied with any particular difficulties: but the latter part, which purfued a track different from that by which we afcended, was fteep and hazardous. We were occafionally ftartled by the diftant rumbling of thofe Avalanches, which are (particularly during the heats) detaching loofe maffes of ice or ftone, and precipitating them with violent explofion. Thefe mountains are not without their luxuries. We were prefented in different ftations of the defcent with ftrawberries and goats-milk of delicious flavour. Thofe who have felt the heat can alone imagine how grateful thefe refrefhments proved.

ed. Having at length effected our descent, we traversed a valley through which flowed the Arveron;—this, like all the bottoms in the neighbourhood of these mountains, was strewed with those fragments of stone, which once occupied a higher situation. Our guide now conducted us along this uncouth track to one of the noblest objects in nature —the source of the Arveron. It is a recess hollowed out by the hand of nature, and all the colours that enrich it are of her own pencilling. Imagine the openings of a mighty cavern—scooped in the centre—and over-arched by various masses of ice in forms the most wild, yet the most majestic. — Picture to yourself the purest tints, blending into each other with the most enchanting softness, and the most regular gradation. From the centre of this cave thus artfully formed,—thus sublimely coloured,—imagine a torrent issuing with violence, and tumultuously rolling among masses of rock, which obstruct the channel and spread its

## LETTER XLVI.

waters into foam. If the picture be not entire, throw into the canvas the surrounding scenery;—the vale of Chamouni decorated in all the charms of industry and culture;—the hoary magnificence of the Glaciers;—and the sombre majesty of those stubborn rocks, which retain no trace of vegetation:—let the setting sun throw his last rays over this groupe;—and then tell me, whether it be enthusiasm to class this with the noblest productions of nature.

I must remark, from some conversation I had this day,—that the Savoyards participate those discontents, which seem to have become so general in Europe. The yoke of the Catholic church is a cause of great dissatisfaction, and they treat with ridicule the idea of papal supremacy. They speak of the riches which the church amasses, as an unmerited exaction from their labours; and even consider the *disme*, or tithe, as a very high price for occasional absolution. This I was rather surprized to hear: but there is

another

another and very ferious fubject of difcontent, in the preference given by the court to Piedmont, to the prejudice of Savoy. The Savoyards affirm, that they are treated with neglect; that their inferiority is marked by an exclufion from pofts of diftinction and emolument; and that in all cafes where honour, profit, or authority are annexed to any places at the difpofal of the government, they have the mortification to fee a Piedmontefe preferred. The *greateft* ferment prevails in thofe parts which border on the lake, or connect with Geneva. The frequent communications which thefe have with the inhabitants of the Pays de Vaud— many of whom are ftrongly inclined to French principles—have contributed to the diffufion of that fpirit of revolt, which reigns among them. At the mineral fprings of Thonon and Evian there are occafional fetes, and this keeps up a perpetual intercourfe between the Savoyards and the inhabitants of the other fide of the lake; and *ça ira* has

has been trumpeted at their feftive meetings with no fmall fhare of applaufe. The clergy in the neighbourhood of Chamouni are by no means numerous; at Salenche and its environs they abound, and exhibit all the marks of fovereign pride.

At firft entering Savoy, I was embarraffed to conceive how the land could be divided; as it difcovered no vifible partitions. I was however told, that it is parcelled out with great accuracy, and preferved fufficiently diftinct,—though in many places by imaginary boundaries. Land is here preferred to every other fpecies of property; each man is emulous of acquiring a portion; and fuch are the happy manners of the valley —a ftick or ftone,—the moft *trifling* mark ferves to define the *meum* and *tuum;*—and, with few exceptions, his property is facred from violation.

# LETTER XLVII.

THE evening after our defcent from Montanvert, I amufed myfelf with walking about in various parts of the valley, and gazing at the different furrounding objects of magnificence. It was within a quarter of an hour of fun-fet that finding myfelf fomewhat fatigued, I ftretched along a bank, watching the decline of the fun— now about to retire among the Glaciers. The Aiguille de Midi, the Dome, and Mont Blanc were at that time richly illuminated; and I waited with anxious curiofity the iffue. The rays of light gradually paffed from the Dome and the Aiguille, till the former was enveloped in fhadow, and the points of the latter glittered only at the extremities. All this time Mont Blanc poffeffed a large portion of folar luftre; and, after

the

the Aiguilles were enveloped in the gathering fhades of evening, the rays of the parting light ftill refted on the fuperior mountain.

It was this day determined by four of us to continue our expedition along the valley, and vifit as much as fhould be convenient of this extraordinary country. We were joined the following morning by two other gentlemen, whofe intentions co-incided with our own; and under the conduct of Pierre Balmat, feverally mounted upon mules, we began at an early hour to afcend the Col-de-Balme. This is a mountain which bounds the valley of Chamouni, and over which is the fhorteft paffage into the Pays de Valais. A more ufual, becaufe more practicable track is over the Tête Noire. The afcent of the Col-de-Balme is attended with little difficulty. The greater part is—and all may be—made upon mules. The defcent is hideoufly fteep; and, though the track is fufficiently ferpentine, yet it is not defcended without confiderable fatigue.

. From

From the summit of this mountain we enjoyed a very noble and extended view. M. Sauffure calculates that it rifes 1181 toifes, or 7086 Englifh feet, above the level of the Mediterranean. On completing our defcent we found ourfelves in the valley of Trent, fo called from a torrent of that name which iffues from a contiguous Glacier. On the higheft part of the Col-de-Balme there is a ftone, defining the limits of Savoy; and from this land-mark commences the territory of Valais. We turned a little into the valley of Trent, in order to ftop at the village of that name, and give fome repofe to our mules. Our guide conducted us to a fmall hut, where the good folks did all in their power to entertain us. They fucceeded better with the mules than with their riders; for all the effufions of honeft hofpitality could not atone for the poverty of their fare. They fet before us a difh of honey and fome bottles of meagre and acid wine.

This

## LETTER XLVII.

This village is very curiously situated, at the bottom of immense and innumerable mountains,—and composed of an handful of diminutive huts. The largest of these were very little above the size of an ordinary stye, and constructed in a very grotesque style. They resembled a kind of wooden box, set upon four beams, which are laid upon a foundation of uncemented stones; and upon the roots are stones placed, as a provision against the violent winds, which are not unfrequent in these mountainous climes. The people did not appear unhealthy, nor did I see any *goitrous* persons here. The slopes of the mountains bore the marks of industry and fertility : all was simple, and primitive; and we felt our infirmity, when we saw our guides devour as a luxury—what revolted our palates. The shoes of our mules being repaired, and their stomachs replenished, we, passing from Trent over the Forclay, arrived at St. Blanchier in the evening.

# LETTER XLVIII.

THE paffage of the Forclay had nothing in it either formidable, or difficult. Wherever the track paffes,—which it did in many places upon the edge of a precipice,—the imagination was amufed with a flight fence; which was indeed rather a fecurity againft fear, than a protection from danger. The defcent was extremely rough, and ftrewed with a multitude of large and loofe ftones. It took us up nearly two hours to defcend into the valley of Martigny. From the Forclay we enjoyed a very fine view of the city of Sion, the Mont St. Gothard, and the Glaciers of Grindelwald. As our intention was to take Martigny in returning from St. Bernard, we purfued a courfe to the right from the Forclay; this track defcribed a fort of femi-circle round a hollow vale watered by a river, or rufhing torrent, over which clusters of trees hung in the most romantic forms.

We shortly after entered the valley of Entremont. The road by which we passed, ran along the steep declivities which flanked the valley to the right; and on either hand of us were mountains of correspondent height and magnificence. The Drance—a very powerful torrent which takes its rise from the Glaciers round St. Bernard—rolls down the valley with noisy impetuosity. It was between seven and eight o'clock when we entered the village of St. Blanchier. Our guides conducted us to a species of Inn, where we were to pass the night. We found our landlady very untractable: all our *toute-suites* were coolly returned with *tout-à-l'heures*. We had not however in the issue, reason to complain of any thing but the pertinacity and dilatoriness of our hostess; for in her own good time, an excellent and smoaking supper was introduced. Our night passed well, and the morning found us suf-

ficiently

ficiently recovered to refume our march. We obtained fome bowls of lufcious milk of our landlady, who began to improve upon us by acquaintance; and having mounted our mules, we put ourfelves in motion for St. Bernard.

Very foon after iffuing from the village of St. Blanchier, we entered upon a part of the valley of Entremont, beautiful beyond defcription; and this continued with little variation to St. René, a courfe of three leagues. Between Martigny and St. Blanchier the whole fcenery was wild,—the mountains rocky and barren,—and the torrent below us obftructed by prodigious maffes of ftone. On the contrary, from St. Blanchier to St. Pierre all is fmooth, harmonious, fruitful. The mountains are ranged in the nobleft and moft beautiful forms, and connected with the utmoft regularity. Their fides are clothed with a charming verdure of various hues according to the different fpecies of cultivation. The Drance rolls along

along in one continued stream of foam, and fills the valley with its echoes. I thought, as I beheld these scenes, that the fables of Romance and the visions of Arcadia were more than realized to my senses. My imagination seemed not to experience a want, nor could I figure to myself one absent charm which could improve this wonderful valley. All the varieties of nature were here deliciously blended. Here were viewed all the different shades of verdure, and every artful distribution of culture. Add to these, the sinuous channel of the torrent,—its frothy surface,—its hollow roar,—and then say what is there left for poetry to feign?

Between St. Blanchard and St. Pierre we passed two villages—the first of which is Orsieres, the last Liddes. As we entered the first of these, we passed the Drance by a wooden bridge. They appeared in this part of the valley to be in a way of refinement. Some few houses were undergoing repairs, and fitting up in—what I presume may have been

been—the ſtile of a century paſt in the civilized parts of the world; and what may paſs for modern taſte, in a valley, where the viſits of the ſun are but juſt long enough for the purpoſes of exiſtence. It appeared much the faſhion along this valley to conſecrate the houſes by pious inſcriptions. I obſerved upon many doors, which had been lately painted, the names of ſaints inſcribed, or ſome religious motto. Juſt upon the part where in a mercantile town would have been advertiſed the name and occupation of the inhabitant, were inſcribed on many doors the three names *Jeſus—Marie—Joſeph*.

We now paſſed from Orſieres to Liddes, having the Drance to our right. Liddes is romantically ſituated in the narroweſt part of the valley, the mountains of which approach ſo near each other as almoſt to compreſs and entomb it. In paſſing through this place, we overtook one of thoſe good induſtrious Penitents who travel far for the benefit

nefit of their fouls. The pious pilgrim was in a garment refembling that which honeft Bunyan has defcribed his hero to have received from one of the *fhining ones*. It was variegated with the brighteft colours,—adorned with fhells, mottoes, and portraits of the moft fuccefsful interceffors in behalf of thofe who practife pilgrimage and penance. He bore a tall ftaff, his feet were bare,—that is to fay the upper parts,—and thus he was about to crofs the rugged flints of St. Bernard; in order to vifit the holy fhrine of Loretto, and—in the fpirit of antient fuperftition—" to feek him dead who lives in Paradife."

## LETTER XLIX.

IT was about ten o'clock when we entered the village of St. Pierre; and, as the Convent of St. Bernard was but three leagues diftant from this place, we determined

mined upon making our visit immediately, and returning to St. Pierre in the evening. We requested our hostess to prepare us a supper. The good woman talked of honey and goats-milk;—we questioned her upon the articles of bread and meat; she assured us that there was neither butcher nor baker in the town, but that she would send up to the mountains to kill a sheep for our accommodation. It was indeed our fate, wherever we stopped, to spread slaughter and devastation. We had scarcely entered our quarters at St. Blanchier, when the most dismal screams assailed us from the hen-roost. Scarcely had we quitted St. Pierre, on our route to St. Bernard, before we saw a remorseless clown, deputed to that service by our hostess, scaling the mountain, and seizing the affrighted and defenceless sheep. We blushed for the disorders we had introduced into these Arcadian regions, where all was innocence as in the age of Gold, and the peaceful reign of Saturn. Here the flocks seemed proprietors of the mountains, and the wants of men were fatisfied without the effufion of blood; here the woods appeared facred to folitude and filence.—

> —Where the rude axe with heaved ftroke
> Was never heard the nymphs to daunt,
> Or fright them from their hallowed haunt.

In leaving St. Pierre the track divides—that to the left, opening into the Valforey; that to the right, conducting to St. Bernard. From thefe oppofite directions iffue two ftreams, which are feverally denominated from the Valforey and the St. Bernard; and which uniting a little below, form that torrent which pours along the valley of Entremont. St. Pierre is the laft village of the Valais in this route; and from this to the Convent of St. Bernard, they eftimate three leagues or hours. Soon after leaving the village, we entered upon a coarfe and rugged plain, ftrewed with fragments of ftone, which had been wafhed down from

the

the heights; and from this we continued to afcend over rocks of fhapelefs afperity. In paffing thefe I was indebted to my mule, whofe dexterity in running up the fteep declivities excited my aftonifhment, and I ought to add, my gratitude. The moft provoking property of thefe animals is, that they will always coaft upon the precipice. I more than once laboured to force my mule to abandon this dangerous fyftem, but he taught me acquiefcence, by either making a full ftop, or, if I perfifted, in betaking himfelf to a fit of kicking. I am perfuaded that no one ever reached the heights of St. Bernard in this mode of travel, without having learnt more of paffive obedience and moral refignation, than he would ever have acquired from Sir Robert Filmer, or the Whole Duty of Man.

We had now climbed about two leagues and a half over a very rugged and flinty track, difcovered rather by the induftry of cur guides and the recollection of our mules,

than

## LETTER XLIX.

than by any veſtiges of former footſteps. We at length croſſed the torrent which takes its riſe a little above us, and now entered upon the moſt dreary and melancholy ſcenes. The mountains on every ſide were rugged and naked, except where the ſnow continued undiſſolved the whole of the year, nearly a quarter of a league. Before we reached the Convent, we paſſed through a track of ſnow, many parts of which were more than a foot deep. This ſnow liquidates very ſlowly: it is a part of the mountain expoſed to the north, and which enjoys but for a few moments the rays of the ſun. A few years paſt it continued undiſſolved the whole of the ſummer; and the pious fathers began to feel alarm, leſt it ſhould accumulate and form a Glacier.

We arrived by three o'clock at the door of the Convent. Our guide demanded admittance, when one of the order came to the door, and invited us to enter and partake of the refreſhment of their " pauvre hoſpice."

hofpice." He was indeed particularly forry it fhould have been a day of penance, and feared left the kitchen could not afford us a fuitable repaft. He accompanied us over the Convent, fhowed us the feveral apartments, library, chapel, &c. We were feated in a gloomy faloon, after due obfervation of the rarities of the place; and a very frugal meal was ferved up,—the brother of the order himfelf waiting upon us. We urged him to partake with us—he excufed himfelf, by faying—that he had dined at their ufual hour of half paft ten. We entreated him not to ftand; he refifted our entreaties, by affuring us—that it became him, and fupplicating us to receive the hofpitalities of the Convent " au nom de " Dieu"

## LETTER L.

OUR venerable hoft had, in the interval of preparation for dinner, conducted us round the environs of the Convent, and wretched indeed was the fcenery which furrounded thefe pious fathers. The whole mountain is of fo obdurate and untractable a nature, that no art or labour can render it a fubject of cultivation. There were two or three fmall interftices between the rocks, in which thefe induftrious men had difpofed fome mould imported from the foil of St. Pierre; by means of which—with the greateft difficulty—they raife a few vegetables. The whole crop would have fcarcely filled an ordinary plate: but elevated into thefe regions of cold and folitude, they have recourfe to any little expedient which may occupy their hopes, and diffipate the *ennui* of perpetual imprifonment. Theirs is indeed
a fate,

a fate, though self-imposed, beyond the rigors of the severest punishment.

> ———From the cheerful ways of men
> Cut off, and for the book of knowlege fair
> Presented with an universal blank
> Of Nature's works, to them expunged and rased.

The good father who performed the honours of the place, told us, that he had been twelve years in this Convent; and, though he was not in reality more than thirty years of age, his countenance was so haggard, so fallow, and so sickly, that he appeared quite a veteran. We asked him after the rest of his comrades; he said, they were gone "se promener."—It is diverting to hear of a promenande, in regions where every step leads to fresh dangers, and every change of scene is only an aggravation of horrors. He spoke of a journey to St. Pierre, as a boy would of his holidays; and made as much of an excursion to Martigny, as an Englishman would of a trip to Newmarket.—"On y va," said he, " des fois pour *s'egayer*."

He

He shewed us a small lake near the Convent, in which they had attempted to keep some fish; but the coldness of the water almost instantly killed them. This lake is, he said, seldom free from ice, and was frozen over last year so late as the month of August. Indeed the water he gave us to mix with our wine was prodigiously cold. He assured us it was two degrees below the standard of freezing. We were shewn a spot upon which once stood a temple of no mean fame, and the ground is still scattered with fragments of stone.

It has been a subject of much dispute among the learned what route Hannibal pursued in crossing the Alps. An attempt has been made from the evidence collected on these ruins, to fix this route in the passage over St. Bernard. This opinion is not new, as M. Saussure has remarked. It was prevalent in the time of Livy, and he opposes it as destitute of foundation. Pliny was afterwards of opinion, that he passed by by the Mons Jovis, or Penninus. The latter of thefe appellations is referred to the Celtic word *Pen*, which fignifies high. M. Sauffure fpeaks of numerous ex-votos, which he has himfelf feen; the greater part of which are of bronze, and bear infcribed, fome, JOVI PENNINO; others, JOVI POENINO. From the latter of thefe it has been concluded, that Hannibal erected a temple here to the God of his country, in teftimony of gratitude for the difcovery of the paffage. The ftatue of the Jupiter in queftion, is proved to have been deftroyed by Conftantine, from a pillar which now ftands at the foot of the mountain at St. Pierre: it is infcribed to Conftantine the younger.

St. Bernard was a Savoyard, and archdeacon of Aofte in the year 962. Since his time the *Hofpice* has been twice deftroyed by fire. This inftitution was formerly very opulent; it poffeffed lands in Sicily, England, the Low Countries, &c. of which it is now

now pretty well fhorn. For its fupport at prefent, it is in great meafure indebted to the alms collected in different parts of the country. There is upon the mountain near the Convent, a ftone, which marks the boundary of the Vallais on the one fide, and the king of Sardinia's eftates on the other. The contiguity of this Convent to the latter has produced fome altercations; and, at the beginning of this century, the king of Sardinia difputed with the Swifs the right of nominating a Provoft, or Head. This, after much oppofition, was decided in favour of the Swifs; who deemed it of importance, that a foreign king fhould not nominate to a benefice within their dominions,—particularly to one fo important, as that of St. Bernard has always been efteemed.

I know not the precife number of this fociety: they are all regular Auguftines: the Provoft is elected by the Chapter, and confirmed by the Pope. He refides at Martigny. Next to him, is a Prieur Clauftral, who acts as Prefident, and refides at the Convent. Befides thefe, there is a Sacriftan, who has the care of the chapel; a Cellerier, who fuperintends the provifions; a Clavandier, who diftributes to travellers; and an Infirmier, who takes charge of the fick. Ufually not more than eight or ten refide; and powerful muft be that motive which determines men, who can exift elfewhere, to fuch a mode of life.

## LETTER LI.

THE principal duties of thefe Bernardines fall in the feafon when fnows and ftorms are moft frequent. At that time they are conftantly in the habits of watching occafions for the exercife of their hofpitable functions: a fervant, whom they call the Maronnier, goes before the travellers who pafs this way during the perilous feafon, with a large dog, peculiar to the mountain. This dog is of an enormous fize, and of

fingular

singular sagacity. We saw two of them at the Convent. These dogs have the wonderful talent of discovering the way through fogs and snows, as also of scenting out the bodies of those who have perished by the severity of the cold. During the whole of the winter, the brothers at the Convent are employed in searching for miserable objects who have lost their way, or have been buried in the snows, by the terrible *avalanches* which happen in the severe season. Each is furnished with a stick pointed with iron. With these they found, wherever the dogs direct; and by shaking, chafing, and other remedies, they frequently restore those who are fortunate enough to be found before animation is totally extinct.

The height of this mountain is estimated at about 7542 English feet perpendicular above the level of the Mediterranean. The nature of their situation exposes them to a thousand maladies. Indeed they looked like the family of death. It was so cold in the Convent, that they requested permission to kindle a

fire

fire for us; and yet it was the third of August. I confefs to you, I could not view their fituation, nor hear the detail of their fufferings, without afking myfelf the queftion, whether the fervices rendered to fociety by thefe men were at all proportioned to the pain with which they are effected. I am of opinion that few would, in modern days, undertake a pilgrimage over St. Bernard, if they were not fure of *three* \* days entertainment on the way: and I cannot think highly of an inftitution calculated only to keep alive an almoft obfolete fuperftition. M. Sauffure has taken fome pains to defend this inftitution in its prefent ftate; and certainly if, as this author affirms, the paffage of St. Bernard is of great importance to the Vallais on one fide, and the Lombards on the other; if the communication between thefe two divided countries be of fuch reciprocal advantage; the labours of thefe religious, and their

\* So much is allowed by charter to every pilgrim.

feclufion

seclusion from society, merit the approbation of the world.

There was something so unusually dreary and ungenial in the aspect of this place, that we were impatient, after due gratification of our curiosity, to leave it. We had ordered our mules; and while these were preparing, the skies blackened prodigiously, and a heavy storm of hail and thunder came on. The monks were urgent with us to pass the night in the Convent; but we were unanimous in wishing to take our leave of these grim and stormy regions. We descended through a deluge of rain, from which we shortly issued, and left behind us the storms and the hail, to drench the Convent of St. Bernard. Doubtless these fathers must be actuated by some powerful principle, in fixing their abode in these regions of misery: by their voluntary sufferings here, they no doubt hope to mitigate the pains of purgatory hereafter. I know not what purgatory is, but I should think it almoſt worth hazarding, rather than endure the penance of a reſidence during life upon the mountains of St. Bernard. Milton has attempted to give us ſome idea of another place; and I could not diſmiſs the images from my recollection, when I turned my eyes upon this miſerable ſcene,

> " A diſmal ſituation, waſte and wild;
> " Regions of ſorrow, doleful ſhades; where peace
> " And reſt can never dwell;—hope never comes,
> " That comes to all."

Deſcending partly upon our feet and partly upon our mules, we arrived in the evening at St. Pierre. The activity of our hoſteſs and her co-adjutors—for it appeared by the buſtle that ſhe called in the aſſiſtance of the neighbourhood—had prepared our ſupper. On the following day we had, on our way to St. Blanchier, an opportunity of ſeeing the full diſplay of muliſh reſiſtance. A watch had been left by one of the party at St. Pierre. We were now a full league from the place, and the guide was directed to return

# LETTER LI.

turn in search of it. The guide prepared to return, but his mule said, "NO."—At every effort the *former* made, the *latter* added his "VETO." He used every measure of violence, but he might as well have attempted to flog the Trojan horse into a gallop. Much manœuvring was displayed on both sides; at length victory declared in favor of the beast, and the great Pierre Balmat—who had so often conquered mountains—was himself compelled to yield to the invincible stubbornness of his mule.

# LETTER LII.

THE appearance of St. Blanchier is picturesque indeed, but partakes too much of the horrid. It stands upon the borders of the Drance, at the confluence of three vallies, and in the very heart of mountains, which project in awful forms over its cottages, and seem to menace its

its destruction. It was a festival with the inhabitants; the church bell was ringing a hollow sound, and the peasants were crowding the porch, in order to consecrate the festivities of the day by an act of devotion. As we passed through this village, we were alarmed by an explosion, the effect of which among the mountains was tremendous. We took it for thunder, and its echoes were prolonged by the reverberation of the rocks with which we were enclosed. A volume of smoke issuing from a distant eminence convinced us, that it was but the report of gunpowder.

Martigny, where we reposed ourselves and mules, is considered as of some importance in the Vallais; they called it a city, and spoke of it in high terms. It has, however, from the figure it makes, no great pretensions to distinction. It is the head-quarters indeed of business and gaiety in this country. Our landlord introduced us into a very spacious room, in one corner of which sat a man, whose figure and manner

rather

rather excited our curiofity. We had taken from the table a large pair of flappers, and were feverally offering our conjectures upon their ufe, when, obferving our embarraff-ment, the ftranger came up, claimed the flappers, and told us, they were " pour at-" traper les papillons."—The inn-keeper informed us when he had retired, that it was a German baron, whofe *penchant* for butterfly-hunting was extraordinary; that he expofed himfelf to a thoufand dangers and fatigues in this whimfical purfuit; " et, Mef-" fieurs, (continued he,) ce baron là mettroit " huit jours pour attraper un feul papillon."

Our hoft was a lank meagre man: his figure was remarkably tall, ghaftly, and puritanical: his head was crowned with a white cap, which did not diminifh the folemnity of his appearance. He harangued us the whole of dinner upon the different purfuits of mankind. He treated the butterfly-hunter with the moft farcaftic contempt.—" A fellow, faid he, who runs
" over

"over bogs, lakes, and brambles after a shadow; a phantom; a being that is not touched without falling to pieces; a thing that has neither body nor foul." Our landlord argued, and we fed; and his harangue finished only with our dinner. We then refumed our journey to Bex.

I have not feen during my excurfion many goitrous or idiotic perfons. At Salenche I faw fome few of the latter; and in different other places I have obferved the former. You know the opinions of medical men are much divided upon the probable caufes of thefe wens, and of the concomitant diforder of idiotifm. Thefe phænomena have by many been referred to fnowy or calcareous waters, which are here drank by the inhabitants—by others to the marfhy air, &c. but M. Sauffure affirms, that in the higher parts of the mountains, where the fnows and ice for the moft part prevail; and in the vallies open to the plains, where the marfhes are principally found; neither wens nor idiocy are common. These are almost solely to be met with in the vallies elevated a little above the plain. In order to account for this phænomenon, M. Sauſſure ſuppoſes, that the warmth which the encloſed air receives in this ſituation, relaxes the fibres of infants; and produces theſe inflations of the neck, and that *inertia*, which is the ſtrong characteriſtic of the Cretin. This he eſtabliſhes, by remarking, that on the ſide of the valley, where the heat from direct and reflected rays is greateſt, theſe diſorders moſt abound; inſomuch that it is now cuſtomary for thoſe whoſe circumſtances are not too contracted, to ſend their wives to lie-in, and their infants to be nurſed upon the mountains; and this experiment has, in no inſtance, failed of preſerving the health and faculties of the children.

## LETTER LIII.

WE were now entered into the valley of the Rhône, and shortly arrived upon that plain, consecrated to fame by the cascade of the Pissevache. The body of water rushes between the divided projections of a rock, whose summits are rounded off, and overspread with a picturesque umbrage. Its waters dash with the force acquired by a fall of near three hundred feet against the rocky fragments below, and remount in a cloud of foam. In comparison of these stupendous phænomena of nature, how little are the atchievements of art!

St. Maurice, through which we now passed, is the last town of the Vallais; and is famous for having been the Agaunum of the ancients, where the massacre of the Theban Legion happened. The Roman bridge

## LETTER LIII.

bridge of one arch, built acrofs the Rhône, is ftill in exiftence. Their excellencies of Berne, whofe territory here commences, have a fmall garrifon in the place; and fome frivolous queftions, of our names, country, defigns, &c., put by a few invalids, notified our entrance upon this fovereign foil. We arrived in the evening at Bex, and finally difmiffed our guides. Before I take my leave of them, let me commend their activity, fidelity, and gratitude. Men more ready to ferve, and more difpofed to be fatisfied, I have never yet met with: their underftandings are in general good, their information found, and their manners pleafing and ingenuous. This is an eulogium due to the guides of Chamouni.

Bex is famous for the falines, or falt works, which are carried on in its neighbourhood. We vifited thefe the following day, having obtained permiffion from the fuperintendant. Our char-a-bancs carried us to the foot of the mountain which contains

tains thefe falt fprings, and a guide conducted us to the mouth of thofe caverns by which we were to enter the heart of the mountain. I muft obferve, that it is now one hundred and twenty years fince thefe fprings were difcovered; and the Seigneurs of Berne, who are the proprietors, have fpared no expence to derive from them every poffible advantage. The great Haller had for fome years the fuperintendance of thefe works, which are now under the direction of Mr. Wild. It was fuggefted to the republic, that there muft be fome bed of falt funk deeply under the mountain; becaufe, in proportion as they dug into the earth, the water ran more copious, and was more ftrongly impregnated with falt. An experiment was therefore made at an immenfe coft; and upon digging below the bed of the Rhône, they heard the found of a fpring, to which they feemed faft approaching. This animated their labours: they penetrated to the fpring, and

to

to their infinite mortification found it perfectly *sweet*.

A labourer met us at the entrance of the mountain, and furnishing us with frocks and lamps, conducted us along a narrow passage bored through the solid rock, and lined with sulphureous matter. After viewing in our way the reservoir, we continued along this channel, which kept ascending, till we came to the centre of the mountain. Here a large wheel of thirty-six feet diameter was playing with the ease of a clock wheel, and the sky was visible above, the mountain being here pierced from the summit to the centre. We now descended from this eminence, retracing our former steps, till we came to another bore of the mountain which opened a passage to the right. This, our guide told us, penetrated one thousand feet, and we should, he added, find the workmen extending it still farther. We entered upon it, but had not gone many paces before we felt a great difference in the atmosphere.

mosphere. As we advanced, we found the air still less fit for respiration: our lamps went out frequently, and we felt a painful pressure upon the lungs. Yet here the poor labourers were employed in chisselling the hard rock, and hewing out a passage, in an air poisoned by sulphureous exhalations, and to us—unfamiliar with its vapours—totally suffocating. We were at this moment, as the guide informed us, four thousand feet deep in the mountain. These poor people have but eight batz, or about one shilling per day. Their day consists of eight hours; at the expiration of which, the set that goes off, is succeeded by another, without interruption; so that the works are never suffered to stand still. We hastened to emerge from this dismal dungeon; and were on our way, when a hollow sound rumbled through every cavity of the mountain, and was conveyed to our ears in thundering claps. We were thrown into alarm, and imagined that the sulphureous air had kindled from the lamp,

and

and occafioned the explofion; nor did we find ourfelves much relieved by the intelligence of our guide, that it was *only* occafioned by fome labourers below, who were blowing up parts of the rock with gunpowder.

## LETTER LIV.

SUCH was our exterior when we left the hollow windings of the Salt Mountain, that we were obliged to perform half a dozen luftrations before we were reftored to humanity. What will not curiofity atchieve? A more difagreeable expedition could not have been undertaken. A frock, thick-fet with greafe, hanging over our shoulders— our heads bent, to watch our footfteps over the rank fmoke of a lamp—noxious exhalations hovering round the walls—and a contaminated air entering into our lungs.— Such were the circumftances attending our defcent

defcent into thefe abodes of mifery and horror. Speaking in the language of a traveller, it is one of thofe objects which it is more pleafant to *have* feen, than to *fee*.

Bex is a town of no great extent, pleafantly fituated, in a foil that has enriched its inhabitants to a degree incommodious to the traveller. Their indifference to further gain is fuch, that they will rather fuffer their cattle to continue unemployed, than let them out to ftrangers at a reafonable payment. The grand eatable at Bex is potatoes. Thefe they grow of an enormous fize, and a very admirable quality. They ufually ferve them up, dreffed in various ways, in the fame courfe. Some troops were entering this town, at the moment in which we were quitting it. The occafion was fufficiently whimfical. A difpute had arifen among the inhabitants, refpecting the church pews. This quarrel had at length affumed a ferious fhape, and a holy war was expected. Their Excellencies of Berne had

been

## LETTER LIV.

been requested to march some troops into the town, in order to quell those religious feuds, and reduce this church militant to a peace establishment. I suspect that the spirit of discontent, which is gaining so rapidly among the provinces dependent on the government of Berne, has excited them to this measure of precaution; and the struggle for church pews, has only afforded the pretext for putting it in execution.

We now passed by Aigle and Villeneuve to Vevai. This was a very delicious part of our journey. It was on this day that we regained our view of the Lake of Geneva, at the extremity of which Villeneuve stands. Between Bex and this last mentioned place, we saw the entrance of the Rhône into the lake. There is nothing peculiarly striking in this, beyond the consideration, that this river continues its course through the Lake till at Geneva—a distance of more than forty miles from the point of entrance—its waters are again collected into a stream, acquire a

## LETTER LIV.

new velocity, and move in a rapid current towards the fea.

We paffed the Chateau de Chillon, as we drove to Vevai. It is a very beautiful ornament to this part of the Lake, and reminds one forcibly of antient fable. This Chateau is built upon a ftupendous rock, running far into the Lake; on the other extremity of which are the heights of Milleray, immortalized by the pen of Rouffeau. It was in this Chateau that the bailiffs of Vevai had their antient refidence; and, previous to the introduction of artillery, this fort was confidered as impregnable. The garrifon has lately been augmented by the providence of the Bernois, who do not view, without ftrong fymptoms of apprehenfion, the eclat which the French revolution has obtained in the different provinces dependent upon their authority. We paffed the night at Vevai—a very lively little town upon the banks of the Lake, furnifhed with

very

## LETTER LIV.

very agreeable promenades—and the next morning arrived at Laufanne.

I have now brought my journal of this expedition to a conclufion. Nine days were fpent in accomplifhing this object; and fuch has been our induftry, that we have in the courfe of this fhort period gone over a track of near two hundred miles. I retrace the journey with great fatisfaction. The fcenes with which it has been crouded, will never perhaps, in my experience, meet a parallel. Where fhall I feek again the contiguous elements of heat and cold? Where fhall I find the tranfparent pyramids of Boiffons, or the icy magazines of Montanvert? What climes will fhow me a parallel to the chryftal arches over the Arveron, or the magnificent varieties of the valley of Entremont? Where, in its darkeft moments, fhall the mind borrow more fombre colours, than from the caverns and perforated rocks of Bex, or the flinty deferts of St. Bernard? My foul is chilled when I confider the wretches who toil in the one, or refide on the other. But Heaven has moulded us to every variety of fituation; and, when the wifhes of man are bounded by his wants, there are few fituations which can exclude pleafure; when they are not, no condition can banifh pain.

## LETTER LV.

Laufanne, Aug. 26, 1791.

WHAT a wonderful country is this! He who has fojourned on the banks of the Leman Lake, will tell you, that the fcenery around prefents an ever-fruitful, ever-varied picture to the eye. The wonders of the univerfe feem here to be combined in one magnificent groupe, and all the fublimities of nature collected into a focus. Each recovering day gives birth to fome new beauty. The clouds are diftributed into more fantaftic forms. The mountains are
illumined

illumined with a richer luftre, and the trees are embrowned with deeper and more vivid tints. But it is in the rocks of Millerai that enthufiafm delights to dwell—thofe rocks where the wild and difconfolate St. Preux uttered his accents of defpair. Oft as my eye fixes upon thefe awful precipices, the lover of Heloife is prefent to my view. I fee him frantic with the agonies of difappointment, meditating, amidft thefe frowning heights, the rafh refolve, as he furveys the gulph below. His notes of anguifh feem ftill to live in faint and languid echoes—
" Les rochers font efcarpés, l'eau eft pro-
" fonde, et je fuis au defefpoir."

I fhould tell you, perhaps, that thefe mountains face directly that part of the Lake upon which our villa is planted; and it is among the chief amufements of the place, to pafs *en bateau* to the very mountains themfelves. The paffage is eafily effected in three hours; and a romantic repaft is made on the fhelving declivities of Millerai. The baths

baths of Evian form the principal rendezvous; and here, on the Sunday evenings, the fong and the dance are celebrated. Numbers pafs the Lake from Laufanne and its environs, to partake of thofe feftivities in Savoy, which the rigid police of the country denies them at home.

It has been remarked by many travellers, that Switzerland would form a very noble fchool of painting; and it is a matter of aftonifhment to thofe who furvey the very rich and exuberant fcenery of this country, that it fhould not yet have excited the labours of the pencil, and that the canvas fhould not hitherto have glowed with its original beauties. The author of the " Ta-
" bleau Pictorefque de la Suiffe" indulges in the warmeft raptures upon contemplating the general ftate of the country—which he calls an abftract of the known world ; and then, adverting to the manners and genius of the inhabitants, he breaks out into the moft indignant ftrain of invective: " Et
" pour

" pour qui cette superbe et magnifique ga-
" lerie? pour qui cette etonnante et riche crea-
" tion? pour un peuple insensible, apatheque,
" et froid—pour un peuple qui ne sent rien,
" qui n'imagine rien, qui ne pleure jamais,
" qui rien n'affecte; pour un peuple inca-
" pable d'emotions vives, de passions pro-
" fondes; pour un peuple qui ne connoit
" jamais le delire, l'enthousiasm de la poesie,
" de la peinture; ni les transports, les de-
" lices, les douces fureurs, les accens frené-
" tiques et brûlans des sentiments pas-
" sionnés."

Those who have studied more closely the manners of this people than I have been able to do, will better decide how far this delineation of character is accurate. A very different, and far more favourable picture of this nation, is drawn by the masterly pen of the Chevalier Mehegan, which I am disposed to believe does them no more than strict justice. " La habite un peuple sim-
" ple, bienfaisant, brave, ennemi du faste,
" ami

"ami du travail, ne cherchant point d'ef-claves et ne voulant point des maîtres." Society is unquestionably in many families upon a very civilized footing, and all the *agremens* of polished life are cultivated with success. The peasants preserve for the most part the sturdy traits of antient character. They live principally on vegetable diet; are frugal, industrious, and, generally speaking, inoffensive. Their habits of economy are not wholly exempt from the meaner foibles to which it is allied. Frugality too often degenerates among them into a sordid attachment to gain, and renders it difficult to dispute the truth of that characteristic proverb—"Point d'argent, point de Suisse."

## LETTER LVI.

*Laufanne, Sept. 20, 1791.*

THE harmony of this place muft now fuffer interruption. Political intrigues have been carried on, to introduce fome changes into the government, and, as it is rumoured, to effect a revolution, upon French principles. Great rejoicings were made at Rolle, a town not far diftant, upon the anniverfary of the French Revolution. At this feftival were found fome of the moft confiderable people in the Pays de Vaud; and toafts' were drank, which carried no fmall terror to the ruling Powers. Since this memorable day, a very high tone of language has been held by many, whofe influence in the country is great; and in private parties and public affemblies, no fcruple has been made, of reprobating ariftocracy, and holding up to ridicule the government

of

of Berne, which they ſtile "Le gouvernement "d'Ours."

There were not wanting among the females of the higher rank, thoſe who eſpouſed warmly the cauſe of France, and carried into public upon their head-dreſs the national colours. The air of "ça ira" was demanded upon every occaſion when muſic was to be had; and this was danced to in their numerous aſſemblies, with a degree of enthuſiaſm which threatened ſerious conſequences. The Geneveſe have for ſome time paſt prohibited this dance; and thoſe who have ſeen the effects it produces when performed in the ſpirit and with the vivacity of the nation from which it is derived, will not conſider the proſcription of ſuch an air as a meaſure of contemptible precaution.

At Lauſanne the government ſlumbered, or ſeemed to ſlumber. The libraries were reſorted to for political diſcuſſion. There the French gazettes were read and debated. To ſo great a licence had the ſpirit of the people

## LETTER LVI.

people proceeded, that the tranfactions of France were not commented upon without fome bold application to their own government; and projects of reform, nay even of revolution, were more than whifpered. At length the alarm was given, and the energy of the ruling Powers was awakened. It is not, indeed, to be fuppofed, that they continued idle fpectators of the game that was playing. It had, however, the appearance of neglect, nay even of timidity. This might be done with the defign of fuffering the plot to attain maturity, in order to meet the full mifchief, and crufh, with more fuccefs, the partizans. News was quickly circulated, that the Bernois were now marching three thoufand men, and feveral pieces of artillery, towards Laufanne, where they fhortly arrived, and were encamped before the town. Meafures the moft vigorous were adopted, both civil and military. Laufanne had all the appearance of a befieged town: Cannon were planted at the gates, with lighted matches,

matches, in a state of preparation. A species of inquisition was instituted; and no ceremony was used in quartering a sufficient number of soldiers in the houses of those who were suspected to have been concerned in the intended revolution. Some people of consideration were arrested; and, if report may be credited, their treatment was marked with the most rigid severity. The Chateau de Chillon is the Bastile of the country: to this prison have been consigned, those who were considered as principals in the plot; and informations are still paid for at the price of fifty crowns.

What this plot was, which has brought a camp to our gates, and an inquisition into our houses, I am not able to inform you. The government of Berne does not make manifest the details of its proceedings, and some people have affected to regard the whole as a bubble. This, however, must be said, that very strong symptoms of discontent were discoverable for some time

previous

previous to the arrival of the troops; and the general turn of converfation demonftrated, that fome movement might fhortly be expected. It is I think fufficiently clear, that the lower ranks of people in this country never felt themfelves interefted in the projected revolution. The punifhments have entirely fallen upon families of a certain rank; and the peafants are obferved to continue their labours of hufbandry, without occafioning or receiving moleftation.

Indeed, the grievances alleged have never appeared to me capable of interefting the community at large: they are principally felt by perfons of condition, and relate, for the moft part, to civil and military rank. As a province dependent upon Berne, it enjoys not the full privileges of the fuperior country; and officers are impofed upon them, both in the civil and military departments, to the exclufion of thofe among the natives who afpire to fuch rank. This is what I have heard ftated by one who had the reputation

putation of being a principal in the conspiracy, as the most formidable species of oppression. However invidious and unjust this may be—however it may wound the pride, and provoke the resentment, of the higher classes—it cannot be supposed that a rough and hardy peasantry, who are not oppressed by taxes, nor abridged in the enjoyment of the fruits of their labour, should take any interest in reforms, which sought the redress of such grievances. The influence of their lords, and the eclat of the French revolution, might seduce the abject and capricious; but the wiser, and by far the greater part, would continue, as they appear to have done, firmly attached to the government, under which they enjoy tranquillity and protection.

## LETTER LVII.

Laufanne, Oct. 2, 1791.

THIS country is now in its full beauty: all the floping parts towards the Lake are covered with vines, the grapes of which are advancing faft to maturity. The vines are remarkably low, and planted very thick. They are fupported by fticks; and fuch indeed is their exuberance, that they ftand greatly in need of fupport.

As I have underftood, the cultivation of the vineyards is done upon this principle. The farmer undertakes the whole of the labour and expence; in recompence of which he receives half the nett profit made upon the produce. This fecures the eftates from pillage. The farmers are very active in protecting the vineyards, which lie fufficiently expofed to depredation. It is difficult to make an excurfion, in any direction, without paffing through many acres covered with vines; and the heat of the weather, added to the very feducing afpect of the fruit, renders it not a little difficult to abftain from acts of plunder. As the vintage is now approaching, more than ordinary diligence is ufed to guard this facred property; and men, fuitably armed, are on the watch day and night.

The heat here is very oppreffive, except when the *Bife*, which is a north-eaft wind, blows. This is extremely fharp; and paffing over the fnowy mountains, comes charged with a very penetrating cold. Though we have now been a confiderable time in this part of Switzerland, and are indeed looking forward to our departure, I have not had opportunity to make any excurfion beyond the Glaciers and the Lake of Neuchatel. But indeed the whole of Switzerland has been fo accurately delineated in the journals of Mr. Coxe, and fo warmly painted by the

Marquis

## LETTER LVII.

Marquis de Langle, that I could not flatter myself with being able to tread to advantage the same ground, without borrowing largely from the induſtry of the one, and the animation of the other.

Such is the ſeverity now adopted by the government of Berne, that the French language is in many regiments forbidden to be ſpoken. Some gentlemen, lately returned from an excurſion into the heart of the country, related to me, that upon entering an inn where the officers of a Swiſs regiment were quartered, they requeſted as uſual to be ſhewn the room where the company ſupped. They were ſcarcely entered, when the Commandant demanded of the landlady in a very angry tone, " Qui ſont ces Meſ- " ſieurs là ?" " Ce ſont des Anglois," replied the matron. He looked ſtern, and with ſome degree of harſhneſs rejoined, " il eſt " defendu à mes officiers de parler Fran- " çois ;" and they ſupped together without exchanging a word. Proſcriptions are now going on with great difpatch; but all is conducted with fo much fecrecy, that it is difficult to arrive at a knowledge of particulars. Thus much however is certain, that fociety has very confiderably fuffered by thefe political machinations; and many individuals of the firft character have been put under arreft. This change of meafures in the ruling powers has abridged very greatly the freedom, and even the convenience of ftrangers. The libraries are put under a new law: all the gazettes from France, deemed dangerous or offenfive, are profcribed; and a notice has been affixed to the walls, prohibiting the difcuffion of political queftions—threatening the librarian with a fevere penalty, if he neglected to fee the order enforced. The uniformity of my prefent mode of life, and the ftrict military law under which we now are, will not allow me to tranfmit to you more interefting details—and the dulnefs of the place muft be my apology for the dulnefs of the letter.

# LETTER LVIII.

Laufanne, Oct. 16, 1791.

I TOLD you in my laſt, that the pleaſures of reſidence in the Pays de Vaud had been very much abridged by the colliſion of political intereſts. It was my fortune to have fallen under the particular patronage of the obnoxious party, and the deſtruction of their conſequence has thrown me very much upon myſelf for amuſement. Societies are indeed not totally annihilated; but all the frank and open intercourſe of life is at an end : the ſhadow yet ſtalks abroad, but all the delicious ſubſtance is extinct. If any deſigns of a revolutionary nature were ever ſeriouſly projected, it is difficult to ſay whether the weakneſs of the projectors or the wiſdom of the governors appears to have been the greateſt. Diſguiſe is conſidered ſo
eſſen-

essential to plot, that nothing but respect for the pointed cannon of their Excellencies of Berne can prevail upon me to believe, that half a dozen families of indiscreet enthusiasm had really conceived the design of detaching the province they inhabit from its alliance to the mother country. The ruling powers have at all events stolen a march upon them; and whether the necessity may have been real or imaginary, it is certain that the government has sustained no loss of influence by this interference.

The livery of nature is now changing rapidly in this delicious country, and the completion of the vintage has stript the long hills of their best ornaments. With the swallow I am now lingering in impatient anxiety for the signal of departure to a warmer and more cheery clime. The cabals of state, by arresting the stream of amusement, have driven me to the elements of a new language; and I shall hope to mix with a new people, not indifferently prepared

## LETTER LVIII.

prepared to enjoy their fociety. My mind is big with that expectation which books and reports have taught me to form of the country to which we tend. Endeared by the fame of its heroes and its poets, and exalted by the character of its local beauties, it now fills up the void which banifhed pleafures have left; and my mind embraces, in thefe its moments of folitude and feclufion, a thoufand fairy vifions.

Some deduction muft doubtlefs. be made from anticipation, and proportionable allowance muft be admitted for circumftances of change and deterioration. Such would, however, deftroy the pleafure of anticipating at all, which is then only exquifite, when it fees no limit; and as I have yet to encounter a few more blafts of the cutting life, before I approach the *reality*, I am yet anxious to preferve the *vifion* entire.

Your amufement cannot have received any fpecial addition by my late communications. The uniform progrefs of my days opens no difcovery in circumftance or reflection; and you have little to expect on the fcore of novelty, till the Alps are between us.

## LETTER LIX.

Turin, Nov. 7.

I WAIT your congratulations on having paffed the Alps. I feel as though we had performed no mean atchievement. Unluckily fo many have been beforehand with me, and fo many are likely to follow, that my travelling pride muft fuffer, I fear, on the reflection, a great abatement.

We lingered too long upon the northern frontier to find a ready paffage over this mountainous barrier. It was not till the evening of the 28th ult. that we determined upon this enterprize. The *Bife*, which is a very favage kind of wind, had

blown

## LETTER LIX.

blown for some days, and carried off the last remains of autumn. Our friends had severally struck their tents, and had quitted our neighbourhood in succession. Solitude, a barren soil, and the blasts of winter, now prompted our final resolve, and at the close of the day we bid adieu to the environs of Lausanne, and, passing the night at Morges, arrived the next morning at our old quarters in Geneva. As friendship is said to divide the pains and double the pleasures of society, we agreed to unite with two agreeable companions, of whom we had some previous knowledge, and who were, as we found, loitering between resolution and apprehension in the hotel at Geneva. The remainder of my day in that city was passed in seeking out those from whom I had on former occasions received marks of hospitable attention. Madamoiselle A. had arrested me at Rolle in the interim of preparation for breakfast. I profited of an hour's conversation with her on the state of French politics.

politics. Her talents for drawing had enabled her to indulge her veneration for some of the leading characters at Paris, whose portraits, in some cases from recollection, in others from engraving, she had designed with much spirit. These she descanted upon as she severally exhibited them with enchanting volubility. "Voila "des gens," said she, "comme il y en a "peu!" On La Fayette she was most liberal in her encomiums. "C'est un homme "fait exprès pour la revolution." My time was limited. Our political dialogue was interrupted by mutual adieus and reciprocal professions, "d'une amitié la plus sin- "cere."

Geneva was rendered unusually gay by a vast influx of company from the neighbourhood to attend the comedy. This is, to be agreeable to report, the last season of theatrical indulgence; and, by a decree of the Council, no dramatical exhibitions are hereafter to be tolerated within the jurisdiction

of

of the republic. Theatres are, according to Rouffeau, only juftifiable in great cities; and I am of opinion with the puritanical legiflators of Geneva, that the permiffion of a theatrical corps, in a town regulated even by the ftricteft police, may yet ferve as a paffport for the introduction of thofe vices which the indolence and the diffipation of this profeffion are too well calculated to encourage.

But I have detained you too long at Geneva, impatient as you muft no doubt be to pufh acrofs the Alps. Bear then with this delay in the outfet, and I promife you that my narrative fhall now move with as little interruption as the inequalities of the way will allow.

LETTER LX.

REPORTS had reached us the night previous to our departure from Geneva, that heavy falls of snow had been observed on the route, and that dispatch was necessary, lest the pass should be rendered impracticable. We made therefore every preparation to enter upon Savoy at an early hour, but were after all compelled to put up for the night at a village called Frangy. This is about sixteen miles from Geneva. Here we had early experience of that inexpressible misery characteristic of the inns of Savoy. The rooms into which we were conducted were strewed with clods of grass and dirt, and the supper was made up of vile morsels steeped in garlic. Our next day's journey brought us to Chamberri. The air was clear, and the mountains began to

be

be diſtinctly viſible. Aix les Bains, which lies between Frangy and Chamberri, arreſted our attention for half an hour. This town is remarkable for the excellence of its hot ſprings. They are ſulphureous, and reputed to poſſeſs very ſalubrious properties. The baths are very commodiouſly conſtructed. Excepting ſome emigrants who have ſought aſylum here, very few ſtrangers were to be ſeen.

Chamberri, where we next lodged, is, as you know, the capital of the duchy of Savoy. Its ſituation is not among the leaſt of its beauties, commanding noble and varied views of hills, plains, and vallies. I ſaw the town in a diſadvantageous hour. It was a ſaint-day, and the rain fell hard. Theſe were two circumſtances equally unfavourable to the reſpect of a trading town, which is only rendered cheerful by the ſpirit and activity of commercial occupation. The ſhops were cloſely barricadoed, and no doors were ſeen open but thoſe of the churches.

churches. Here I followed the multitude, and encountered a host of beggars, more ragged, importunate, and clamorous than any of the fraternity of mendicants I ever met with. I ought to remark, that, agreeably to custom, this should have been the first stage from Geneva; and the accommodations here are at least such as ought to silence complaint. Our third day brought us to Aigue-belle, in the course of which we passed through Montmelian, sufficiently known in the contiguous countries for the excellence of its wines. It is at Chamberri that the valley opens which conducts to the foot of Mount Cenis. Down this valley the river Aar pursues its course, and moves with considerable rapidity. In some points it is worked into foam, and breaks its way with all the violence of the most impetuous torrent. In the journey of this day the Alps began to open upon us, till on our arrival at Aigue-belle they showed themselves in all their majestic and tremendous forms.

Our fourth day brought us to St. Jean de Maurienne, where we found no contemptible quarters.

From St. Jean to St. André, for we were now roving amidſt the reſidences of the ſaints, we toiled the fifth day. The valley, as we advanced, gradually narrowed, and the mountains as regularly augmented in number, height, and horrors. The torrent of the Aar we paſſed a variety of times, in the courſe of this day, upon wooden bridges, of what appeared to us the lighteſt conſtruction. We hinted ſome apprehenſions reſpecting our ſafety, but were aſſured that their ſtrength was ill-judged of by their appearance. The road was as little calculated to inſpire confidence. It coaſted almoſt uniformly along the moſt hideous precipices, exciting at times lively emotions of terror, and exhibiting, through a frightful alternation of aſcents and declivities, all the varieties of difficulty and danger.

## LETTER LXI.

It was not till the evening of the sixth day that our procession arrived at Lannesbourg at the foot of Mount Cenis. Nothing but miserable sights of human infirmity had occurred in this latter part of the valley. From St. Jean de Maurienne to Mount Cenis I saw little besides sallow countenances and emaciated forms. St. André appeared, indeed, the head-quarters of goitrous idiotism and wretchedness. Mountains on either side seemed to compress, within a most gloomy and insalubrious sort of dungeon, these woe-begone inhabitants, who called to my mind

> the wasteful host
> Of pain and sickness, squalid and deform'd.

You will readily conceive that great falls of snow could not much improve a track which

## LETTER LXI.

paſſed over the declivities of mountains. Sixteen miles performed between the hours of ten and four, will enable you to judge of our pace and patience. The diverſity of ſhapes and magnitudes, which the vaſt cluſter of Alps, among which we were now moving, preſented, under a deep coating of ſnow, made a very curious appearance.

In a village through which we paſſed, ſome violent ſhouts excited our curioſity. We found they were occaſioned by an event of great importance to the inhabitants,— the ſhooting of a bear, which had made frequent deſcents upon this wretched hamlet, and borne off conſiderable booty; till the loſs of an infant, whom he was ſuppoſed to have ſtolen, enraged the peaſants, who purſued this inhuman depredator into the ſavage wilds in which he reſided, and, at the moment of our arrival, Bruin was dragging in triumph through the village.

The approach to Lanneſbourg offered a curious ſpectacle. The valley through which we had been journeying for some days, and which had gradually narrowed, now appeared to terminate; and the mountain over which we were to pass seemed to oppose, by the trackless snow which inveloped it, an insuperable barrier. We entered Lannesbourg before the day closed, and were instantly surrounded by a number of men, who demanded permission to pull our carriages to pieces by royal authority. I respect governments wherever I go, and would not wantonly pour contempt upon any of his Sardinian Majesty's subjects; but I think in my conscience, that an assemblage of more ill-looking wretches never acted under government authority. A commissioner soon showed himself at the head of these raggamuffins, and throwing out a tariffe, in length " a full cloth-yard or more," gave us our choice of travelling accommodations, with the prices settled by order of the police. Our negociation with him was expedited by the pressing desire of finding

the

the comforts of a blazing fire, and a trout fifhed out of the Lake of Mount Cenis. A very converfible madamoifelle, the daughter of the landlord, attended on us at fupper, and did credit to the vivacity and naïveté of the Savoyardes.

The hotel, which is newly fet up, ftands a very fair chance of fucceeding; for, in addition to the bad reputation under which the other labours, of being the worft and moft impofing inn in Chriftendom, I have no where feen a little fyren better calculated for detaining travellers, who are not violently preffed to crofs the mountain.

## LETTER LXII.

IT was not by the aid of mules and porters, fedans and fledges, that the hero of Carthage made his *entrée* into Italy: and yet I much queftion whether the Carthaginian foldiers complained more emphatically of cold,

cold, fatigue, and inconvenience, than we did. I am impatient to carry you over this mountain, or I could expatiate very largely upon the murmurs I uttered and heard in the afcent from Lannefbourg. The air was indeed impregnated with particles of intenfe cold, and made its way through all the armour with which we were provided. One hour brought us upon the plain, when, to recover from the effects of thefe feverities, we were conducted to a fhed, in which a fire recovered us to fomething like good humour. From this fhed we were feverally drawn in a fledge to the fouthern extremity of the plain, by mules who trotted with confiderable fwiftnefs through the fnows. The poft is fituated a mid-diftance on this route, and was carefully announced to us by the guides and muleteers. At the Grande Croix, in the extremity of the plain, were fome objects upon which I could not but beftow a fhare of attention. To the right was the lake fo celebrated for

the

the excellence of its trout; to the left, the hôpital.

This hôpital was founded, like that of St. Bernard, for the relief and refreshment of those pilgrims whom devotion might induce to seek the shrines of Loretto, or solicit the benediction of Christ's vicar. At some distance stood the " Chapelle de transis"—a cœmetery constructed for the burial of those who may chance to perish on these pious expeditions. Numerous huts are also raised upon different parts of this mountain, the residence of shepherds during the summer, as very excellent pasture is found in the bosom of those rocks which inclose the upper level, and whose points rise to a very considerable height. In fact, when upon this plain, which covers the summit of the mountain, we seemed to be in a valley, enormous ridges of rock rising on either side, some of which appear to bear the snows of ages. It was from this point, the beginning of the " descente des Echelles," that

that we entered the sledge, in order to slide down in the whimsical fashion in usage here, when the sides of the mountain are incrusted with snow. A hundred travellers have told you what this mode is, and by what expedients and under what fears it is effected. I shall not, however, be deterred from telling you what I found it. You are then to imagine me seated in a sledge. To this sledge are fastened two sticks pointed with iron, in the form of a shaft. The guide seated in the front, by the assistance of these shafts, and his feet, which are also eminently serviceable, hastens or retards the motion of the machine, conducts it along precipices with wonderful dexterity, and makes, as occasion requires, yet oftener to show his skill, the most sharp and difficult turns. In some parts we descended with vast rapidity; and the zig-zag course which these ingenious conductors sometimes pursued, in order to pass each other on the way, was really diverting.

This

## LETTER LXII.

This was a very pleasant as well as novel descent. The objects by which we glided composed an assemblage of wild and grotesque scenery—a torrent amongst these issuing from the brow of that plain which we had quitted, precipitated its stream in the form of a beautiful cascade. Ten minutes brought us to the miserable village of Ferriere, the regular descent to which is called an hour. The sledges were discharged here as no longer useful, and the remainder of the distance to Novaleze performed on foot. The whole of this descent is estimated two hours or leagues, for time and space stand for each other in these countries; and thus reckoning the commencement of the rise from Chamberri, the height which is ascended by a track of twenty-five leagues, is descended in two. In this calculation, the perpendicular height of the mountain may be reckoned at more than seven thousand English feet. Our journey, though fatiguing, abounded in objects of curiosity and interest.

The memory of the great hero who, two thousand years ago, fought his way through this valley, was frequently a prop to my declining patience. What were our toils, in comparison of those sustained by men who had to scale the towering rock under the pressure of arms, exposed to the surly tempest, with no resources but the habit of combating danger, and the hopes of future conquest!

While I was entering my sledge at the point of descent, I eyed the opening through which Hannibal, probably, pointed out to his exhausted followers the spoils that awaited them in the delightful plains of Lombardy: for all circumstances conspire to fix the passage of the Carthaginians into Italy across the Mont Cenis. The line of separation between Savoy and Piedmont is the little Doria, a stream which rises in the Lake of Mont Cenis, and afterwards uniting with the great Doria, the waters of both are borne to the Po, at a little distance from Turin. At Novaleze, our carriage dissected

at

at Lannefbourg was very dexteroufly and completely re-conftructed,—a fubject of juft congratulation, when it is confidered how much more difficult it is to reftore than to deftroy. The courfe of the little Doria conducted us to Suze, a town agreeably fituated, and in high reputation among the inhabitants on the northern fide of the Alps; who furnifhed us with no article of luxury or convenience, but what they pretended to import from the fruitful treafures of Suze. This town has the reputation of being founded by Pompey. A triumphal arch is among the monuments of antiquity which it ftill preferves, and which is by Gruter carried up to the time of Tiberius. Our equipage paffed rapidly through this place, in order to reach the inhofpitable village of St. Ambroife; but in this the convenience of the horfes was much more confulted than that of their mafters, the ftages of our journey being regulated by the diftribution of the pofts.

# LETTER LXIII.

THE road in paffing from Rivoli, the laft village on the route to Turin, gradually opens into a confiderable width, and announces with much magnificence the approach to a great capital. Turin cannot be too handfomely fpoken of as a town. Regularity and beauty are terms appropriate to its character. I was extremely diverted by the appearance of the inhabitants. Drefs, air, countenance, and language were full of novelty. Etiquette here holds fovereign fway. I faw numbers, whofe thread-bare fuit could fcarcely maintain its place, fqueezing with the utmoft formality a *chapeau bras*—a burnifhed fword vibrating by their fide.

Turin wears all the marks of a vigilant police. Every quarter of the town is tranquil in the night. I went the morning after my arrival to view the palace. His Sardinian majefty was there, and we could not be admitted till he fhould fet off for his *maifon de Chaffe*. The firing of guns, and the beating of drums, fhortly announced his majefty's intention of quitting the palace. All who were on the fpot drew themfelves up in order and formed an alley, through which his majefty and his fuite paffed. This obtained me a fight of the monarch; but the fqueeze was fo great, that I had little leifure to take cognizance of the royal features.

I am not in general very curious in examining the interior of palaces, except fo far as they are reputed to enclofe the works and monuments of art. I was however unexpectedly gratified in this inftance, by the uncommon fplendor and rich decorations of the apartments. The number of them was prodigious, and they formed a labyrinth almoft as intricate as that of Crete. I
fhall

shall only mention a few of those rarities which struck me most forcibly:—Victor Amadeus, an equestrian statue. This monarch himself, in bronze, is mounted upon a horse of marble, trampling upon the bodies of slaves in chains, with all the wild barbarity of a conqueror and a tyrant. One stands astonished at the corruption of that mind, which can find a feast in such base and unfeeling adulation. " Parcere subjectis," was the favourite maxim of Henry IV. of France; and the arts are miserably degraded, when they are employed to celebrate the abettor, rather than the vanquisher of tyranny, and to immortalize him who imposes, rather than him who breaks the chains of servitude.—The four seasons, by Albani, were curious objects of speculation. There appeared to enter much ingenious composition into these works of the pencil, and you will readily perceive, that a fine imagination can alone embody those phantoms of the mind. I know not whether Albani has executed these

these pieces as well as he ought; but I cannot conceive how he could have executed them better. The portrait of Charles I. of England, and his children, is a fine *morceau*, from the animated pencil of Vandyke. But my attention was very highly engaged by a small groupe which passes for the *chef d'œuvre* of Gerard Dow. The subject is a dropsical woman seated in a chair. The physician is examining the water. The maid servant is at the same time administering a spoonful of physic to the patient; and casting her eye upon the afflicted daughter at her mother's knee. Every circumstance, the most minute, is expressed with an accuracy, and a finish, which surpasses conception. This piece is said to have cost the late king twenty thousand livres.

# LETTER LXIV.

TRAVELLING, like age, is garrulous; and merely to see, without relating, is but to have half seen. I have made my debut as an Italian connoisseur, and am now about to appear in my new character of an antiquary. My knowledge is about equal in the one and the other science; but a man cannot travel south of the Alps, without either being, or becoming so much of both, as to take off that stupid stare with which a perfect novice regards the works of art.

From the palace of his Sardinian majesty we went to the university, situated in that very handsome street, the Strada di Po. The university is announced by a portico, bearing the inscription, " Regium Athe-" næum," and consists of an extensive range of buildings, comprehending various objects;

jects; among which the "Mufeo del Re," or "the King's Mufæum," was pointed out to us as an object of importance to travellers. This Mufæum forms indeed a very extenfive and valuable collection of antiques in every kind, ftatues, bufts, and ancient fragments. Among a great variety of elegant works in bronze, were a delicious little figure of Venus in the whimfical attitude of cutting her toe-nails: this is executed with the moft perfect accuracy and beauty. The famous Tripod, which contracts or increafes its dimenfions at pleafure. A foot of a horfe of the natural fize, of the moft exquifite execution: this, together with the leg of a man, fuppofed to be its rider, were purchafed by accident of a founder who had employed the other parts to make bells, and was about to convert thefe precious relics to the fame ufe. There are alfo fome thunders of Jupiter, which yet retain ftrong veftiges of the brilliant gold with which they once glittered: to thefe muft be added, vafes

vafes of filver, and fepulchral lamps, in all the forms which ingenuity could fupply.

The collection of Egyptian antiquities is alfo extremely curious and valuable: numerous penates, talifmans, &c. are here depofited. The objects which were held up as of the greateft eftimation, were, " a head of " Ifis, and the Ifiac table." The firft is of bronze admirably executed, and covered with hieroglyphics. The fecond, or Ifiac table, is confidered as one of the moft precious monuments of ancient times, which Italy preferves. It is of red copper, nearly four feet long, and fomething more than two in width. Ifis, who is reprefented fitting, forms the principal figure in this table, which thence derives its name. She is fupplied with two bulls horns as fymbols of fecundity. It appears to have been, in its original ftate, adorned with filver plates, as fome of thefe ornaments ftill remain; and it is like the head of Ifis before named, and, indeed, any relic of Egyptian origin, co-

vered

vered with hieroglyphics. This myfterious table has furnifhed a wide field of difcuffion and enquiry for the learned, to whom hieroglyphics yet continue an inexplicable language. The moft rational opinion yet offered, refpecting the defign of this table, is, that the Egyptians, who came to fettle in Italy, formed it, in order that the epocha of their worfhip, their ceremonies, habits of their priefts, &c. might not pafs into oblivion. This folves, however, no part of thofe myfterious fymbols which croud the table; for, after all the efforts of antiquarian refearch, or happy conjecture, the Egyptian continues, in refpect to his hieroglyphics, yet mafter of the field.

The collection of medals appeared to be numerous and well arranged; the greater part of thefe, and of the valuable antiques in general, with which this mufæum abounds, were taken from the ruins of " Induftria," a well-known colony of the Romans, whofe fcite and veftiges were not discovered till the year 1745. The attendant at this musæum was an Abbé, intelligent and polite, who declined any gratuity offered, as contrary to usage. The stranger is, however, permitted to indulge his liberality to the servants at the door, the objects of whose bows and forward civilities cannot easily be mistaken.

I thought to have drawn the curtain upon Turin in this letter, but the musæum has carried me beyond the bounds I had prescribed, and I have too much respect for the Italian opera to mention it in a postscript.

## LETTER LXV.

THE Italian opera is the touchstone of fashion; and no man, who has any regard for his reputation, would venture to dislike what good breeding obliges him to approve. The serious Italian opera is, in
the

the judgment of profeffional men, better prefented on the Englifh than upon the Italian ftage. This arifes from the liberal encouragement given to all the fingers of reputation, and from the very expenfive decorations which thefe exhibitions receive in a country whofe refources and prodigality feem to keep equal pace with each other.

The Buffo, or Comic Opera, is that which a ftranger will vifit to moft advantage in Italy, this being the fpecies of compofition in which modern fingularities are held up to ridicule; while the ferious opera reforts to fome tale of ancient hiftory, choofing, for the moft part, that into which the greateft number of fplendid characters can enter. I went, the evening after my arrival at Turin, to the Theatre di Carignano, and was agreeably entertained with a comic reprefentation of La Serva Inamorata. My knowledge of Italian is as yet but very flender; neverthelefs, without underftanding any confiderable portion of the dialogue,

I found an excellent fcholium in the gefture, play of the mufcles, and mufical expreffion, with which the whole was accompanied. To judge from the only two fpecimens I have as yet had, the Italians have a very extraordinary talent at mufical inflection upon fubjects of humour; and can render, with the greateft effect, by artificial modulation, the eafy familiarities of colloquial wit. On a foreign ftage the fame freedom is not felt, becaufe it is with reafon fuppofed, that what will be ill underftood where humour is concerned, cannot be highly relifhed; and every attempt to methodize or accommodate, muft in fuch cafes deftroy thofe features of nature which he who ftudies mankind would wifh principally to find.

Italian dancing has been frequently commented upon with great feverity: and indeed, the meafure of cenfure has never yet reached the demerit of the performance. Such outrageous ftrides, jumps, and fomerfets,

merfets, I never before had witneffed, as were exhibited in the ballets annexed to the operas. The dance formed a direct contraft to the fong, and produced in me as lively emotions of difguft, as it did in the audience of applaufe. A dance of favages round a cannibal banquet could not have been more wild and extravagant. I could not but feel aftonifhed, that a people, who excel fo decidedly in the arts of mufical expreffion, fhould judge fo corruptly on a fubject which appears to turn upon principles fo nearly analogous.

## LETTER LXVI.

I HAVE fpoken with fufficient emphafis of the general beauty of Turin, and I ought to add, that the details will not fuffer by examination. They reckon 110 churches in this capital, of which many are of great architectural beauty.

The

# LETTER LXVI.

The *place* or square which precedes the palace prefents a magnificent appearance. Eight streets there concentre; and continued arcades, or piazzas, favour the expofition of every kind of merchandize. The place San Carlo divides, at nearly its centre, the Strada Nuova, and adds confiderably to the fplendour of the city. The promenades are delicious. They confift in an efplanade between the town and the citadel, and alfo in a beautiful diftribution of the ramparts. The streets are for the moft part wide, clean, and regular; and many of the houfes are conftructed upon a grand fcale.

The Po, near the city, appears not yet to have recovered from the commotion into which the mufe of Ovid has thrown it. Addifon tells us, on the authority of fome botanifts, that larch-trees, and not poplars, are thofe which fhed a gum, and are found on the banks of the Po. And Apollonius could not have been very accurate when he tells us, that the thunderbolt of Jupiter fo affected

affected the waters, as to render it fatal to a bird to fly acrofs the ftream. But this was a favourite image with the poets; and the lake of Avernus was not efteemed by Virgil fufficiently corrupt without this quality. There is a pleafure of no common magnitude in contemplating thofe realities which have been wrought by claffic fancy into fuch fplendid vifions. It would afford a ftill higher pleafure, if it were poffible to diveft them completely of the veil which covers them; for after all that Hefiod, Apollodorus, and ftill more rationally Ariftotle, and others, who have improved upon this fyftem, have taught us, the fable of Phaeton, and the combuftion he occafioned, is one among thofe amufing myfteries whofe machinery is enchanting, whofe moral is obvious, but whofe precife meaning has perifhed with the records of the times.

The fpirit of trade feems to be very active at Turin, if any judgment may be formed from the lively buftle of the ftreets. Articles

ticles of English manufacture are vended in every part of the town, and a very considerable traffic is reported here to be carried on with Great Britain. How greatly is the state of empires changed since Virgil pronounced the Britons " penitus toto di- " visos orbe?" I am aware that their insular situation formed a part of that sentiment; but the very striking contrast which modern Britain presents to the more general construction of the expression, I am called upon continually to remark. Briareus-like, she now extends her hundred arms over the different districts of the continent, and maintains, by the vigour of her commerce, and the extent of her political influence, a connection with every nation of the globe.

## LETTER LXVII.

Feliffano, Nov. 11, 1791.

AT the end of two days journey, we have got into a miserable village, and though shivering with an aguish cold, contracted amidst the snow of Mount Cenis, I shall endeavour, by attention to my journal, to forget my maladies. Imperious circumstances, rather than choice, shortened my stay at Turin; and as I had foreseen that our departure might be precipitate, I had availed myself of every opportunity to gratify my curiosity upon objects of interest and information. Being either too little or too great to quit without notice the capital of Piedmont, in attempting to cross the bridge over the Po, we were suddenly commanded to halt, and take off a pair of horses, it being contrary to the established rules of the place to suffer one man to drive out four horſes. This was rather a trial of pride than of patience, for the remainder of the town was of no great length;—and our horſes being again put to, we proceeded in quiet pace along the banks of the Po.

It was morning, and all that remained of dying vegetation was illumined by a clear and temperate funſhine. Although the ſeaſon of the year has greatly abridged the beauties of the ſcenery, objects were not wanting to inſpire the landſcape with intereſt. A charming diſtribution of country villas covered a wide and variegated tract. The Alps, at diſtance, preſented their ſnowy ſummits in a vaſt and ſtupendous chain, while beſide us rolled in peaceful motion the turbid waters of that ſtream, conſecrated to claſſic fame. Imagination was not idle in theſe moments ſo favourable to fancy. All the fictions which had crowded my childiſh memory embodied themſelves before me; and I ſeemed to be moving over enchanted ground, till I arrived at Villa Nueva.

## LETTER LXVII.

Nuova. I muſt tell you, that I never yet entered any town at ſo late an hour. For upon aſking the *padrone* of the inn the time of the day, he aſſured me it was leaſt 3 and 20 o'clock.

On remarking to our hoſt that this was a ſmall village, he replied, with ſome degree of diſpleaſure, *padrone!* This word *padrone* is a term of moſt comprehenſive ſignification; inſomuch that I, who am but an *inceptor* in the language, feel ſome difficulty in determining the intention of the party by whom it happens to be uſed. In the ſalutation of friends, I have obſerved *padrone* enquired on the one part, and the ſingle term *padrone* returned on the other; and, in this caſe, it implies the " How do " you do ?" and the " Pretty well, thank " you," of the Engliſhman. But the ſenſe in which my hoſt employed it was, as I have ſince underſtood, a very common and a very civil one; namely, " I beg your par- " don." In order to impreſs me more
strongly

ftrongly with the importance of the place, he added, that it contained a convent. I was not quite fatisfied with this proof; but fearing that my Italian might not bear me out in the difpute, and dreading the confequences of an attack upon the church, I fuffered myfelf to be beaten out of the field. It was in our plan of this day's journey to reach Aleffandria, but the inevitable flownefs of our pace, from the extreme badnefs of the road, and the counfel of an old man, who was queftioned upon the remaining diftance, determined us to ftop at Feliffano for the night. Two beds of ftraw, with fcanty coverlids, juft leave fpace for a ricketty table, upon which my pen is now moving; and the chilling winds, which enter by the papered cafement, are playing moft wantonly about my fhoulders.

If ever you fhould be tempted to crofs the Mont Cenis, at a period when the fnows are almoft knee-deep, and one or both of your boots may happen to admit water,

water, let me caution you not to exchange your carriage for your feet. A raging fever of laſt night, and a thouſand aches and ſhiverings all this day, enable me to aſſure you that the pains attending on ſuch indiſcretion, are as ſevere as thoſe which puniſh ſome of the moſt important follies of human eccentricity.

## LETTER LXVIII.

Caſtel San Giovanni, Nov. 13, 1791.

OUR hoſt at Feliſſano made up in attention, for the deficiences of his miſerable accommodations. Aleſſandria, through which we paſſed in our road to Tortona, detained us no longer than was neceſſary to procure a dinner, for which we paid at a rate which left no room for regret on the part of the landlord. The country from Aleſſandria is for the moſt part flat, and in

a ſtate

a state of high cultivation to Tortona, where we arrived in the evening.

I am not in the habits of retailing the articles of provisions which I find on the way, but our yesterday's fare may serve as a specimen of what I am given to understand is considered as an excellent Italian supper. A dish of macaroni was our first service. This was followed by a saucer containing some scraped parmesan. A plate was then introduced with some morsels of pigs liver, and a second adorned with omelettes and garlick. Three small birds, and a handsome desert, closed this *petit souper*, which, however deficient in weight and essentials, may, in the language of the Latins, be at least allowed to have been " *numeris* abso-" luta fuis."

Horace has told us of some meals in his time, in which variety appears to have been not less consulted. Nasidienus's supper made certainly a better figure; and was on that account more deserving of recital: but I think

think that, taken upon a small scale, the gusto of antient times is not badly preserved in the modern arts of Italian catering. As I have brought Horace upon the stage, in vindication of my bill of fare, I shall make him do me another service before I dismiss him. His visits to Mæcenas were frequent, and their repasts convivial. Some animating topic had engaged him at one of these " noctes coenæque Deum ;" and inattentive to the objects of sense, which were doubtless set before him in profusion, he imprudently swallowed some garlick. How he felt upon that occasion, his muse has amphatically told us. My feelings are so perfectly in unison with his, upon all that relates to this nauseous vegetable, that though I am not prepared to consider it as a sufficient punishment for the crime of parricide, yet I can never see it cordially digested without exclaiming,

O dura messorum Ilia!

# LETTER LXIX.

Piacenza, Nov. 14, 1781.

A VERY diverting Signora, who attended upon us at Tortona, gave us the firſt ſpecimen of the Italian face, ſuch, at leaſt, as I have béen taught to expect it. It is not beauty, or rather it is not lovelineſs; but it poſſeſſes great ſymmetry, and there is much in it to excite admiration. I remarked to the Signora that the town muſt be dull, as I underſtood from her that it could boaſt no theatre. She replied, that at preſent there was indeed but one battalion of ſoldiers at Tortona, but that their uſual compliment was three. One was gone off towards France, and another into Savoy. I found by this, that a red coat was not without its charms beyond the Alps; and that the Signoras of Italy were of an opinion,

nion, not peculiar to this country, that "where troops were quartered, there could be no want of amufement."

Our journey from Tortona to Caftel San Giovanni, where we ftopped laft night, brought the Apennines before us: but the country is in general fo flat, as to furnifh little variety. I would not fay, of any part of Italy, that it is uninterefting. It was the theatre of all that is great in hiftory for many ages; and not a fpot of it exifts that has not been the feat of fome celebrated event. The claffic enthufiafm of Mr. Addifon was able to difcover fome veftiges of its antient grandeur, even in the rudeft parts of this country. "There is," fays he, "fcarce any part of the nation that is not famous in hiftory, nor fo much as a mountain or river that has not been the fcene of fome extraordinary action." I could however learn nothing of Caftel San Giovanni from any of its inhabitants. The place feemed funk in wretchednefs and poverty; yet an old wall, mouldering into ruins, appeared to commemorate some lost importance. The strolling ecclesiastics, of whom I enquired respecting those ruins, could give me no information, though they appeared to have sufficient leisure for antiquarian studies. No less than eight churches and three convents were enumerated in consequence of my enquiries; and notwithstanding the deplorable wretchedness which covered the inhabitants, it was easy to see that the honour in their estimation outweighed the burden.

Indeed, I could not but be strongly impressed with this infatuation, upon passing a few minutes in their cathedral. It was curious to observe the contrast that appeared between the worshippers and their shrines. While the one were covered with rags, the other were invested with costly ornaments. Columns of marble supported the altars, while the thread-bare cloke scarcely covered those who knelt and crawled around it. On the

## LETTER LXIX.

the one, precious odours were afcending in votive clouds; from the other, proceeded only the vile fcent of garlick. Yet the countenance of the worfhipper fpoke a fentiment above content. He eyed, with fomething more than complacency, the range of coftly ftatues which enkindled his devotion, and feemed to forget the depth of his mifery in the fervor of his prayers. How ftrong is the grafp of fuperftition, when it has once faftened upon its victim! The comforts of life really feemed to thefe deluded people, a very mean price for the religious trumpery they received in exchange, and the privilege of worfhipping at a golden altar: content to exift upon macaroni, and to ftretch their bodies upon beds of ftraw, provided their faints and demi-gods may feed upon frankincenfe, and inhabit fhrines of alabafter!

# LETTER LXX.

Parma, Nov. 15, 1791.

I KNOW not how a town can be viewed to lefs advantage than during a fall of undecided rain. By undecided rain, I mean that diftillation which fcatters a dufky mift over all the works of art. Such was the ftate of the atmofphere upon my arrival and during my ftay at Piacenza; and perhaps it is to this that I owe the impreffion of dullnefs which I have brought away with me from that town. It is not, however, without its ornaments.

The Piazza Publico (which is a fquare) partakes of the grand; it is difficult, however, to be fatisfied with more than one of its fides. Two noble equeftrian ftatues commemorate in bronze, at two angles of this fquare, the virtues of Aleffandro I. and

his

his fon. I ought to have admired, as books inftruct me, the painted cupola of the cathedral; but, alas! the height of the cupola, and the gloom of the cathedral, had ravifhed thofe beauties from my fight. I was obliged to content myfelf with gazing upon an object which had the advantage of a better light—I mean the dial; as this was the firft I had obferved defcribed after the Italian method of keeping time, and prefenting on one circumference the twenty-four hours of the day. I was very much pleafed with a fmall painting of the Virgin and Child in a glafs frame, and hung over one of the altars in the church of St. Francifco il Grande; it had fo much in it of fweetnefs and nature, that I cannot but hazard a word in its praife, though I have not yet found it in that lift which travellers are inftructed to admire. A very elegant altar in the fame church attracted my particular curiofity; it was defigned with art, and finifhed with beauty. The richeft marble,

marble, and the pureſt alabaſter, were here expended with equal ſymmetry and profuſion. I was anxious to know what Saint or Martyr claimed this altar. If it were my lot to be canonized, I know not a ſhrine I ſhould more earneſtly covet. A little invocation, and ſome few inſcriptions, ſoon led me to its lawful claimant, who was no leſs a perſonage than St. Anthony, the great apoſtle to the fiſhes. All the good things in the province of Milan ſeem conſecrated to this powerful Saint, whoſe head-quarters are at Padua. He was ſpoken of in very high terms upon the tablets which beſtrewed this altar, and repreſented as very dear to Jeſus Chriſt, and a great favourite of the Holy Virgin.

The church of San Agoſtino is a riſing ornament to the town of Piacenza, and promiſes to end in a building of great taſte and beauty. The ſide aiſles are fitted up in a very elegant ſtile, and the new front which it is now receiving, preſents the out-

line

line of a noble façade. The Auguſtines, to whom this church belongs, are in poſſeſſion of vaſt property. It is at their expence that this church is now receiving its finiſh. "The façade," ſaid an old mendicant, "has already coſt 14,000 ſechins."—"What then," ſaid I, "theſe gentlemen "are rich?"—"Rich!" ſaid he, "richiſ-"ſimi-ſono i noſtri principi."

As the diſtance from Piacenza to Parma was not conſiderable, we paſſed from thence in the afternoon, and entered Parma in the duſk of the evening. The country in the whole of this route was delectable; not a rood of ground was to be ſeen, but what poſſeſſed the higheſt degree of cultivation.

## LETTER LXXI.

Parma, Nov. 16, 1791.

MY ſpeculations of to-day upon the curioſities of this place have been ſo extenſive, that though I burn with impatience to communicate, I fcarcely know whether the late hour at which I attempt this fketch will allow me to complete my report. It was a grand day at the cathedral, fo that I had the pleafure of hearing high mafs performed. The church of San Giovanni Evangelifta, which I next entered, was very highly ornamented, and the pencil of Correggio has pourtrayed upon its cupola fome animated figures; that of St. John is eminently beautiful.

The academy afforded me a large field of amufement. A variety of mifcellaneous paintings and defigns is here preferved, and fome curious fragments of antiquity; amongft which was a very noble head of Jupiter. But the principal ornament of this academy, and one of the greateft ornaments of Europe I might add, is the *chef d'œuvre* of Correggio preferved here with great care, and ftill in high prefervation. The groupe is formed by the Virgin, who has the Infant in her lap. Mary Magdalen

len is to the left of her, having her head reclined. St. Jerome, an angel, and the Infant Baptist, enter into the composition, and a more exquisite production never issued from the school of painting. I did not think it possible for imagination to pourtray a countenance of such delicacy, grace, and sweetness. She seemed to be occupied in affection, veneration, and rapture. These passions were blended like the mellow colours of the immortal painter into the happiest unity. The bold figure of St. Jerome, the attitude, the solidity and sainted gravity of his countenance, composed a striking counter-part to these softer passions. The infant was vivacious and benign. The Magdalen pensive and dejected; melancholy veiled the full lustre of her countenance, and preserved the proprieties of her character. The angel was what an angel should—I had almost said, all that an angel can be. Such is this wonderful painting. If I might make so free with the terms of art, I would say, that it has all that softness, finish, keeping, and vigour can contribute to animate the works of the pencil. Days and years might be spent in admiring it; and genius might exhaust the power of language in its praise. A copy is now taking of this inimitable groupe, which promises to catch some portion of its spirit. But, alas! such are the imperious limits of this art, that no transcript can be made of its excellencies; and the pencil of the artist can alone perpetuate his own fame.

The theatre which joins the academy is sufficiently known as a building of wood, particularly constructed for the conveyance of sound without echo or confusion; and reports of travellers are perfectly correct as to this fact: for upon experiment made in a whisper at one end, the words were distinctly heard at the other. The form of the theatre is light and elegant. It is now, however, falling into decay, and the sole

LETTER LXXI. 347

use to which it is at present applied, is the occasional exhibition of Naumachiæ, for which the arena is very conveniently adapted. I could descant upon a second production of Correggio's, to which I was introduced after quitting the academy, but I am fearful that my epithets would scarcely hold out through another description; and, indeed, to speak the truth, it succeeded the other too rapidly to find a particle of admiration disengaged.

I have been relaxing this evening at the theatre, being previously acquainted that a tragedy of Shakespeare's would be performed, and wishing to know in what manner our immortal bard would be handled by these cognoscenti. The tragedy was nothing less than Amletto (Hamlet); and, alas! my poor countryman has seldom fallen into worse hands, since Voltaire attempted to translate him. The jokes and the idle play of words which were the side-arms of this poet, were all that this caterer

for

for the Italian ſtage had reliſhed or underſtood. Theſe were laviſhed, and not without effect, upon the audience, who ſeemed to have taken the whole for a burleſque, and expreſſed their approbation of theſe flights of humour with tremendous peals of applauſe. It was only in ſome moment when Hamlet himſelf occupied the ſtage, that any thing like gravity appeared in the houſe. Then, indeed, a call of ſilence was raiſed and echoed from different parts, and attention was erect till Hamlet, who was dreſſed in black, and brandiſhed a white handerchief in his hand, had done ranting. So much for Italian tragedy.

It is painful to ſee ſuch inattention to the convenience of travelling in countries of ſuch wealth and fertility. A ſmall deduction from the palace would clear the peaſant's path. Almoſt all the rivers in theſe opulent duchies, are deſtitute of bridges, and ſome are not paſſed in ferry-boats without danger.

# LETTER LXXII.

Bologna, Nov. 18, 1791.

UPON commencing our route to Modena, we entered upon the old Æmilian way. I amufed myfelf, during this part of our journey, with reading a letter of Pliny to Trajan, in which he mentions the Cura Viæ Æmiliæ as an object of great advantage, and thanks the Emperor for having given the appointment to a friend of his. It was fome addition to this train of pleafurable images to be informed, that on paffing through Reggio, I was viewing a place which, befides its antient fame, was revered as the birth-place of Ariofto. Modena is a delicious town, and has every advantage of buildings and fituation. Taffoni, in his poem of the *Secchia Rapita*, has given a very

very animated and juft defcription of this his native place:

"Modana Siede in una gran pianura," &c.

The cathedral is rather fingular than handfome, and fufficiently fombre for all the purpofes of occult devotion. One of thofe who ftand in the place of Levites, and ferve about the altar, offered to conduct me to fome objects of curiofity. They confifted of a number of antient maufoleums, whofe infcriptions were not difficult to decipher. My guide was however fo intolerably ftupid, that I got no information from him as to their hiftory. They were all found in the town, he affured me; and when I afked him how long it was fince their difcovery, he talked to me of more centuries than I fhould chufe to repeat. All that I could draw from him was, that they were "tro-
"vati nel piazzo," (found in the fquare,)
"tranfportati qui," (conveyed here,) "&
"tutti di marmore," (all of marble.) This laft

last he repeated with great energy. He next introduced me, having previously lighted two candles, into a chapel, which he called the Chapel of San Geminiano.

This saint, of whose history I cannot inform you, is in great estimation among the Modanese, as Petronius is at Bologna. Tassoni, in his poem before quoted, calls the former *Gemignani*, as he does the latter *Petronj*, from these respective saints:

"Che tolsero a' i Petronj, i Gemignani.
Canto I.

This chapel was sufficiently curious. There were two very well executed portraits in it. I wished to know the artist, but the only answer I could get was " San Geminiano," and " tutto di marmore!" My guide now led me to the back part of that monument, on which the portraits were hung, and pointing to a small door, resembling the entrance into a vault, he rehearsed a history respecting it, which I was far from thoroughly comprehending. He spoke of creeping and
crawling

crawling upon his knees, and accompanied his words with geftures, which made me conclude that this was the opening into fome fubterraneous paffage. He afked me, if I would enter it? I made no objection; on which he unlocked the door, and pointed to the infide. I was furprifed on looking, to find that it was but a fmall area under the monument or vault, the roof of which was fupported by fix or feven marble pillars, at fuch intervals as to leave room for a perfon to crawl on his knees. Upon feeing me hold back, he explained the whole of the myftery, by telling me " Chi vuol' " obtenere una grazia di Dio bifogna fer- " pere qui." (He who would obtain a bleffing from God, muft creep through here.) And ftooping down, I obferved that this operation had actually worn a channel upon the marble. I afked him how long it had been the fafhion to creep among thefe pillars? He told me, five hundred years. Whether his chronology was accurate or

not,

# LETTER LXXII.

not, I had no opportunity to afcertain. The man feemed not a little aftonifhed at my retiring without making this religious tour. Unfortunately he detained me fo long in his recital of miracles performed at this tomb, and in the exhibition of a moft marvellous and wonder-working crucifix, that I loft the opportunity of feeing the *Secchia*, which is preferved among the archives of this cathedral.

It paffes for a fpecies of miracle, that the mere theft of a bucket fhould become the foundation of a war; and it does at firft fight prefent a fubject of furprife, that the blood of nations fhould be fpilt for " un " infelice e vil fecchia di legno." It is however to be feared, that in reviewing the wars of Europe, too many cafes will be found, in which fo valid a pretext cannot be affigned for the effufion of human blood.

## LETTER LXXIII.

*Florence, Nov. 21.*

BOLOGNA is a town, the remembrance of whose beauties will not readily be effaced from my mind; and yet I have seen so small a portion of them, and been compelled to take so rapid and cursory a glance, that I almost blush to attempt any thing like an enumeration of its curiosities.

The churches are usually in all places the first object of attention: and I had heard so much of the celebrity of St. Luke at Bologna, that I immediately requested to be conducted thither. The path to this church is a continual ascent; but pilgrims of all ages, and labouring under whatever infirmities, seemed to tread it without reluctance or fatigue. The church bears the name of the Madonna di San Luca, from

the

## LETTER LXXIII.

the famous portrait of the Virgin, painted by the hand of the Evangelift, and which it is the boaft and glory of the Bolognefe to poffefs. A portico of three miles conducts the pilgrim to this object of adoration. This portico has considerable beauty, and ftill more convenience, as it affords at once the means of fhelter and of reft. It was raifed by voluntary contribution; fix hundred and forty-eight arcades compofe the whole range; all of which were built at different periods by the zealous devotion of private perfons, or different corporations, and they were conftructed in reference to each other, fo as now to compofe an uniform piazza to the entrance of the church, adorned with frefcoes, fome of which have no fmall merit.

The church is an elegant building, and bears on its walls fome tablets, commemorative of miracles performed by this marvellous picture. This ineftimable treafure is provokingly covered with a cafe, ornamented

with jewels, and different offerings of devotion; fo that I could only judge of St. Luke's pencil by its miraculous effects. A ftring of beads, which I purchafed to efcape the fufpicion of herefy, entitled me to a little tract, written by the Abbé Calindri, from which I learned the very high value fet upon this precious depofit, the folemnity with which it is venerated at Bologna, and the innumerable benefits which have been derived by this city from its refidence among them. The Abbé, fpeaking of the annual ceremony of carrying this image in proceffion, fays, " Molte altre volte é ftato, " &c. *i. e.* This ceremony has alfo been
" performed in cafes of public emergency,
" as was the cafe in 1779, on account of
" repeated earthquakes. The confequence
" was, that though thefe fhocks were fo
" violent, and fo frequent as to agitate the
" country for three years, the city of Bo-
" logna fuftained no fenfible mifchiefs from
" this fcourge, which, during its continu-
" ance,

## LETTER LXXIII.

" ance, committed such ravages in the cir-
" cumjacent cities."

The Abbé, full of the authenticity and influence of this magical picture, has annexed to his abridged account of this history, the means by which it passed into the hands of those who founded the present church. As such a curiosity may not often come before you, I will endeavour, for your amusement, to put this portion of monkish Latin into a decent English dress*. " In

---

* Anno Domini millesimo centisimo sexagesimo, Die octava intrante Madis. Actum in Monte de Guardia sub heremitico Domne Azoline & Beatrixie, presentibus Domno Rambertino de Guezis, Domnus Marcheximus Ottonellus, Judex; Domnus Angelettus de Ursis, et alii plures testes; Domnus G. Episcopus Bonon dedit et assignavit supradictis Azoline et Beatrixie unam capsulam de ligno, cum tabula, ubi picta est imago Beate Marie manu beati Luche Evargeliste, quam portavit de Constantinopoli, in civitate Bononie Theoclys Kennya hermitanationis Grecus ibi presens ad conservandam, tenendam, et custodiendam in heremitatico de monte de Guarda pro se et earum successoribus, in dicto heremitico ad honorem Dei et dicte imaginis. Prenominati Dominus Episcopus et Theoclys heremita hoc instrumentum assignationis ut super legitur scribere rogaverunt. Ego Vitalis Biblicie Dei gratia dicti Domni Episcopi notarius interfui; et hanc cartam instrumenti consignationis rogatus scripsi et sigillavi cum sigillo dicti Domni Episcopi indictione octava.

" the

" the year of our Lord 1160, and the 8th
" day of May, in the Monte di Guardia, at
" the hermitage of the ladies Azolina and
" Beatrice, and in the prefence of Signior
" Rambertino de Guezi, Signior Marche-
" fino Ottonello, Judge, Signior Angioletto
" del Orife, and many other witneffes,
" Gerard, Bifhop of Bologna, gave and
" affigned to the aforefaid Azolina and
" Beatrice, and their fucceffors, a box, con-
" taining a tablet, upon which is an image
" of the bleffed Virgin, painted by the hand
" of St. Luke the Evangelift, and brought
" by Theocles, a Greek hermit, then and
" there prefent, from Conftantinople, to
" have, to hold, and to keep in the hermit-
" age of Monte Della Guardia, to the ho-
" nour of God, and of the faid image.
" The afore-named bifhop of Theocles,
" the hermit, have called upon me to make
" out the foregoing inftrument. I there-
" fore, Vitale di Beliefa, by the grace of
" God notary of the faid bifhop, have
" written in their prefence, and at their in-
" ftance,

## LETTER LXXIII.

"ſtance, this inſtrument of conveyance,
"and have ſealed the ſame with the ſeal
"of the ſaid biſhop, in the 8th indic-
"tion."

I muſt allow you to take a moment's refreſhment after ſo tedious a journey through the ſcrolls of ſuperſtition. And as the whole reſembles ſo ſtrongly the ſtructure of a fable, I think you will not object to its uſual appendage—a moral! I am free to confeſs, that I could neither view, nor can reflect upon the whole, without concluding, that when religion is addreſſed to the ſenſes rather than the underſtanding, there is nothing too ridiculous to become the object of adoration; and, for my own part, I can diſcern in the rationality of this ſpecies of devotion no difference between the tomb of Mahomet and the croſs of Calvary—the image of Diana that fell down from heaven, and the portrait of the Virgin painted by Saint Luke.

## LETTER LXXIV.

AMONG the advantages I derived from my vifit to St. Luke, were the extenfive, varied, and delicious views which I obtained of Bologna and the environs, from different points of the arcades. Numerous villages are fcattered over the circumjacent country, which is adorned with the richeft cultivation. The next object of attention which I found in my excurfion, was the grand and beautiful church of St. Paul. It is not eafy to imagine a more impreffive piece of fculpture than that which ftands before the grand altar, and reprefents the decollation of St. Paul. The hand of the executioner is raifed to ftrike, and the neck of the calm and intrepid apoftle is bared to receive, the blow. This group is difpofed with fuch juft attention to light and eleva-

## LETTER LXXIV.

tion, that no part of the effect produced by the energy of the artift is loft.

The academy (L'Inftituto) being only viewed to advantage during a clear light, was the next fcene to which my intelligent and managing lacquey conducted me. This is a collection which, as it might not be curforily viewed, fo it ought not to be lightly criticifed. Among the more valuable treafures of this mufeum were a large variety of defigns and fketches, by different mafters of the Bologna fchool. I know fcarcely any pleafure equal to that of tracing the growth of a noble thought from the rude outline to the laft perfection. In viewing the random fketches of the pencil, one is enabled to feparate genius from art, and to difcriminate between imagination and mechanifm. I wifhed to have dwelt longer upon the contemplation of thefe draughts, but I was obliged to obey the fummons which called me to the Hall of Antiques, where my eye was loft in beholding ftatues, and limbs of ftatues,

tues, pigmean heads, coloffal feet, Roman wells, idols, tablets, and tomb-ftones. I had fcarcely time to wonder, before I was hurried into a library, faid to contain twelve thoufand volumes, befides MSS. With the fame rapidity, I laftly vifited various cabinets of minerals, petrefactions, and philofophical inftruments, halls of wax-work, chambers of fortification, and naval tactics.

Of palaces I faw but one, viz. the Sampieri, where the Labours of Hercules, by the Caraccis, the Crucifix in ivory, by John of Bologna, and other productions, attracted their portion of admiration; but my attention was chiefly fixed upon three paintings. The firft of thefe was the very affecting fcene of Abraham difmiffing Hagar, by Guercino. All the emotions which their refpective fituations could infpire, have been attended to by the painter. Sternnefs on the one hand, and diftréfs on the other, were never expreffed in a manner which could fpeak more powerfully to the feelings.

## LETTER LXXIV.

ings. There are dufky tints in the colourings of this mafter which affort well with the graver fubjects. The fecond was a portrait of Chrift, and the Pharifee who brought the tribute-money. The countenances could not be infpired with jufter expreffion; plaufibility and artifice reigned in the one, caution and penetration prevailed in the other. The painter appeared to have nicely ftudied the fhades of fentiment and character, and to have well diftinguifhed between fubtilty and fagacity, between the fpecioufnefs of art and the fobriety of truth. The laft is a painting, whofe fame is not confined to the fpot which contains it. I mean the celebrated production of Guido, in which St. Paul is reprefented rebuking St. Peter. Any other performance would have acted in vain upon my nerves, whofe vibrations began to fail, exhaufted by repeated impreffions of the fublime; but this was irrefiftible. The firft glance quickened my fenfes, and all my powers of admiration fuffered a refurrection.

I declare

I declare to you, that in contemplating this interefting work, I feemed to enjoy an interview with the very perfonages whofe portraits were expreffed on the canvafs. And what an interview! With what chara&ers! and on what occafion! Two apoftles whofe equals for piety and chriftian heroifm are yet to be fought—men who, from the fimilarity of their views, their motives, and their labours, muft have entertained for each other the higheft reciprocal affe&ion and efteem— are here found in a fituation the moft critical and interefting. " I rebuked him to his " face, faid St. Paul, for he was to be " blamed." I thought I faw in the countenance of the firft, an inflexible attachment to virtue and to truth, which filenced the pleadings of private feeling; and obliged him to reprove the errors of a man, unequalled perhaps in the chriftian church, excepting by himfelf. In the latter I marked manly forrow and fober penitence. While the former flood with his hand raifed, his finger pointed, and his attitude bold, the

latter

# LETTER LXXIV.

latter fat with his head reclined, refting upon his hand, and his eyes turned with confufion from the countenance of the rebuking apoftle. So much life, vigour, and intereft, fuch an union of fentiment and pathos, I have never yet feen in the productions of the pencil: and I am much deceived if the impreffion which this excited, will ever be furpaffed by any of the mafter-pieces of art which may yet lie before me. However that be, I cannot but felicitate myfelf upon having acquired that fund of noble images which the recollection of this painting fupplies: and if I could with the pilgrims perfuade myfelf that the fight of a picture would quiet my confcience, and fettle my faith, I fhould make no fcruple of turning my back upon the Madonna di San Luca, and feeking my abfolution at the Palazzo Sampieri.

## LETTER LXXV.

BOLOGNA is reputed to contain as many paintings as Rome itself, and some are of opinion, even more. The churches of Giovanni in Monte, that of the Dominicans, St. Agnes, Corpus Domini, and Petronius, were the chief of those which, in addition to the Cathedral and that of St. Luke, I had leisure or even disposition to visit.

The first of these could not be neglected. Respect for the Cecilia of Raphael carried me there, and I was repaid by the sight of a countenance full of serenity and beauty. The church of the Dominicans contains the Massacre of the Innocents, by Guido. This is held to be one of his best productions, but it is a subject which excites horror. The church is one of the handsomest buildings in its kind that I have ever seen. A very elegant

gant tomb of pure marble here pretends to preserve the relics of that Saint to whom the church is consecrated. The guide unlocked a small door, in order that I might apply my hand to the place where the body lay, and obtain, as I supposed, full demonstration of the fact. In compliance with his wishes, I made the experiment, but not feeling all that anxiety to be convinced, which he showed to convince me, I did not obtain sufficient evidence to remove my infidelity. I ought to observe that the Dominicans have lately possessed themselves of a very beautiful painting, representing the death of the Virgin. It is a production full of sweetness and delicate expression, and may be regarded as a valuable acquisition to the treasures of this monastery. The martyrdom of St. Agnes has given sufficient celebrity to the church of that name: and the powers of Dominichino are in this bold design very ably and successfully exerted. St. Petronius had nothing to shew me but the meridian line drawn by Caffini, and the figure of that fon of Mars whofe hand was arrefted in an attempt to wound the Virgin. The hiftory is given at length by Moore.

The opera was very brilliantly fupported by fome fingers, who will, I prefume, in due time, follow the fortunes of their brother Sepranos, in England. Crefcentini is the favourite, and the Dilettanti have great expectations from his promifing talents. Bologna is indeed the fchool of Italian mufic: and as the air is foft and temperate, the voice muft have an advantage the lofs of which is much felt in England.

I regret that the fhortnefs of my ftay fhould have deprived me of the power of communicating more extenfive information upon the interefting curiofities of this delightful town. Its general afpect is ftrongly prepoffeffing, and its details are fubjects of ftudy. We left it yefterday morning, and began to afcend the Appennines. Thefe mountains are diverfified by a rich and laboured

LETTER LXXVI.

boured cultivation; and the two days paffed between Bologna and Florence were enlivened by fcenes of magnificence and beauty. The lambent and fulphureous flames of Pietra Mala, rifing near the village of that name, and conftantly burning, lighted us as we approached Cavigliaro, the boundary of our firft day's journey: and early in the morning of the fecond, we defcended amid the rays of the rifing fun upon the turrets, palaces, bridges, gardens, and all the majeftic fcenery of this celebrated capital.

LETTER LXXVI.

Florence, Nov. 25, 1791.

THERE is nothing that requires more art than a juft felection of local curiofities. It is difficult to difcern the faireft where all are fair, and to fix upon the moft ufeful where

where none are without their ufe. Florence abounds fo greatly in objects of intereft to travellers, is fo rich in natural fcenery, monuments of architecture, and cabinets of art, that the mind is rather diftracted than directed, by thofe catalogues which undertake to do the duty of guides. Whether I have yet vifited one tenth part of its nominal, or digefted one hundredth part of its real beauties, I am not anxious to know; my time has been wholly employed in feeing, and much of what I faw has filled me with wonder. The gallery,—the great monument of Tufcan liberality, and the firft refort of ftrangers,—has furnifhed me with a large fund of ftudy and amufement. The princely bounty of the Grand Duke, who has enlarged the falary of the guides, to throw open the gates of this invaluable mufæum, is a subject which calls for the traveller's eulogium. All who have croffed the Appennines, have indulged in the praife of this gallery; and, though the rarities of its cabinets have been

fo

so often and so variously served up, I cannot deny myself the pleasure of reporting to you in what manner I was affected by them. The Tribune, which is usually the *last* displayed, was that into which I accidentally entered *first*. I knew not the name of the cabinet, and had followed some strangers. " This (said our conductor) is the Tribune, " and here," pointing to a statue that stood before us—" is the Venus de Medicis." Thus taken by surprize, I remained for some time in silent contemplation of this " statue " which enchants the world," and which is considered as the perfection of sculptural art. Carrying my speculations back to the first rudiments of this wonderful production, I pictured to myself, with the Abbé Du Palli, the birth of this design in the mind of the sculptor, and the enthusiasm which fired him when he first viewed the mass. Kindling as I gazed, I traced the progress of the chisel through all the stages of its formation. I admired the genius which actuated, the art which guided, and the delicacy which managed the sculptor's hand. Such circumstances must combine to give perfection, and perfection is the only attribute which can characterize this statue. The Arrotino or Whetter, who stands to the left of the Venus, is a subject both of admiration and perplexity. Position of body, cast of countenance, and circumstance of occupation, denote some mystery which they do not develop. He is resting on one knee, and whetting a knife or cutting instrument. His head is elevated inclining to the left, as though he were listening to something said. It is curious to observe what ingenious conjectures have been indulged upon the history of this Arrotino: he is listening to Cataline's conspiracy, he overhears the plot of Brutus's sons to restore the Tarquins: it is Cincinnatus; it is Manlius Capitolinus; and lastly, as though there were not already sufficient hypotheses to obscure the fact, the Abbè Palli has found out that it is the Scythian who assisted at the duet between Apollo and Marſyas, and who afterwards flayed the latter. Now, that he is liſtening, cannot be diſputed: and that he may be liſtening to the Catalinarian or the Tarquinian faction, are conjectures equally probable. And whether or not he repreſents the Scythian who was to flay Marſyas, it muſt be owned his heart ſeems ripe for a murderous deed. The hiſtory of this character is, in ſhort, among thoſe records which have ſlipped through the fingers of time, and whoſe place can only be ſupplied by fancy and conjecture.

## LETTER LXXVII.

Florence.

As I have ventured ſo far into the field of deſcription, it would be treaſon to the remaining ſtatues not to allow them ſome ſhare of encomium. The Wreſtlers, ſo oft and

and so deservedly admired, is a most beautiful and energetic production of the chisel; the mind of the artist must have been filled with the justest conceptions of human proportions and anatomical accuracy. My ignorance of antient sculpture had led me to form false and vulgar expectations of this groupe. The figures are of a moderate size and a perfect form; and exhibit an happy union of beauty and strength, of grace and vigour, of muscular force and personal comeliness. The inter-twining of the limbs is most artfully rendered, and evinces at once the power of the superior, and the disadvantage of the fallen combatant: while the countenances respectively express, by emotions of confidence and agony, the triumph of the victor and the despair of the vanquished. The dancing faun is certainly the most facetious and mirthful character ever brought out of marble. This grotesque figure is presented with one leg elevated, in the attitude of dancing. His head is inclined with

much

much natural expreffion, and in his countenance is painted a lively image of luxurious joy. Every lineament difcovers the abfence of folicitude and the annihilation of care. It is indeed a charming ftatue, full of antient thought, and in perfect unifon with the feftive imagery of the Grecian mufe. I might now conduct you, as I was conducted myfelf, through a feries of cabinets feverally furnifhed with diftinctly arranged curiofities. Among others were thofe that contained collections of precious ftones and minerals wrought into a thoufand varieties of form. Here were columns, vafes, and urns of agate, rock-cryftal, lapis lazuli; and, in fhort, a large profufion of antient and modern valuables, diftributed and afforted with great tafte. The cabinet of portraits was not among the leaft interefting of thefe fecondary departments. Thefe portraits are of different painters, painted by themfelves. Madame Le Brun and Angelica Kauffman are not among the leaft attracting. The

very

very noble urn di Medicis, on which is reprefented, in relievo, the facrifice of Iphigenia, forms a grand central ornament to one of thefe faloons. The Cabinet of the Hermaphrodite, and the Hall of Niobe, containing this defcendant of Jupiter and her fourteen children, are treafures of ineftimable value. Amongft a variety of urns, fepulchral fragments, and different *morceaus* of antiquity, are the known and celebrated bufts of Alexander the Great, and Brutus, the laft of which may well deferve a place amongft the productions of the Grecian fchool. Thefe bufts have alfo fet the learned afloat upon the occean of conjecture. The firft of thefe is the buft of a coloffal figure, and bears in the countenance a ftrong expreffion of agony. What circumftance this alludes to in the hiftory of Alexander is the queftion at iffue. " He fighs for new worlds," fays Mr. Addifon. " He is difturbed, *beyond a doubt*, fay " others, with remorfe for the murder of " Clitus." There is certainly an expreffion

of

of pain in the countenance more deeply coloured than the fretful emotion of pining discontent could inspire; and such as might be expected from the man, who had rashness enough to kill, and sensibility sufficient to repent. The bust of Brutus has also furnished work for the critics. The bust is excellent, but *unfinished*. All the mystery is, why should Michael Angelo have left it in this state? Cardinal Bembo has assigned a reason which will scarcely please beyond the pale of a court.

Dum Bruti effigiem sculptor de marmore ducit,<br>
In mentem sceleris venit, et abstinuit.

But Michael Angelo has left many unfinished works. All his figures upon the tombs in the chapel of St. Lorenzo, are uncouthly and imperfectly sculptured. Perhaps this great man, enamoured with the rougher strokes of his chisel, and pleased with the expression of his outline, would rather leave the bust unfinished, than efface the bolder parts by an addition of the last polish.

LETTER LXXVIII.

Florence.

THIS city appears conſtructed, in all its parts, to fill the eye of the traveller with pleaſure. The ſtreets, which are paved with even flag-ſtones, chiſeled as occaſion requires, for ſafety—are generally clean; and where they open upon the Arno, are illumined by wide and varied views, extending on either ſide of this noble ſtream. The entrance from Bologna is not improperly called a deſcent upon the town: for at the diſtance of ſome leagues the whole appears extended below the brow of the Appennines; and the traveller ſeems to be plunging from the lofty precipice into the boſom of thoſe viſtas and parterres, which interſect and adorn the vale below. A triumphal

umphal arch receives him at the foot of this descent, and announces his entrance into the Tuscan capital. The palace Pitti, residence of the Grand Duke, is sombrous in its aspect, but has an air of Gothic majesty. The interior is noble, and adorned with all that art, riches, and good taste can contribute to dignify the palatial residence. Here Pietro de Cortona has lavished the finest touches of his pencil upon the ceilings; and among the pendents is preserved the Madonna of Raphael, to which the connoisseurs assign the highest rank. It is but justice to the patron of this palace to say, that it is exhibited with the same liberality as the gallery: and that strangers are conducted through all its chambers with an attention and respect, which in other places is considered as involving the expectancy of an exorbitant fee. The palace Ricardi is a structure of noble architecture, raised, for the most part, upon the designs of Michael Angelo. It is impossible not to be delighted with the very elegant and masterly pieces

of

of Luca Giordano which cover the spacious roof of the grand saloon. Of the four Evangelists painted by Guercino, each had its proper merits; but the portrait of St. John was a faithful transcript of the Evangelist's pen. It was a countenance animated with as much fire and intelligence as can consist with sweetness and sensibility. Of other palaces I can only speak from a view of their exterior, and the reports of others. Their inhabitants are reputed to hold an high rank in polite accomplishments; and, those who have leisure to cultivate their society by a longer residence, bear testimony to their domestic hospitality. Amusements of every description are in this city at their zenith. Their opera has indeed its seasons, and the tide of gaiety its flux and reflux; but from what I have seen—and still more from what I have heard—no city has a fairer ground of pretension to detain those travellers, whom *ennui* and *hypochondria* have driven to seek the cure of their melancholy from the hands of pleasure.

# LETTER LXXIX.

*Florence.*

THE cathedral of Florence is a very large and ponderous edifice, conſtructed of black and white marble, and therefore preſenting a very ſhadowy aſpect. The ſtatues of the twelve Apoſtles, and the noble baſſo relievos which ſurround the altar, hardly compenſate the gloom which over-hangs the general maſs. The braſs gates which adorn the baptiſtery, an octagonal building detached from, but belonging to this cathedral, were by Michael Angelo deemed worthy of opening and ſhutting the entrance to Heaven. Next in order is the church of San Lorenzo. Here, in the chapel of the princes, are the two celebrated tombs of Michael Angelo. They are, like his buſt of Brutus, imperfectly sculptured; and prefented to me little beyond the rude outline. Two figures of bold defign adorn each of thefe monuments—the firft of which reprefent Day and Night—the fecond Crepufculum and Aurora. The chapel di Medicis in this church is defervedly efteemed amongft the ornaments of Florence. It contains fix tombs conftructed upon the defigns of Michael Angelo. The form of the chapel is octagonal; and the monuments are, in point of defign and execution, ftriking and magnificent. Oriental granite of the moft beautiful vein, lapis lazuli, coral, and, in fhort, every fpecies of ftone and mineral is here difpofed and arranged by the hand of a mafter. And were the chapel completed in a ftyle fuited to the original plan, the world would not be able to fhew fo perfect a model of tafte and magnificence. The church of Santa Annuntiata is adorned with fome handfome altars of marble, and paintings of no mean execution. The *bas reliefs* in bronze

## LETTER LXXIX.

bronze by Jean de Bologne, compofe rather an interefting than fplendid ornament to the Chapelle de La Vierge, in which an image of high character is depofited. The flagellation of Chrift is, among thefe brazen tablets—an extraordinary effort of genius, replete with vigour and fenfibility. Among the contiguous cloifters are fome admirable frefcoes. The wafteful hand of time, and expofure to the damps and dews have brought into decay a beautiful Madonna of Andrea del Sarto, whofe buft and epitaph are affixed againft the walls of this cloifter. The church of the Dominicans is of inferior reputation to the convent. This contains a grand elaboratory for balfams, fimples, &c. and is efteemed to produce fome of the beft effences and perfumes which ever fhed their fragrance around the perfons of beau or belle.

The church of San Spirito, prefents a bold defign of folid but fimple architecture. It is as yet fo little advanced, that the paintings it contains are perfectly eclipfed. It promifes,

mifes, however, to exhibit in its finifhed ftate that fpecies of grave and decent edifice, which correfponds with the rational idea of a Chriftian Temple. My regifter of the churches fhall clofe with that of the Santa Croce. It had for me only two objects— the firft of which was the monument of Michael Angelo—a monument worthy of the fubject. Three of his fcholars united to form this memorial of their illuftrious preceptor—equally fkilled in the rival arts of painting, fculpture, and architecture. The tomb of the great Galileo was the fecond. A fimple buft and tablet of marble record his memory. Peace to his afhes! May no facrilegious hand deftroy the pile on which his name is infcribed! may his memory for ever flourifh! and may it appear from the concurrent plaudits of all fucceeding ages, how perifhable are the decrees of fuperftition and error, how immortal the difcoveries of reafon and truth!

LETTER LXXX

Foligno, Dec. 1.

IT was not without great reluctance that I left Florence, after so short a stay. An offer of introduction to some of the principal inhabitants, rendered this abrupt departure still less palatable; but change and reverse are the lot of man, and the chances of travel, like those of life, are not all in favour of the adventurer. It was by a tardy movement of more than two days, that we reached the antient and venerable town of Peruggia.

The journey to Rome, by this route, is less frequently taken, than that of Sienna, as it is a track extremely circuitous; but those who study the wear and tear of horses and carriages, prefer this route, as more than compensating for its length, by the superiority of its roads. Among the curiosities of this place, are to be seen many of the productions of Pietro Perugino, the master of Raphael, whose best and greatest works are here preserved. At the church of San Francesco, is one representing the Resurrection, on which I fixed with a great degree of admiration. The outline was faithfully sketched; and there appeared a great degree of accuracy and chasteness in the drawing, and disposition of the colours. In what I had ever before seen of this master, there was so great a dryness and formality, that it was difficult to trace, without a deeper knowledge of the art than I can pretend to, any thing like the touches of an able and animated pencil. But from this and other specimens at Peruggia, it appears, that Raphael may have stood considerably indebted to the lessons of his preceptor. Superadding to his own genius the principles of Pietro, he has shewn the sublime effects which result from the union—too seldom existing—

of

## LETTER LXXX.

of ſtrong talents and attentive ſtudy. This church was rich in excellent paintings. From viewing ſome deſigns, more remarkable for their quaintneſs and antiquity, than their merit, I paſſed to the contemplation of an aſſumption of the Virgin, which paſſes with me for the beſt Raphael I have yet ſeen. The Virgin is repreſented in Heaven, and Jeſus Chriſt placing the crown upon her head. The Apoſtles below are collected about her tomb, and gazing upwards with countenances full of attention and rapture. There was in this painting a ſort of expreſ- ſion, which made its way more ſucceſsfully to my admiration, than the Cecilia at Bo- logna, or the Madonna at the Palace Pitti. I had formed very erroneous conceptions of the pleaſure I was to derive from the pro- ductions of Raphael—expecting to know them at firſt ſight, and to worſhip them al- moſt by inſtinct. Painting has however its myſteries, I find—and it requires ſome ſtudy and knowledge of its principles, to be able to admire what is moft excellent. Like the fifter arts of poetry and mufic, it feems to hide its excellencies from thofe who are ignorant of its laws. A good painting feems therefore to ftand very much in the predicament of a good poem, and a well wrought concerto. Some fimple delineation fhall fafcinate in the *firft*, beyond a regular and ftudied production; while in the *laft*, an artlefs tale and a popular air fhall pleafe more, than the ftately mufe of Milton, and the learned melodies of Pergolefi.

At a palace belonging to the noble family of Della Penna, I was gratified with the fight of fome of the beft and moft finifhed pieces, from the hand of Salvator Rofa. Numerous productions of this extraordinary mafter were fhewn me, in which all the wild and grotefque fancies which genius could create, were brought upon the canvas. To thefe were added four landfcapes in his beft ftile, two of which prefent nature in lefs uncouth forms, and are in all refpects deferving of the higheſt eulogium.

I was completely occupied, during the time we paſſed in this town, with the various and valuable ſpecimens of art which I had opportunity to viſit. The town is ſufficiently gloomy in its afpect—the marks of antiquity, defertion, and decay, are ſtrongly viſible in all its extent: and it is among the very few cities in Italy which are ſtruck out of the liſt of the travellers route. It is however certain, that though little viſited, it wants not its importance in the ſcale of art. Its churches and its palaces have indeed little to boaſt of ſplendor or ornament: the intelligent traveller will, neverthelefs, be repaid, for entering apartments ſeldom inhabited, and churches little frequented, by defigns and ſtudies appropriate to this place, and of a clafs which is in vain fought for in cities of greater reſort.

# LETTER LXXXI.

Terni,

FROM Foligno to this place, the road was flanked on either side, by sloping lands of rich and laboured cultivation. Foligno is a town of some traffic, and much fraud. The British minister resident at Florence, (Lord Harvey,) was by some accident passing on this route. Whatever be the subject of his journey, it is certain that he went *incog*. to the confines of Rome, and is returning to Florence by this little-frequented route. The politicians of this place are greatly perplexed to account for his Lordship's appearance amongst them; under such circumstances, they regard it as full of mystery. He paid us a visit with much politeness, and I had an opportunity of laying before him a specimen of that sort of information which

## LETTER LXXXI.

the politicians of Foligno poſſeſſed. For in a newſpaper of the place, which I was not a little ſurprized to meet with, it was hinted with ſome confidence, that an union was in agitation of the crowns of England and France, by the marriage of the Prince of Wales with Madame Royale. This may ſerve to ſhew you, how much theſe people are admitted into the ſecrets of ſtate.

I roſe early on the following morning, in order to obtain, before my departure from Foligno, a ſight of the Madonna of Raphael, preſerved in the convent Des Comteſſes. My guide and myſelf had concerted the hour and the means, but alas! when I approached the door of the chapel and demanded admittance, a number of Franciſcans, who were aſſembled at their devotions, growled refuſal.

From Foligno to Spoletto the track conducted us through a country whoſe beauties have not diſappeared in the month of December. The air was ſoft, the ſky deliciouſly ſerene above us, and every where around

around were scenes of that ornamental description, which confound, in the traveller's eye, all diſtinction of ſeaſons. In proportion as we advanced, the ſtate of the country ſtill improved; mountains of the moſt picturesque forms preſented themſelves. Emboſomed upon the heights of theſe, were caſtles, monaſteries, and towns, interſperſed with olive gardens, the bloom of whoſe fruit reflected in various hues the rays of the ſun. We alighted on our route, to view the little temple by the road ſide, conſecrated, as the lovers of antiquity affirm, to the god Clitumnus; and as men of leſs enthuſiaſm, and therefore probably of more judgment, ſay, to ſome modern Divinity. Spoletto was the boundary of this day's journey, and the hour of our arrival was ſufficiently early to viſit the Gothic Aqueduct, which here connects the mountain of St. Francis with Spoletto. It is a ſtupendous building of ten arches, the loweſt of which is eſtimated to ſtand more than ſix hundred feet above its

founda-

## LETTER LXXXI.

foundation. Its hiftory is carried back to the times of Theodoric, and it forms in its prefent ftate, an object of great magnificence. The mountain againft which it refts, has many wild and picturefque beauties. A loofe and irregular fhrubbery overfpreads it from the fummit to the narrow channel below; and intermixed with the maffes of ftone which hang upon its flopes, the tangling fhoots exhibit thofe light and negligent ornaments, which art can never fuccefsfully imitate. I was given to underftand that a portrait of the Virgin by St. Luke, was among the ineftimable rarities of Spoletto—but I heretically contented myfelf with the report of its miraculous properties; and, glancing fimply at the pompous infcriptions which announce the pride of this place, as the " caput umbriæ," and the town fo celebrated by the flight of Hannibal—compofed myfelf to an anticipation of thofe beauties which I was to fee in the Cafcade of Terni.

LETTER LXXXII.

Citta Castellana.

THE Cascade of Terni is formed by the fall of the Velino into the Nera, (anticntly the Nar—" Narque albescentibus aquis—in Tiberim properans." *Sil. Ital.*) The Velino is a pretty considerable river of a navigable depth, and takes its rise in Monte Abruzzo; separating, in its passage to the point of descent, the town of Rhieti, from its suburbs. There are many circumstances attending this Cascade, which render it not only an object of astonishment to the traveller, but of interest to the naturalist. The river Velino once formed a marsh in the valley of Rhieti, highly prejudicial to the country, and whose waters had the singular property of petrifaction. This circumstance is attested by Pliny: " In lacu Velino lignum dejectum lapideo cortice induitur." The channel

## LETTER LXXXII.

nel through which the Velino now paſſes, in its way to the point of deſcent, was dug by order of Clement VIII. The calcareous particles with which the water is impregnated, have here concreted in their paſſage, and overlaid the whole ſuperficies of this bed with a ſubſtance reſembling the ſolidity of marble. Hence this level has acquired the name of Piano del Marmore, or the Marble Level; and the Caſcade itſelf, La Caduta del Marmore, or the Marble Caſcade. The track from which it is approached from the town of Terni, is ſingularly pictureſque. Cut for the greater part out of the ſolid rock, it purſues a winding courſe, and furniſhes, by a gradual yet conſtant aſcent, numerous and varied views of the ſurrounding ſcenery. The rapidity of the river in that channel, which is hewn out of the rock to give paſſage to its waters, is ſcarcely to be imagined. It is here that the ſpectator is uſually conducted firſt, in order that he may ſee the quantum of force with which this

body

body of water haftens to its fall. It is impoffible, to regard without dizzinefs, the extreme velocity of this part of the current. Stones of confiderable weight are buoyed up by the rapidity of the motion. The next point of view, is that which from a fmall terrace conveys to the eye this powerful ftream, precipitated from the extremity of its marble level with all that violence which it has already acquired by the compreffion of its waters. The ftream thus precipitated is received in a rocky bafon, fcooped out by the force of the waters, and from whofe bafe it is difcharged to a fecond receiver, amidft a vaft profufion of foam and uproar. Defcending thus with a rapidity regularly diminifhed by the re-action of two fucceffive rocks, the river enters the Nera, and proceeds to join the imperial Tiber. A fcene of greater and more terrific magnificence cannot be pictured by the imagination. The force and velocity of the current, in the point preparatory to its defcent, is moft tremendous.

ous. It is difficult to decide—so different are the calculations upon this subject—its accurate measurement. The Pere Carrara has fixed its total height from the Piano del Marmore to the level of the Nera, at 1871 Roman palms. The tumult of its waters, reverberated in a thousand directions;—the frothy clouds which issued from the valley;—the arching rocks which overhung the gulph;—and the luxuriant shrubs which scattered their delicate shades;—formed together a picture of romantic sublimity, too impressive to be easily supplanted by any scenes of secondary beauty.

## LETTER LXXXIII.

*Rome, Dec. 7.*

IT was between Spoletto and Terni, that we passed the highest point of Appennine upon this route, and we have been since regularly descending. I could not pass through Terni,

## LETTER LXXXIII.

Terni, without feeling an emotion of classical pleasure. It was the birth-place of Tacitus, and the mind is forcibly impressed with scenes thus connected with those it has learned to admire. Johnson has expressed, in his masterly imitation of the Roman poets, the same sentiment:

> Struck with the spot which gave Eliza birth,
> We kneel, and kiss the consecrated earth.
>
> Imit. Sat. 3. Juv.

Our route from Terni lay along the beautiful valley which connects this town with Narni. The waters of the Nera, gracefully discomposed, and rendered musically sonorous by the influx of the Velino, roll along this charming vale, in their way to the point of junction with the Tiber. The ruins of the great bridge, which once connected the two opposite mountains, and over which passed the high road to Peruggia, stands at no great distance from the town of Narni. The only entire arch which now remains, discovers it to have been, whatever were its form,

form, of bold and fublime conftruction. Blocks of ftone compofed without cement, and compacted into an apparently folid mafs, convey an high idea of the perfection to which the arts were carried in the age of Auguftus. What was once Otriculum, is now a little dirty poft town, and preferves more of its name than its fubftance,—ftill retaining the appellation of Ocricoli. Numerous veftiges of ruined monuments are vifible in its environs, and different fides of the roads yet fhew the remains of antient fabrics, and heaps of crumbling materials. The very ferpentine courfe which the Tiber purfues, engaged particularly my attention in paffing from Narni. The level furface of the country allowed the eye to obferve the flexions of this ftream over a confiderable fpace. The beauties of cultivation gradually difappeared as we approached Citta Caftellana. It was from this miferable town, once the capital feat of the Falifci, and taken by Camillus, A. U. 359, that we yefterday finifhed our

journey

journey to this metropolis. Scenes of natural beauty had been for some time receding; and now, in proportion as we advanced, the aspect of the country increased in that deformity which neglected agriculture and reduced population have introduced into the most fertile and productive soil under the Heavens. A few scattered huts, and these for the most part sinking into ruins, serve rather to heighten the picture of desolation; and to awaken a more lively degree of sensibility in the bosom of the contemplative traveller. At length the dome of St. Peter's rising amidst this weary waste, indicated our approach to ROME, which received us by an entrance majestic, and expressive of the genius of this antient capital.

END OF THE FIRST VOLUME.

The following valuable BOOKS are printed for T. CADELL, Jun. and W. DAVIES (Successors to Mr. CADELL) in the Strand, 1796.

---

HISTORY, VOYAGES, AND TRAVELS.

THE History of England, from the Invasion of Julius Cæsar to the Revolution in 1688. By David Hume, Esq. A new Edition, printed on fine Paper, with many Corrections and Additions; and a complete Index, 8 vol. Royal Paper, 4to, with fine Impressions of the Plates, 10l 10s

*⁎* Another Edition, on small Paper, 4l 10s

✚✚✚ Another Edition in 8 vol. 8vo, with the Plates, 2l 16s

The History of England, from the Revolution to the Death of George II. forming a Continuation of Mr. Hume's History; with Plates. By T. Smollett, M. D. 5 vol. 8vo, 1l 15s

The History of Political Transactions and of Parties, from the Restoration of King Charles II. to the Death of King William. By Thomas Somerville, D. D. 4to, 1l 5s

The History of Scotland, during the Reign of Queen Mary and of King James VI. till his Accession to the Crown of England; with a Review of the Scottish History previous to that Period; and an Appendix, containing Original Papers, 2 vol. 4to. By William Robertson, D. D. 5th Edition, 1l 10s

*⁎* Another Edition in 2 vol. 8vo, 14s

✚✚✚ Another Edition in one volume, 7s 6d

The History of the Reign of the Emperor Charles V. with a View of the Progress of Society in Europe, from the Subversion of the Roman Empire to the Beginning of the 16th Century. By W. Robertson, D. D. Embellished with 4 Plates, elegantly engraved, 3 vol. 4to, 3l 3s

*⁎* Another Edition in 4 vol. 8vo, 1l 4s

The History of America, vol. I. and II. By W. Robertson, D. D. Illustrated with Maps, 2l 2s

*⁎* Another Edition in 3 vol. 8vo, 1l 1s

An Historical Disquisition concerning the Knowledge which the Antients had of India, and the Progress of Trade with that Country, prior to the Discovery of the Passage to it by the Cape of Good Hope. With an Appendix, containing Observations on the Civil Policy—the Laws, and Judicial Proceedings—the Arts—the Sciences,

A

and Religious Inftitutions of the Indians. By William Robertfon, D. D. Illuftrated with Maps, 4to, 18s

*⁎* Another Edition in one vol. 8vo, 8s

The Hiftory of Greece. By William Mitford, Efq. Vol. I. and II. 4to, 1l 19s in boards.

*⁎* The two Volumes include the Hiftory of Greece from the earlieft Accounts to the End of the Peloponnefian War; and it is intended to continue the Hiftory till the Reduction of Achaia into a Province of the Roman Empire.

The fame Work in 4 vol. 8vo, 1l 8s

*⁎* The third Volume in 4to, is now in the Prefs.

The Hiftory of Ancient Greece, its Colonies and Conquefts; from the earlieft Accounts till the Divifion of the Macedonian Empire in the Eaft: including the Hiftory of Literature, Philofophy, and the Fine Arts. By John Gillies, LL. D. F. R. S. with a Head of the Author, and Maps adapted to the Work, 4 vol. 3d Edit. 1l 8s

A View of the Reign of Frederic II. of Pruffia, with a Parallel between that Prince and Philip II. of Macedon. By J. Gillies, LL. D. F. R. S. and S. A. 8vo, 7s

The Hiftory of the Reign of Philip II. King of Spain. By Robert Watfon, LL. D. Profeffor of Philofophy and Rhetoric at the Univerfity of St. Andrew, 2 Edition, 2 vol. 4to, 2l 2s—Another Edition in 3 vol. 8vo, 18s

The Hiftory of the Decline and Fall of the Roman Empire. By Edward Gibbon, Efq. 6 vol. which complete a Period of Hiftory from the Age of Trajan and the Antonines, to the taking of Conftantinople by the Turks, and the Eftablifhment at Rome of the Dominion of the Popes. Adorned with a Head of the Author, and Maps adapted to the Work, 6l 6s in Boards.

*⁎* The 4th, 5th, and 6th Vol. may be had feparate, to complete Sets, 3l 3s in Boards.

✢✢✢ Another Edition, complete in 12 vol. 8vo, 3l 12s

Alfo an Abridgment of this Work for the Ufe of young Perfons, 2 vol. 8vo, 14s

The Hiftory of Rome, from the Foundation of the City by Romulus, to the Death of Marcus Antoninus, 3 vol. 8vo, 1l 1s  This Work, with the Abridgment of Mr. Gibbon's Hiftory, forms a complete Roman Hiftory, in 5 vol. 8vo.

The Chronology and Hiftory of the World, from the Creation to the Year of Chrift 1790, illuftrated on 56 Copperplate Tables, with 16 Maps of Ancient and Modern Geography. By the Reverend John Blair, LL. D. 3l 13s 6d

The History of France from the Accession of Henry III. to the Death of Louis XIV. preceded by a View of the Civil, Military, and Political State of Europe, between the Middle and the Close of the Sixteenth Century. By Nathaniel William Wraxall. Vol. I. II. and III. 4to, 3l 3s in Boards.

Memoirs of Great Britain and Ireland, from the Dissolution of the last Parliament of Charles II. until the Capture of the French and Spanish Fleets at Vigo. By Sir John Dalrymple, Bart. 3d Edition, with Appendixes complete, 3 vol. 1l 16s

The History of England, from the Earliest Accounts of Time to the Death of George II. adorned with Heads, elegantly engraved. By Dr. Goldsmith, 4 vol. 1l 4s

An Abridgment of the above Book, by Dr. Goldsmith, adorned with Cuts, for the Use of Schools, 3s 6d

An Ecclesiastical History, Ancient and Modern, from the Birth of Christ to the Beginning of the Present Century. In which the Rise, Progress, and Variations of Church Power are considered, in their Connexion with the State of Learning and Philosophy, and the Political History of Europe during that Period. By the late learned John Lawrence Mosheim, D. D. Translated, and accompanied with Notes and Chronological Tables, by Archibald Maclaine, D. D. A new Edition, corrected and improved, 6 vol. 2l 2s

A Summary of Geography and History, both Ancient and Modern; containing an Account of the most illustrious Nations in Ancient and Modern Times; their Manners and Customs; the local Situation of Cities, especially of such as have been distinguished by memorable Events. With an Abridgment of the Fabulous History or Mythology of the Greeks, &c. &c. The whole chiefly designed to connect the Study of Classical Learning with that of General Knowledge. By Alexander Adam, LL. D. Rector of the High School of Edinburgh. Illustrated with a new Set of Maps, 9s

Roman Antiquities; or an Account of the Manners and Customs of the Romans; respecting their Government, Magistracy, Laws, Religion, Games, Military and Naval Affairs, &c. &c. Designed chiefly to illustrate the Latin Classics. By Alexander Adam, LL. D. 3d Edition, 7s 6d

Bibliotheca Claffica; or a Claffical Dictionary, containing a full Account of all the proper Names mentioned in ancient Authors. To which are fubjoined, Tables of Coins, Weights, and Meafures, in Ufe among the Greeks and Romans. By J. Lempriere, A. M. of Pembroke College, Oxford. 2 Edition, 9s

A Philofophical and Political Hiftory of the Settlements and Trade of the Europeans in the Eaft and Weft Indies. Tranflated from the French of the Abbé Reynal, by J. Juftamond, M. A. A new Edition, carefully revifed, in 8 vol. 8vo, and illuftrated with Maps, 2l 8s

Sketches of the Hiftory of Man, by the Author of the Elements of Criticifm. 3d Edition, 4 vol. 1l 8s

An Account of the Voyages undertaken by Order of his prefent Majefty, for making Difcoveries in the Southern Hemifphere, and fucceffively performed by Commodore Byron, Captain Wallis, and Captain Carteret, in the Dolphin, the Swallow, and Edeavour. Drawn up from the Journals which were kept by the feveral Commanders, and from the Papers of Jofeph Banks, Efq. and Dr. Solander. By John Hawkefworth, LL. D. Illuftrated with Cuts, and a great Variety of Charts and Maps (in all 52 Plates). 3 vol. 4to, Price 3l 12s

An Account of a Voyage towards the South Pole and round the World, performed in his Majefty's Ships the Refolution and Adventure, in the Years 1772, 1773, 1774, and 1775. Written by James Cook, Commander of the Refolution. In which is included, Captain Furneaux's Narrative of his Proceedings in the Adventure during the Separation of the Ships. 2 vol. Royal 4to, with Maps and Charts, Portraits of Perfons, and Views of Places, drawn during the Voyage, by Mr. Hodges, and engraved by the moft eminent Mafters, 2l 12s

A Journey from Prince of Wales's Fort, in Hudfon's Bay, to the Northern Ocean. Undertaken by Order of the Hudfon's Bay Company, for the Difcovery of Copper-Mines: a North - Weft Paffage, &c. in the Years 1769, 1770, 1771, and 1772. By Samuel Hearne, 4to, with Charts and other Plates, 1l 11s 6d

The Environs of London: being an Hiftorical Account of the Towns, Villages, and Hamlets, within 12 Miles of that Capital; interfperfed with Biographical Anecdotes. By the Rev. D. Lyfons, A. M. F. R. S. 3 vol. 4to, 4l 14s 6d in Boards.

Travels in Portugal, through the Provinces of Entre Douro e Minho, Beira, Eftremadura, and Elem-tejo, in

BOOKS PRINTED FOR CADELL AND DAVIES.  5

the Years 1789 and 1790: confisting of Obfervations on the Manners, Cuftoms, Trade, Public Buildings, Arts, Antiquities, &c. of that Kingdom. With 24 Plates of Views, &c. By James Murphy, Architect, 4to, 1l 11s 6d

Travels through Spain, in the Years 1775 and 1776. In which feveral Monuments of Roman and Moorifh Architecture are illuftrated by accurate Drawings taken on the Spot. By Henry Swinburn, Efq. 2d Edition, 2 vol. 14s

Travels in the Two Sicilies. By Henry Swinburn, Efq. in the Years 1777, 1778, 1779, and 1780. With a Map of the Two Sicilies, and 22 Plates of Views, &c. 2d Edition, 4 vol. 1l 8s

Travels through various Provinces of the Kingdom of Naples, in 1789. By Charles Ulyffes, of Salis Marfch-lins. Tranflated from the German, by Anthony Aufrere, Efq. and illuftrated with Plates, 8vo, 9s

*<sub>*</sub>* This Volume forms a proper Supplement to Mr. Swinburn's Travels in the Two Sicilies.

Travels into different Parts of Europe, in the Years 1791 and 1792. With Familiar Remarks on Places, Men, and Manners. By John Owen, A. M. late Fellow of Corpus Chrifti College, Cambridge. 2 vol. 16s

Travels in Switzerland, in a Series of Letters to William Melmoth, Efq. from William Coxe, M. A. F. R. S. F. A. S. Rector of Bemerton, &c. 3 vol. with a large Map of Switzerland, and other Plates, 1l 7s

Travels into Poland, Ruffia, Sweden, and Denmark, interfperfed with Hiftorical Relations and Political Enquiries, illuftrated with Maps and Engravings. By William Coxe, A. M. F. R. S. &c. 5 vol. 3d Edit. 1l 17s 6d

A new Volume, being the 3d in 4to, and the 5th in 8vo, of the above Work, with a Map of Southern Norway, and other Plates, may be had feparate.

An Account of the Ruffian Difcoveries between Afia and America; to which are added, the Conqueft of Siberia, and the Hiftory of the Tranfactions and Commerce between Ruffia and China. By William Coxe, A. M. F. R. S. Illuftrated with Charts, and a View of a Chinefe Town. 3d Edit. 7s 6d

A complete Tranflation of the Count de Buffon's Natural Hiftory, from the 4th Edit. in 16 vol. 4to, with occafional Notes and Obfervations. By William Smellie, Member of the Philofophical and Antiquarian Societies of Edinburgh. Illuftrated with 300 Copperplates, 9 vol. 4l 1s

A new Tranflation of the Count de Buffon's Natural Hiftory of Birds. Illuftrated with near 300 Engravings, and a Preface, Notes, and Additions by the Tranflator, 9 vol. 4l 1s

A new Syftem of the Natural Hiftory of Quadrupeds, Birds, Fiſhes, and Infects. With about 150 Copperplates, 3 large volumes 8vo, 1l 16s

A Tour through Sicily and Malta, in a Series of Letters to William Beckford, Efq. from P. Brydone, F. R. S. 2 vol. Illuftrated with a Map. 3d Edition, 12s

Obfervations and Reflections made in the Courfe of a Journey through France, Italy, and Germany. By Hefter Lynch Piozzi, 2 vol. 14s

Obfervations made in a Tour from Bengal to Perfia, in the Year 1786-7; with a ſhort Account of the Remains of the celebrated Palace of Perfepolis, and other interefting Events. By William Francklin, Enfign on the Hon. Company's Bengal Eftabliſhment, lately returned from Perfia. 2d Edit. 8vo, 7s

A View of Society and Manners in France, Switzerland, and Germany, with Anecdotes relating to fome eminent Characters. By John Moore, M. D. 2 vol. 7th Edit. 12s

A View of Society and Manners in Italy, with Anecdotes relating to fome eminent Characters. By John Moore, M. D. 2 vol. 4th Edition, 14s

A Journey to the Weftern Iſles of Scotland. By the Author of the Rambler, 6s

The State of the Prifons in England and Wales, with Preliminary Obfervations, and an Account of fome Foreign Prifons and Hofpitals. By John Howard, F. R. S. 4to, 4th Edit. with all the Plates complete, 1l 5s

An Account of the principal Lazarettos in Europe; with various Papers relative to the Plague, &c. by the fame. 2d Edit. with all the Plates complete, 1l 5s

DIVINITY.

Ifaiah: a new Tranflation, with a Preliminary Differtation, and Notes Critical, Philological, and Explanatory. By Robert Lowth, D. D. F. R. S. Londin. & Goetting. late Lord Biſhop of London. 3d Edit. 2 vol. 8vo, 14s

Jeremiah and Lamentations: a new Tranflation, with Notes Critical, Philological, and Explanatory. By Benjamin Blayney, D. D. &c. &c. 4to, 1l 5s

BOOKS PRINTED FOR CADELL AND DAVIES. 7

The Four Gofpels, tranflated from the Greek; with Preliminary Differtations, and Notes Critical and Explanatory. By George Campbell, D. D. F. R. S. Principal of Marifchal College, Aberdeen. 2 vol. 4to, 2l 10s

Sermons on feveral Subjects. By the Right Rev. Beilby Porteus, D. D. Bifhop of London. 6th Edit. 2 vol. 13s

*⁎* The fecond Vol. may be had feparate, 6s in Bds.

An Introduction to the Study of the Prophecies concerning the Chriftian Church, and in particular concerning the Church of Papal Rome. By Richard Hurd, D. D. now Lord Bifhop of Worcefter. 3d Edit. 2 vol. 7s

Sermons preached at Lincoln's Inn Chapel, between the Years 1765 and 1776. By Richard Hurd, D. D. Lord Bifhop of Worcefter. 2 Edit. 3 vol. 18s

The Works of the Right Rev. Jonathan Shipley, D. D. Lord Bifhop of St. Afaph, 2 v. 8vo, with a Portrait, 12s

Sermons by Hugh Blair, D. D. one of the Minifters of the High Church, and Profeffor of Rhetoric and Belles Lettres in the Univerfity of Edinburgh. 19th Edition, 4 vol. 1l 8s

*⁎* The 4th Volume may be had feparate, 6s in Boards.

Sermons by William Leechman, D. D. with fome Account of the Author's Life, and of his Lectures. By James Wodrow, D. D. 2 vol. 14s

Sermons by the late Rev. John Dryfdale, D. D. F. R S. Ed. one of the Minifters of Edinburgh, &c. &c. With an Account of his Life and Character, by Andrew Dalzel, M. A. F. R. S. Edinburgh, Profeffor of Greek, &c. in the Univerfity of Edinburgh, 2 v. 14s

Sermons by George Hill, D. D. F. R. S. Ed. Principal of St. Mary's College in the Univerfity of St. Andrew; one of the Minifters of that City, and one of his Majefty's Chaplains in Ordinary for Scotland, 7s

Difcourfes, chiefly on the Evidences of Natural and Revealed Religion. By John Sturges, LL. D. 7s

Difcourfes on various Subjects. By Jacob Duché, M. A. 3 Edit. 2 vol. 14s

Sermons on different Subjects, left for Publication by John Taylor, LL. D. late Prebendary of Weftminfter, Rector of Bofworth, Leicefterfhire, and Minifter of St. Margaret, Weftminfter. Publifhed by the Reverend Samuel Hayes, A. M. 2 vol. 12s

*⁎* Thefe Volumes include the Sermon written by Dr. Johnfon, for the Funeral of his Wife; and

all the Sermons exhibit strong internal evidence of their having been carefully revised, at least, if not wholly written by that eminent Moralist, who had been, for a great Number of Years, in Habits of close Intimacy with the Divine whose Name they bear.

Sermons on the Present State of Religion in this Country, and on other Subjects. By the Rev. Septimus Hodson, M. B. Rector of Thrapston, Chaplain to the Asylum, and Chaplain in Ordinary to his Royal Highness the Prince of Wales, 8vo, 5s

One hundred Sermons on Practical Subjects, extracted chiefly from the Works of the Divines of the last Century. By Dr. Burn, 4 vol. 1l 4s

Sermons by the late Lawrence Sterne, M. A. 6 v. 18s

Sermons on the Christian Doctrine, as received by the different Denominations of Christians, &c. &c. By. R. Price, D. D. LL. D. F. R. S. &c. 2 Edit. 6s

Sermons on various Subjects, and preached on several Occasions. By the late Rev. Thomas Francklin, D. D. 4th Edition, 3 vol. 1l 4s

Sermons on the Relative Duties. By the same, 6s

Sermons to Young Men. By W. Dodd, LL. D. Prebendary of Brecon, and Chaplain in Ordinary to his Majesty. 3d Edit. 7s 6d

Four Dissertations. I. On Providence. II. On Prayer. III. On the Reasons for expecting that virtuous Men shall meet after Death in a State of Happiness. IV. On the Importance of Christianity, the Nature of Historical Evidence, and Miracles. By Richard Price, D. D. F. R. S. 4th Edit. 8vo, 6s

Sermons to Young Women. By James Fordyce, D. D. 2 vol. 6th Edit. 7s

Addresses to Young Men, by the same. 2 vol. 8s

Sermons on Various Subjects. By the late John Farquhar, A. M. Carefully corrected from the Author's MSS. by George Campbell, D. D. and Alexander Gerrard, D. D. 4th Edit. 7s

A Review of the Principal Questions in Morals. By Richard Price, D. D. F. R. S. 3 Edit. corrected, 7s

MISCELLANIES, BOOKS OF ENTERTAINMENT, &c.

The Works of the late Right Hon. Henry St. John, Lord Viscount Bolingbroke; containing all his Poli--

BOOKS PRINTED FOR CADELL AND DAVIES. 9

and Philosophical Works: a new and elegant Edit. 5 vol. 4to,

*⁎* Another Edition in 11 vol. 8vo, 2l 16s

The Works of Francis Bacon, Baron of Verulam, Viscount St. Alban's, and Lord High Chancellor of England. 5 vol. Royal Paper, 4to.

An Inquiry into the Nature and Causes of the Wealth of Nations. By Adam Smith, LL. D. F. R. S. 3 vol. 6th Edition, 8vo, 1l 1s

An Inquiry into the Principles of Political Œconomy; being an Essay on the Science of Domestic Policy in Free Nations; in which are particularly considered, Population, Agriculture, Trade, Industry, Money, Coin, Interest, Circulation, Banks, Exchange, Public Credit, Taxes, &c. By Sir James Stuart, Bart. 2 vol. Royal Paper, 4to, 2l 2s in Boards.

Essays and Treatises on several Subjects. By David Hume, Esq. with his last Corrections and Additions. 2 vol. 4to, 1l 16s

*⁎* Another Edition, in 2 vol. 8vo, 14s

Moral and Political Dialogues, with Letters on Chivalry and Romance. By Richard Hurd, D. D. now Lord Bishop of Worcester. 3 vol. 10s 6d

An Essay on the History of Civil Society. By Adam Ferguson, LL. D. 4th Edit. 7s

Zeluco. Various Views of Human Nature, taken from Life and Manners, foreign and domestic. 2d Edit. 2 vol. 14s

The Theory of Moral Sentiments. By Adam Smith, LL. D. F. R. S. 5th Edit. 2 vol. 14s

The Elements of Moral Science. By James Beattie, LL. D. Professor of Moral Philosophy and Logic in Marischal College, Aberdeen. 2 vol. 8vo, 15s

The Works of Alexander Pope, Esq. with his last Corrections, Additions, and Improvements, as they were delivered to the Editor a little before his Death; together with the Commentary and Notes of Dr. Warburton. With Cuts. In 9 large Volumes, 8vo, 2l 14s

The same in 6 Volumes, 12mo, 18s

A complete and elegant Edition of the English Poets, printed in 75 Pocket Volumes, on a fine Writing Paper. Illustrated with Heads, engraved by Bartolozzi, Caldwall, Hall, Sherwin, &c. &c. with a Preface Biographical and Critical to each Author. By Samuel Johnson, LL. D. 13l 2s 6d

Miscellaneous Works of Edward Gibbon, Esq. With

Memoirs of his Life and Writings, compoſed by himſelf; illuſtrated from his Letters, with Occaſional Notes and Narrative. By John Lord Sheffield. 2 vol. 4to, 2l 10s in Boards.

The Works of Soame Jenyns, Eſq. including ſeveral Pieces never before publiſhed. To which are prefixed, ſhort Sketches of the Hiſtory of the Author's Family, and alſo of his Life. By Charles Nalſon Cole, Eſq. with a Head of the Author. 4 vol. 2d Edition, 1l

Letters to and from the late Samuel Johnſon, LL. D. To which are added, ſome Poems never before printed. Publiſhed from the Original in her Poſſeſſion. By Heſter Lynch Piozzi. 2 vol. 14s

The Lives of the moſt eminent Engliſh Poets; with Critical Obſervations on their Works. By Samuel Johnſon, LL. D. 4 vol. new Edition, 1l 4s

The Life of Milton, in three Parts. To which are added Conjectures on the Origin of Paradiſe Loſt, with an Appendix. By William Hayley, Eſq. 4to, 18s

Anecdotes of ſome diſtinguiſhed Perſons, chiefly of the preſent and two preceding Centuries. Adorned with Sculptures. 4 vol. 3d Edit. 1l 8s in Boards.

\*\*\* The Fourth Volume may be had ſeparate.

The Works of Mr. Thomſon, complete, elegantly printed on a fine Writing Paper, with Plates, and a Life of the Author. 3 vol. 1l 4s

Another Edition, 3 vol. Crown, 18s; or 2 vol. common, 7s

The Seaſons, in a Twelves Edit. Price only 2s 6d

Another Edition of the Seaſons, in a ſmaller Size, printed on a fine Paper, with new Plates, 6s

The Triumphs of Temper: a Poem in 6 Cantos. By William Hayley, Eſq. 6th Edit. 7s 6d

Elegiac Sonnets. By Charlotte Smith. 5th Edit. with additional Sonnets, and other Poems, 7s 6d

The Pleaſures of Memory, with ſome other Poems. By S. Rogers, Eſq. 7th Edit. 7s 6d

The Pleaſures of Imagination. By Mark Akenſide, M. D. To which is prefixed, a Critical Eſſay on the Poem. By Mrs. Barbauld, 7s 6d

The Art of preſerving Health. By John Armſtrong, M. D. With a Critical Eſſay on the Poem, by J. Aikin, M. D. 7s 6d

The Spleen, and other Poems of Matthew Green. With a Critical Eſſay by Dr. Aikin, 6s

The Shipwreck, a Poem, in 3 Cantos. By a Sailor, 6s

*⁎* The seven laſt-mentioned Works are printed in a moſt beautiful and uniform Manner, and are all embelliſhed with very fine Plates.

Eſſays on various Subjects, principally deſigned for young Ladies. By Hannah More, 3s ſewed, 2 Edit.

Adelaide and Theodore, or Letters on Education: containing all the Principles relative to the different Plans of Education, tranſlated from the French of Madame la Comteſſe de Genlis. 3 vol. 3d Edit. 10s 6d

The Moral Miſcellany, or a Collection of Select Pieces, in Proſe and Verſe, for the Inſtruction and Entertainment of Youth. 3d Edit. 3s

An Hiſtorical Miſcellany. 3d Edit. 3s

The Poetical Miſcellany; conſiſting of Select Pieces from the Works of the following Poets, viz. Milton, Dryden, Pope, Addiſon, Gay, &c. 2d Edit. 3s

A Father's Legacy to his Daughters, by the late Dr. Gregory, of Edinburgh. With a Frontiſpiece, 2s ſewed.

The Mirror: a Periodical Paper, publiſhed at Edinburgh in the Years 1779 and 1780. 3 vol. 8th Edit. 9s; or 2 vol. large 8vo, 14s

The Lounger; a Periodical Paper. By the Authors of the Mirror. 4th Edit. 10s 6d; or 2 vol. large 8vo, 14s

The Adventurer, by Dr. Hawkeſworth, 4 vol. A new Edit. adorned with Frontiſpieces, 12s; or 3 vol. large 8vo, 1l 1s

The Rambler, 4 vol. with Frontiſpieces, and a Head of the Author, 12s; or 3 vol. large 8vo, 1l 1s

A complete Edition of the Works of Lawrence Sterne, M. A. containing his Triſtram Shandy, Sentimental Journey, Letters, &c. &c. Adorned with Plates, deſigned by Hogarth, Rooker, Edwards, &c. 10 vol. 2l

The Man of Feeling, a Novel. A new Edit. 3s

The Man of the World, by the Author of the Man of Feeling, 2 vol. 6s

Julia de Roubigne, by the ſame, 2 vol. 6s

Sentimental Journey, 2 vol. A new Edit. with Frontiſpieces, 5s—Another Edit. 3s

Triſtram Shandy, 6 vol. 18s

The Receſs; or, a Tale of other Times. By the Author of the Chapter of Accidents. 4th Edit. 3 vol. 13s 6d

Julia, a Novel, interſperſed with ſome Poetical Pieces. By Helen Maria Williams, 2 vol. 7s

Emmeline, the Orphan of the Caſtle. By Charlotte Smith, 4 vol. 3d Edit. 14s

Ethelinde; or, the Recluse of the Lake, by the same.
5 vol. 2d Edit. 17s 6d

Celestina, a Novel, by the same, 4 vol. 2d Edit. 14s

The Banished Man, a Novel, by the same, 4 vol. 2d Edit. 16s

Extracts, elegant, instructive, and entertaining, in Prose, from the most approved Authors; disposed under proper Heads, with a View to the Improvement and Amusement of young Persons, one vol. Royal 8vo, 14s

Extracts in Poetry, upon the same Plan, 16s

Epistles, elegant, familiar, and instructive, selected from the best Writers, ancient and modern: a proper Companion to the two preceding Works, 9s

LAW.

Commentaries on the Laws of England, in Four Books. By Sir William Blackstone, Knight, one of the Justices of his Majesty's Court of Common Pleas. Twelfth Edition, with the Author's last Corrections, and Notes and Additions by Edward Christian, Esq. Barrister at Law, and Professor of the Laws of England in the University of Cambridge. 4 large Volumes, 8vo, with 14 Portraits, elegantly engraved, 1l 16s

Tracts, chiefly relating to the Antiquities of the Laws of England. By Judge Blackstone, 4to, 1l 1s

A Digest of the Laws of England. By the Right Hon. Sir John Comyns, Knt. late Lord Chief Baron of his Majesty's Court of Exchequer. 3d Edit. considerably enlarged, and continued down to the present Time, by Stewart Kyd, Barrister at Law, of the Middle Temple. 6 vol. Royal 8vo, 4l 4s

Cases in Crown Law, determined by the Twelve Judges, by the Court of King's Bench, and by Commissioners of Oyer and Terminer, and General Gaol Delivery; from the 4th Year of George II. to the 32d Year of George III. By Thomas Leach, Esq. of the Middle Temple, Barrister at Law. 2d Edit. with Additions, 12s

Cases argued and determined in the High Court of Chancery, in the Time of Lord Chancellor Hardwicke, from the Years 1746-7 to 1755, with Tables, Notes, and References. By Francis Vezey, Esq. 2 v. 3d Edit. 1l 1s

The Attorney's Vade Mecum, and Client's Instructor, treating of Actions (such as are now most in Use); of prosecuting and defending them; of the Pleadings and

BOOKS PRINTED FOR CADELL AND DAVIES.   13

Law, with a Volume of Precedents. By John Morgan, of the Inner Temple, Barrister at Law, 3 vol. 1l 2s

The Justice of Peace; or, Complete Parish Officer. By Richard Burn, LL. D. A new Edit. 4 vol. 1l 12s

Ecclesiastical Law, by the same Author, 4 vol. 1l 8s

A new Law Dictionary, intended for General Use, as well as for Gentlemen of the Profession. By Richard Burn, LL. D. and continued to the present Time, by his Son, 2 vol. 16s

A Digest of the Law of Actions at Nisi Prius. By Isaac Espinasse, Esq. of Gray's Inn, Barrister at Law. 2d Edit. 2 vol. 1l 1s

The Solicitor's Guide to the Practice of the Office of Pleas in his Majesty's Court of Exchequer at Westminster; in which are introduced, Bills of Costs in various Cases, and a Variety of useful Precedents. With a complete Index to the whole. By Richard Edmunds, one of the Attornies of the said Office, 7s

PHYSIC.

Domestic Medicine; or, a Treatise on the Prevention and Cure of Diseases, by Regimen and Simple Medicine. By Wm. Buchan, M. D. of the Royal College of Physicians, Edinburgh. A new Edit. 7s 6d

*⁎* This Treatise comprehends not only the Acute, but also the Chronic Diseases; and both are treated at much greater Length than in any Performance of the like Nature. It likewise contains an Essay on the Nursing and Management of Children; with Rules for preserving Health, suited to the different Situations and Occupations of Mankind: and Directions for the Cure of Wounds, the Reduction of Fractures, Dislocations, &c.

Medical Histories and Reflections. By John Ferriar, M. D. Physician to the Manchester Infirmary and Lunatic Hospital, 2 vol. 11s

First Lines of the Theory and Practice of Philosophical Chemistry. By John Berkenhout, M. D. 8vo, with Plates, 7s 6d

The Seats and Causes of Diseases investigated by Anatomy, in five Books; containing a great Variety of Dissections, with Remarks. Translated from the Latin of John Baptist Morgagni, Chief Professor of Anatomy, and Prefident of the Univerfity of Padua. By Benjamin Alexander, M. D. 3 vol. 4to, 1l 16s

A full and plain Account of the Gout; from whence will be clearly feen the Folly, or the Bafenefs, of all Pretenders to the Cure of it: in which every Thing material by the beft Writers on that Subject, is taken notice of, and accompanied with fome new and important Inftructions for its Relief; which the Author's Experience in the Gout, above thirty Years, has induced him to impart. By Ferdinando Warner, LL. D. 3 Edit. 5s

A Treatife upon Gravel and upon Gout, in which their Sources and Connexion are afcertained; with an Examination of Dr. Auftin's Theory of Stone, and other Critical Remarks. A Differtation on the Bile, and its Concretions; and an Enquiry into the Operations of Solvents. By Murray Forbes, Member of the Surgeons Company, 6s

An Account of the Efficacy of the Aqua Mephitica Alkalina, or, Solution of fixed Alkaline Salt, faturated with fixable Air, in Calculous Diforders, and other Complaints of the Urinary Paffages. By W. Falconer, M. D. F. R. S. Phyfician to the General Hofpital at Bath. 4th Edit. 3s

An Enquiry into the Nature, Caufes, and Method of Cure of Nervous Diforders. By Alexander Thompfon, M. D. 2s

A new Enquiry into the Caufes, Symptoms, and Cure of Putrid and Inflammatory Fevers, &c. &c. By Sir William Fordyce, M. D. 4s

Difcourfes on the Nature and Cure of Wounds. I. Of Generals: of procuring Adhefion, Wounded Arteries, Gun-fhot Wounds, Wounds with Sword, &c. the Medical Treatment of Wounds. II. Of Particulars: of Wounds of the Breaft, Wounds of the Belly, Stitching an Inteftine, Wounds of the Head, Wounds of the Throat. III. Of dangerous Wounds of the Limbs. Of the Queftion of Amputation. By John Bell, Surgeon, 1 vol. Royal 8vo, 7s 6d in Boards.

*\*\** In this Book are contained all thofe Accidents of Practice and leffer Operations which do not belong to a Syftem of Surgery, but which, as they occur more frequently, are the more important.—This Book, it is hoped, will be found particularly ufeful to Country Surgeons, and to young Men entering into the Army and Navy.

Engravings explaining the Anatomy of the Bones,

Mufcles, and Joints, with copious Defcriptions. By John Bell, Surgeon, 4to, 1l 1s in Boards.

A Collection of Cafes and Obfervations in Midwifery. By Wm. Smellie, M. D. 3 vol. with Cuts, 1l 1s

PHILOSOPHY, MATHEMATICS, MECHANICS, &c. &c.

Elements of the Philofophy of the Human Mind. By Dugald Stewart, F. R. S. Edin. Profeffor of Moral Philofophy in the Univerfity of Edinburgh. 4to, 1l 5s

Aftronomy explained upon Sir Ifaac Newton's Principles, and made eafy to thofe who have not ftudied the Mathematics. By James Fergufon, F. R. S. Illuftrated with 28 Copperplates. A new Edit. 8vo, 9s

An eafy Introduction to Aftronomy, for young Gentlemen and Ladies, by the fame. 3d Edit. 5s

An Introduction to Electricity, in 6 Sections, by the fame. Illuftrated with Plates, 4s

Lectures on Select Subjects in Mechanics, Hydroftatics, Pneumatics, and Optics, with the Ufe of the Globes, the Art of Dialling, and the Calculation of the Mean Times of New and Full Moons and Eclipfes, by the fame, 7s 6d

Select Mechanical Exercifes, fhewing how to conftruct different Clocks, Orreries, and Sun-Dials, on plain and eafy Principles, &c. &c. By the fame. With Copperplates, and a fhort Account of the Life of the Author, 5s

Obfervations on Reverfionary Payments; on Schemes for granting Annuities to Widows, and to Perfons in old Age; on the Method of finding the Value of Affurances on Lives and Survivorfhip; and on the National Debt. To which are added, new Tables of the Probabilities of Life; and Effays on the different Rates of Human Mortality in different Situations, &c. &c. By Richard Price, D. D. F. R. S. A new Edit. 2 vol. 8vo, 15s

The Doctrine of Annuities and Affurances on Lives and Survivorfhips, ftated and explained. By William Morgan, Actuary to the Society for Equitable Affurances on Lives and Survivorfhips, 8vo, 6s

AGRICULTURE, BOTANY, GARDENING, &c.

The Complete Farmer; or, a General Dictionary of Hufbandry in all its Branches; containing the various Methods of cultivating and improving every Species of Land according to the Precepts of both the old and new Hufbandry; comprifing every Thing valuable in the beft Writers on the Subject: together with a great Variety of new Discoveries and Improvements. 4th Edit. considerably enlarged, and greatly improved. By a Society of Gentlemen, Members of the Society for the Encouragement of Arts, Manufactures, and Commerce. With a great Number of Plates, Folio, 2l 2s

Practical Essays on Agriculture: containing an Account of Soils, and the Manner of correcting them; an Account of the Culture of all Field Plants, including the Artificial Grasses, according to the old and new Modes of Husbandry, with every Improvement down to the present Period; also an Account of the Culture and Management of Grass Lands; together with Observations on Inclosures, Fences, Farms, Farm-houses, &c. Carefully collected and digested from the most eminent Authors, with experimental Remarks. By James Adam, Esq. 2 v. 14s

Every Man his own Gardener; being a new and much more complete Gardener's Calendar than any hitherto published; containing not only an Account of what Work is necessary to be done in the Hot-House, Green-House, Shrubbery, Kitchen, Flower, and Fruit Gardens, for every Month in the Year, but also ample Directions for performing the said Work according to the newest and most approved Methods now in Practice amongst the best Gardeners. By Thomas Mawe, Gardener to his Grace the Duke of Leeds; and other Gardeners. 6th Edit. 5s

An Introduction to Botany; containing an Explanation of the Theory of that Science, and an Interpretation of its Technical Terms; extracted from the Works of Dr. Linnæus, and calculated to assist such as may be desirous of studying the Author's Method and Improvements. With Plates. 3d Edit. with a Glossary, and other Additions. By James Lee, 7s 6d

Synopsis of the Natural History of Great Britain and Ireland: containing a Systematic Arrangement and concise Description of all the Animals, Vegetables, and Fossils, which have hitherto been discovered in these Kingdoms. By John Berkenhout, M. D. 2d Edit. 2 vol. 12s

Clavis Anglica Linguæ Botanicæ; or, a Botanical Lexicon. In which the Terms of Botany, particularly those occurring in the Works of Linnæus, and other modern Writers, are applied, derived, explained, contrasted, and exemplified. By John Berkenhout, M. D. 2d Edit. 6s

Historical and Biographical Sketches of the Progress of Botany in England, from its Origin to the Introduction of the Linnæan System. By Richard Pulteney, M. D. F. R. S. 2 vol. 12s

www.ingramcontent.com/pod-product-compliance
Lightning Source LLC
Chambersburg PA
CBHW021420300426
44114CB00010B/580